ALWAYS LOOKING FOR HOME

INDRA SENA

Other Books by Indra Sena

Memoir

Closet Full of Coke: A Diary of a Teenage Drug Queen

THIS IS A MEMOIR

This book is a memoir. Everything written about here happened, though these are *my* memories from thirty years ago. Some conversations had to be reconstructed but every conversation is *my* memory of what happened and what was said.

I did not write this to expose others and for that reason some names have been changed. I wrote this to tell you about what I heard, saw, and did.

INTRODUCTION

**July 1988
Suburbs, New York**

I was lying on my little sister's grave, crying, because it was not me in that coffin. I deserved to be dead, not her.

Seely followed me around, wanting to be close to me, wanting to be like me. She drove me crazy until we were in middle school, when our mother began drinking heavily and cheating on her second husband. Then our father split with his second wife. Things got even more chaotic and unstable than usual, so we united against our common enemy—our parents. We became closer than ever before.

Our mother left for good when she met her third husband. My father was now living with his pregnant third wife in his mother's tiny house. There really was nowhere for us to go. I was fifteen. She was thirty-three.

Soon, I was living in my own apartment, running an extensive drug operation. My sister had run away from the juvenile group home she was placed in and moved across the street from me into her boyfriend's house. He was a kid from the hood she met at a party I threw.

Later, she got into a car with my drunken ex, because she knew him for years through me.

It seems like I was always pulling on the strings of her fate.

Her death came a month after I was sentenced to time served plus five years probation. The year afterward, I was barely functional and working part-time as a doctor's messenger. Later I left for a fulltime job at Mercedes and learned computers and inventory control. I worked seven days a week, running the inventories on weekends. I left for a job with a computer manufacturer who offered me an assistant manager position. Later, at just twenty-one, I became a manager.

The doctor I worked for saw me reading *Harper's Magazine* while I waited for paperwork. He asked if I was interested in politics and I told him I was. He invited me to a potluck dinner hosted by a local activist group and encouraged me to listen to WBAI out of New York City, a progressive news radio station.

I joined a group who protested nuclear war and went to anti-nuke rallies in New York City lead by Michio Kaku. I went vegetarian and joined a group that fought for animal rights. I ran canned food and winter coat drives, donating everything to organizations for the homeless. I volunteered weekends in a homeless shelter and when I was not there, I was tabling for animals. I had no social life. I knew the only thing I could do was try to make the world better, any way I could. For at least three years, I volunteered every single weekend I was not working, and some weeknights after work.

I left the corporate world once my probation ended and took a job directing a nonprofit, but that did not seem like enough. I needed to find a way to give my whole life over to saving the world, because after I lost my sister I had no other goal except to die. I vowed that every moment I was here, until I died, I would spend working to alleviate suffering on earth, trying to erase some of the damage I had done as a lost, reckless teenager.

FROM WIKIPEDIA.COM

Rainbow Gatherings are temporary intentional communities, typically held in outdoor settings, and espousing and practicing ideals of peace, love, harmony, freedom, and community...

Rainbow Gatherings and the Rainbow Family ... are an expression of a utopian impulse, combined with bohemianism, hipster, and hippie culture, with roots clearly traceable to the counterculture of the 1960s.

Mainstream society is commonly referred to as "Babylon", connoting the participants' widely held belief that modern lifestyles and systems of government are unhealthy, unsustainable, exploitative and out of harmony with the natural systems of the planet.

The Rainbow Family has no leaders, no structure, no official spokespersons, no official documents, and no membership.

Anyone is allowed to attend and participants refer to themselves as "Rainbow Family." The goal was to create what they believe is a more satisfying culture—free from consumerism, capitalism, and mass media—that's nonhierarchical, furthers world peace, and serves as a model for reforms to mainstream society.

PART ONE

TO THE WHITE HOUSE

ONE

July 1990
Finger Lakes National Forest
Ithaca, New York

"Welcome home, Sisters!" a young man called out, gliding towards our car wearing nothing but a flowing skirt of purple gauze trimmed with beads and tiny mirrors.

Sharon, her arms resting on the wheel, turned towards me with an amused smile. The man was now leaning into the driver's window merrily grinning at us.

I smiled at him. "Thank you and, um, peace."

He hugged Sharon, then he skipped around the car and hugged me the same.

"Welcome home," he said again, looking at us with shining eyes, "I'm Bliss."

Bliss looked angelic; head crowned with a wreath of wildflowers bound by colored ribbons that trailed down his back to mingle with dark curls. His long beard reminded me of my father, whom people said looked like Jesus.

Bliss told us where to park and then he was off, hugging the occupants of the car behind us.

We parked and left our shoes in the car, walking barefoot along a pine-needle-lined path following hand drawn cardboard signs directing us towards "Home."

We passed lots of smiling, welcoming people on the trail.

"Welcome home, Sisters," they said, they all said, and they hugged Sharon and me tightly like we were long-lost relatives. They smelled of campfire smoke, incense, sweat, and sage. Some spoke with lilting southern accents, some with the hard-nasal sound of New York City.

Sharon wore a sleeveless tie-dye jumpsuit and round John Lennon glasses. I had on a gauzy blue Indian print dress with bell sleeves. We had met a few years ago at work and discovered we were neighbors. We started spending all of our free time together, declaring ourselves 'best friends'. She was quiet with a serious face and wise blue eyes and rife with skills from woodworking to outback survival. I felt helpless and girlie around her. She was much more grounded than me.

As we crossed a meadow, a small group of unclothed girls called out to us, "Sisters, you gotta go to the showers, they're amazing!"

Sharon and I grinned. We were never around nudists before but we took it in stride, along with most everything here except the latrines; hand-dug trenches designed for use by more than one person at a time.

One of the girls came over to me. Her long blonde hair was nearly white from the sun.

"Here Sister, this is for you. I made it." She held out a sparkling necklace of emerald glass beads and tiny green stones.

"I love it, it is so beautiful," I said, taking the gift. I gave her a hug and she trotted off. I never even learned her name.

"Where do all these people go the rest of the year?" I wondered. Wherever it was, I wanted to move there.

Sharon and I set up a tent and settled into the routines of the Gathering, short for "Rainbow Gathering," an assembly of tree-huggers, radicals, hippies, activists, and other outliers who called themselves "The Rainbow Family."

Sloppy Joe's, a crude open-fire kitchen, offered meals from breakfast to dinner. Loving Ovens repurposed metal barrels into portable ovens where bread, cakes, and warm cookies emerged almost miraculously. Everything here was free; money was strictly forbidden.

Tradition ruled, and each night at dusk people gathered in an expansive meadow with drums and played together until dawn while onlookers danced.

Standing in the shadows watching you feel transported to another time, an ancient time. A time before you kicked it with gangsters and got your little sister killed.

"My name is Bubble. Welcome home Sister," said a hefty woman dressed in a medieval gown. She gave me a brusque bear hug. "These are my husbands; I'm making a harem called Bubble's harem. Come hang out with us … we need some wives too."

I stood in stunned silence. It was late, and I was walking back to my tent with Sharon, but she was lagging behind.

"Come on sis, we gotta get going." Sharon appeared and pulled on my arm. She gave a gentle nod and a half smile to the group, but it wasn't exactly friendly. Sharon was protective of me and it was good. I vacillate between naïve and curious but rarely express caution—even when I should.

"Hare Krishna, Hare Krishna, Krishna Krishna, Hare Hare …"
The chants of the Vaishnavas drifted down towards the trail from a great white teepee that dominated a small knoll. Soft yellow light peeped out between the stitching of the canvas walls. Smoke rose from the peak, a mix of campfire and *Nag Champa* incense.

The Vaishnavas, commonly called 'Krishnas,' were a staple at the Gatherings. Each night they held Kirtan, a prayer service where they played tiny bell-sounding cymbals while chanting and dancing demurely. I began to visit the teepee nightly and chant for hours.

When my sister Seely died I turned to God, the mysterious, invisible figure I spoke to as long as I can remember.

As a child, under the cover of night, I would lie in my bed looking skyward, whispering my abysmal sorrows for hours at a time. I believed I was heard, though the rescue I pleaded for never came.

Mostly, I asked for comfort. I memorized Psalms and prayers I would recite continually in my head when I was scared.

When I was nine, I asked my father, "Daddy, what is God?"

"God is like the sun," he said, "and people are like rays of the sun."

He probably read that in a Carlos Castaneda book but years later I found the same description of God in the Vedas, the sacred texts of Hinduism.

Since Seely died, I read books on Buddhism and Hinduism unceasingly, looking for spiritual answers. One of the core practices I adopted was to ease suffering in others.

For years, I had spent my free time working with the homeless. Now, I dreamed of dropping everything and living with the Vaishnavas in their temple. I would devote my life to God and do nothing except pray and cook food for the poor.

But I was a reprobate. I spent most nights in reggae clubs dancing, cavorting, smoking weed, and charming my way backstage to meet the band.

I had ascetic fantasies but they were trumped by my obsession with guys, and the Gathering was overflowing with them. Within days, I was besotted.

"Hey Sister, you look like a gypsy!" A Brother said. "Are you one?"

"I'm not sure, maybe," I smiled.

"Can you spray some of that holy water on me?"

"Of course," I said, spraying him with a mister I carried around full of rosewater. It was my relief from the hot sun that blazed down on us all day. The swimming ponds were dry, and we had to drive to the river swimming holes.

"Thank you my Goddess," he said, "I'm Thomas. Why don't you come over to my camp for a little while? I'm with a group here from the Southwest."

"Okay, I'll come by later."

Thomas had long wavy auburn hair and wore oval wire frame glasses. He spent most of his time naked, looking like primitive man. He had a wry sense of humor, and highly idealized political views.

I was smitten, and soon I was missing the evening chanting to meet Thomas. We would smoke pot and talk for hours about politics.

Thomas left the Gathering before I did, telling me he'd see me again.

"How? Should I give you my number?"

"No," he said, "I'm going to a protest at the Nevada Test Site and I may end up in jail for a bit but I know we'll see each other again. You should come live with the Rainbow Family, we'll see each other all the time."

I never saw Thomas again, but I did go and live with the Rainbow Family.

TWO

**September 1990
Monongahela National Forest
West Virginia**

"What do you think about getting a VW camper van? I can ask my father to look for one for us," I said to Sharon as we drove to the West Virginia Gathering in my aging sedan.

My father, a mechanic who championed Volkswagens, always kept a few Jettas without plates scattered on his lawn to salvage and then sell; just one of his many endeavors to keep the wolf from the door.

"Oh, wow, I love that idea, those vans are so cool," she said.

"I know, they so remind me of the sixties. Plus, we'll have a little home with us, a retreat for when we need a break from the fray."

"When you need a break you mean," she chuckled. "Sis, this is so exciting! We are really doing it!"

"I know! I can't wait to see where we go. I want to see all fifty states," I said.

After we returned from the Ithaca Gathering, we decided to divest ourselves of our worldly goods to travel the country, following the weather and the Rainbow Family. I used Walt Whitman's poem, *Song of the Open Road,* as my template. Written while Whitman traveled the United States on foot in the mid 1800s, it was remarkably timeless.

Afoot and light-hearted I take to the open road,
Healthy, free, the world before me,
The long brown path before me leading wherever I choose.

Henceforth I ask not good-fortune, I myself am good-fortune,
Henceforth I whimper no more, postpone no more, need nothing,
Done with indoor complaints, libraries, querulous criticisms,
Strong and content I travel the open road.

Once free from probation, the workaday grind at my corporate job felt meaningless. Though I spent my teens as a glamour-hungry coke dealer, I was instantly cured of that craving when I held my little sister's icy hand while she lay on the silk pillows of her coffin. After that, no possession on earth could give me relief or pleasure. I no longer wanted anything: not money or glamour or gold.

But I yearned for family. I craved love and belonging and stability—all the things I never had in the chaos of five marriages, four stepparents, three schools, and the daily looming threat of violence from my mother's routine explosions of rage.

"Welcome home, Sisters!" the guy stoking the fire said. "I'm Mud Bear, this is my kitchen. I make breakfast, dinner, and mud."

"Mud?" I said.

"Yeah, mud is strong coffee, do you want some?"

"No thanks, I don't like coffee," I smiled at him.

He was handsome, like really handsome, with Nordic looks. His long ash-blond hair was tied into a loose ponytail with a leather string. I hugged him and inhaled the smell of sweat and wood smoke. He reminded me of Grizzly Adams. (If I didn't compare the men here to Jesus, I compared them to Grizzly Adams.)

People here tended to use monikers bestowed on them—at times impulsively—by others. I was given many, but in the end, I used my longtime nickname.

"I'm Sena (see-nah), and this is Sharon."

"You know, you kinda look like a bear yourself ... a little bear ... I'm gonna call you Sena Bear."

Clans were created from Native American philosophies incorporated into Rainbow culture. To be part of a clan was to declare yourself part. No one controls clan membership as no one controls who can be part of the Rainbow Family; there were no leaders, no papers to sign, no oaths to take, and no creeds.

After that, many of the bears called me Sena Bear. I was in the Bear Tribe.

Sharon and I brought our backpacks to Mud Bear's camp. That night, after the dishes were washed with heated creek water, Mud Bear took my hand.

"Come sleep with me, Little Bear," he whispered.

"Oh, I don't know, I mean, we just met today."

He smiled and kissed me, then silently went off to his tent.

I slept in my sleeping bag on the ground near the kitchen campfire along with a few other people.

I spent the next day helping Mud Bear prepare the evening meal, a tasteless green bean stir-fry.

Dinner was served in an open field where everyone sat on the ground in an expansive circle. There were around a hundred people and the air was thick with laughter and the smell of patchouli.

Different kitchens arrived with white five-gallon buckets of steaming hot food. Quiet blanketed the field and everyone began to Om, making a chorus of humming that became progressively louder.

After a few minutes, the chanting stopped and a black top hat called "The Magic Hat" circulated for people put donations inside. This was the only place at Rainbow where money was allowed, the donations used to purchase food and supplies from local stores.

Mud Bear and I walked around the circle dishing food into waiting bowls and cups, and even onto the occasional leaf. It was all smiles, happiness, and love. I felt sure I had found paradise.

That night I went to Mud Bear's tent.

"I can tell you're nervous and I think I know why," he said.

"Really? Why?"

"Listen, Sena Bear, I'm a one woman type of man. If you spend the night with me I'm all yours."

"But we hardly know each other."

"I feel like I've known you forever."

"Well, you haven't … "

"Look, I have nothing to hide. You see how I live, tomorrow morning I'll make the mud, and later I'll start on dinner. I want you to be here with me, by my side."

I stayed with him that night and the next day and the next night.

"Sena Bear, what do you think about doing Cop Council? You can hang out with us down at the gate and help us talk to the six-up."[*]

Miami Joe leaned his craggy body on a walking stick taller than him. His face was sooty black from tending the fire, a hand-rolled cigarette dangled from his mouth, and he held a fresh cup of mud. He reeked of campfire smoke.

"We want a pretty girl who's smart and who we like," he said.

"Yeah, Brother, I'd love to help out. I'll come with you now." I kissed Mud Bear, saying I'd return in a few hours.

Cop Council is the intermediate between Rainbow Family and the police. I felt destined to work with the police; in alt culture, a cop is 'the man,' but I once had a DEA agent save my life. After that, to me, cops were just people—some good, and some bad.

The Road Dogs camp was always at the entrance to the Gathering. They served as gatekeepers and they dealt with the parking, locals who sometimes came to start trouble, and the cops. The service they provided was an absolute necessity.

The Road Dogs camp was also called A-camp. "A" stood for alcohol. It was the only place in the Gathering alcohol was tolerated, since it was technically outside of the Gathering.

There were few rules at Gatherings but alcohol was strictly forbidden, for the simple reason that it *always* caused problems.

---

[*] Rainbow slang for police

I hung around A-camp sometimes. Many of them were Nam veterans. I would listen to their drunken war tales and cry with them.

"Hello officers," I smiled at the cops sitting in a parked car near the entrance to the Gathering. "I'm here to talk to you and create reconciliation between you and the Dogs."

"Reconciliation, huh? Well sounds all right but seems to me you're just a kid. Are you eighteen? Parents looking for you, anything like that?" The older, dark-haired trooper smiled a wide grin. You could see the chaw tucked into his cheek.

"No, I'm twenty-three!" I said. "I'll show you my driver's license."

I spent my young life being mistaken for older, but these days I favored floral-print lavender and turquoise dresses and didn't wear a speck of make-up. Suddenly, people thought I was a teen.

I loved my new job; I spent hours leaning into the open window of the state trooper's car answering endless questions about our lifestyle. Overall, they seemed bemused and most of what they asked for was reasonable.

"Now look here, Sena," the trooper said in a West-Virginia drawl, "We have not come and arrested anyone for nudity, we've been understanding, you might say easygoin' ... but when y'all hitchhike into town and cause problems stealing, and smoking marijuana, well it just ain't safe for y'all, and it ain't respectful to the god-fearing people that live in these parts."

"That's reasonable, Officer Moore," I said, "I'll make sure people leaving for town are informed, but I can't control them and for that I apologize. They just want to feel free. But I can assure you they are not stealing."

"Well aren't you in charge somehow? Don't you got some authority or something?"

"No, no one is in charge here. We're anarchists."

"Anarchists? Anarchists?" he chuckled, "Now don't you know what a mess this world would be in without some authority?" He turned to his partner who laughed and nodded in agreement.

I didn't debate; it wasn't my job to convert them. Besides, they had a point. I felt safer with them at the gate. Each day locals would show up feigning interest in the Gathering just to ogle naked women. And it was worse when they showed up at night, drunk.

Late night I hiked the two miles from the parking lot back to the kitchen. As I approached Mud Bear's tent, I heard voices. I listened outside for a moment and realized there was a girl with him. I walked away stunned. I guess I thought our relationship might last more than two nights.

I found a quilted blanket draped over a log near the fire. I wrapped myself up in it and slept in Mud Bear's hammock. In the morning, I stumbled over toward the campfire and sat down on a log next to a gorgeous girl.

"Do you want some breakfast?" Mud Bear asked over his shoulder. He avoided my gaze while tinkering with the coffee pot.

"Okay," I said.

He handed me a bowl of oatmeal then left camp with a bucket in each hand to fetch water.

The girl turned toward me. "I'm sorry Sister, I'm worried something is going on here. Maybe I got in the middle of you and Mud Bear?"

"Well, actually, I think you slept in my sleeping bag last night."

"Oh, no, my Sister, I'm so sorry." She leaned over and put her lanky arms around me.

"It's okay, I mean, I'm okay now. You can be with him."

"No, it's not like that. It's just that him and I hooked up at the last Gathering ... I didn't see you there. We planned to reconnect here but I guess he met you before I got here."

"I guess he did, this is only my second Gathering."

She gazed into my eyes with a steady loving look. Her eyes were clear blue and as round as her face, which was framed with flowing blond hair.

"I'm Lemongrass," she said, giving me a light kiss.

She went back to squeezing and hugging me. When Mud Bear returned, I barely spoke to him. When I went off to A-camp I removed my sleeping bag from his tent.

The rest of the Gathering I avoided Mud Bear, though from time to time I would stop by his kitchen and sit down with some of my friends from my first days there.

Sometimes Lemongrass was there and she'd pull me into her embrace.

A-camp was my new favorite hangout. I didn't drink at all, but my first stepfather put away a case of Black Label a day and my father never drove his Dodge van anywhere without a cooler stocked with fresh ice and Budweiser to drink while driving. I felt right at home.

Evenings I went to dinner circle and then wandered around camp with Sharon afterwards.

"Would you like a free hug?" I called out to a passerby. Sharon and I had joined Hug Patrol, a small group that spent evenings accosting people with offers of hugs. No one minded; in fact, they always said yes.

"Everyone needs more hugs," Sharon said.

I agreed. I knew I needed them desperately and to give them was to get them. I hoped they could touch the empty pit I felt inside.

One night at dinner a tiny woman walked to the center of the circle, clutching the skirt of her emerald gown so it just skimmed the grass.

"My name is Carrie and I've come from Washington, DC," she called out while leaning on a staff. "We have renamed Lafayette Park 'Peace Park' because there has been a peace vigil there since 1981. We need folks to come join us, we need to stop the US from going to war in the Persian Gulf."

Sharon and I decided right then to join the peace vigil. We were already planning to join an action in DC next month. We could join the vigil when it was over.

Where we would go after that was unknown.

THREE

October 1990
Capitol Hill
Washington, DC

"The nineties are gonna make the sixties look like the fifties," the speaker called out, "only this time, we're gonna win, we're gonna win!"

We started chanting, "We're gonna win, we're gonna win!"

The man abruptly walked off stage and the crowd grew quiet. We huddled around the portable stage: an eighteen-wheeler with its side panels dropped down. Then, he was back onstage, standing by the microphone, looking off in a daze.

We were gathered for a marijuana legalization rally. Our goal: to smoke pot on the Capitol steps.

"It is time we have medical marijuana available to those who need it," he shouted into the microphone.

He was Dana Beal, long-time activist and leader from the Youth International Party—the Yippies. His long sandy-colored hair was a tousle; his eyes, glassy and bloodshot, were a tired blue.

"Okay people, we are going to walk across the street to the Capitol and gather on the steps to listen to a couple of speakers, then, after, we will light up and smoke pot on the Capitol steps ... " He stopped mid-sentence to stare off into the distance. Minutes ticked by and then he said, "and after that, we will come back over here to the stage." He then climbed down, trudging in his cowboy boots. The bedraggled crowd formed an untidy line behind him. At one point, the police showed up and scolded us for blocking traffic, then mysteriously disappeared.

"You can jail a Revolutionary, but you can't jail the Revolution!" the speaker shouted. We cheered from above, the endless stone stairs our amphitheater.

Sharon leaned over and said, "I believe he was a black panther."

"Now, he continued, "it's unlikely you will get arrested today but you will take that risk if you smoke marijuana here on the Capitol steps. Let me tell you something, the reason you're not seeing cops is that in the sixties the powers that be realized that the media exposure given to demonstrations, rather than turn the public against the protestors as they hoped, inspired people to join them, resulting in a historic half million people marching on Washington to decry the carnage of the Vietnam War."

So, in order not to further our cause, they were ignoring us. In other words, as Gil Scott-Heron sang, "The Revolution Will Not Be Televised."

It was difficult to hear the speakers, as they did not have microphones. They stood facing us on the steps, yelling to be heard over the din of the city.

Then the moment we all anxiously awaited was here. A speaker called out, "Power to the people! The people demand legal marijuana now!" And with that, he took out a joint and lit it up.

Then, we all pulled out our joints and lit them, pinching the smoldering paper cones between our fingers. A cloud of thick, sweet smoke formed around us while we inhaled again, and again, until the tension of the trip, the city, and the cold slipped far away from our consciousness, until the corners of our mouths were pulled into grins.

We left the steps of the Capitol building, giddy with adrenaline. We danced and skipped, Sharon and I, and we crossed the busy street back to the stage recklessly, dashing in front of cars and holding our hands in the V of a peace sign. People honked and looked annoyed, but occasionally they would raise their hands, fingers locked into a peace sign, grinning self-consciously behind the wheel of a compact car.

Later, we walked towards Peace Park, trailing a scented cloud of marijuana and patchouli oil, and wearing an array of brightly colored clothes. Sharon sported a belt of jangling bells, and I tied a turkey feather in my hair with a leather string. We smiled and laughed, chatting loudly. Most of DC frowned at us in the grim rain. "Damn hippies!" a man shouted as he rushed by.

We arrived at Peace Park and found a small band of ragtag hippies manning a compact folding table with handouts about nuclear war. We looked for Carrie and found her, and she introduced us to Ellen and Thomas, the founders of the vigil. Ellen, a soft-spoken woman with long gray hair asked us how long we were going to stay.

"We are only here for the day but we want to come back in a few weeks and camp with you. We're not sure how long we will be here, but we want to help stop the Persian Gulf War," I said.

"I came to stop nuclear war. I've been here ten years. I was even married here."

I looked at my feet. I felt how soft I was. I spent years volunteering in soup kitchens and working with the homeless but I didn't sacrifice anything.

Now, I had. I gave up my job, my home, and my possessions in order to be a full-time volunteer. To hopefully become part of a community working towards something good, like serving the poor or housing veterans.

But I hoped to stop the war and leave here by late January, when the Rainbow Gathering was happening in Florida. There would be cute guys, and swimming, and sunshine, and weed.

FOUR

November 1990
Lafayette Park aka Peace Park
Washington, DC

A good-looking man in his forties with raven hair walked towards me on a blustery afternoon as I walked across the park to the payphones.

"Hello there miss, I'm Chief. Thanks for being here."

"Chief? Like an Indian Chief?"

"Yeah, I am, and you know who you look like?"

"Who?"

"A Chief's wife."

I laughed at what I sensed was a well-worn joke.

He smiled wide and held out an orange fleece blanket with etchings of Native Americans wearing feather headdresses and sitting atop horses.

"You should have this. Do you know how to wear it?" he asked.

I didn't, so he showed me how to fold the blanket in half and cut a slit near the center.

"Now you can wear it like a poncho," he said.

Soon I was wearing many blankets at once while trying to keep warm on the DC streets, and soon, I would learn that Chief was a homeless alcoholic who, when sober, was wise and charming, but when drunk was confused and incoherent.

Sharon and I had a daily routine. We woke, often on the ground though our van was parked nearby. We rolled up our sleeping bags, locked them in our van, and then walked to the soup kitchen where we volunteered.

After our shift we were allowed to cook our own food: a pot of vegetable stew. We carried the steaming hot food to the park in a large bucket and passed out servings in paper cups.

At noon, we joined a daily prayer vigil near the White House fountain with nuns from the Catholic Workers. They gave us yellow prayer cards with a rose etching and the heading, "A Prayer for Saddam Hussein and George Bush." We read it aloud, praying for enlightenment of the minds of those leaders, "... so that all civilians and soldiers in the Persian Gulf would be protected from the sufferings of war."

Images of the Vietnam War were splashed on the pages of my father's *Time* magazine. There were haunting photos of crying, dirty children with desperate eyes. At times, they were naked and running while in the background palm trees engulfed in flames dotted the landscape.

There were photos of weary soldiers clad in green, flanked by helicopters, marching through fields of high grass. They bent forward, holding large guns with both hands.

On other pages, colorfully dressed demonstrators carried signs. I saw one that said: "No War!"

"Daddy, what's war?" I asked.

"War is a very sad thing, it's a terrible tragedy. It is many people getting hurt."

"Oh," I said, perplexed. "Did you go to the war?"

"No, I got out of it because of you. Your first war protest was in the womb. Because your mother was pregnant with you I was excused from the draft. It means I didn't have to go. It was a time when they left men with children at home."

I still didn't know what war was but those disturbing images were burned into my brain forever.

On a cold Saturday night, we rang the bell at a large Victorian house and the door swung open.

"Hi, we've been protesting down at Peace Park. Carrie said we should come here," I said.

"Yes, come in. I'm Diego, welcome to the Tree House," he said, peering at us from under a black cowboy hat. He was friendly, but his eyes looked troubled.

We walked through the double glass doors and into a large hall where a grand wooden staircase dominated. It was our first visit to the infamous house, a place where activists had gathered for years.

Yippie posters lined the hallways, supporting peace, community, and guns.

"These are hippies that support guns," I said to Sharon.

"Yeah, I see that," she said, "I'm not sure what I think about it." "I'm afraid of guns," I said.

I was shot at point blank as a teenager. The bullets flew past me but the explosion was deafening and left me shaken for days.

I did not grow up around guns even though I'm from the boonies. My father bought a set of hunting rifles when he was a teenager and they never left the wall rack till finally, he sold them.

"I can't hunt, I could never shoot an animal, I just couldn't," he told me as he collected them from our apartment.

Later that night we saw Diego again in the living room sitting on the floor with a circle of people around him where he rolled joints and preened. "I gotta tell you guys about the time I blocked the entrance to the DOJ!" he said, licking the glue on a rolling paper.

"Now, it was summertime," he continued, "and, I was .... I mean, I was trying ... " His eyelids closed, and he dropped his chin, nodding off. A girl next to him elbowed him in the ribs and he woke up for a minute. "Yeah, what was I saying?"

"The story about the DOJ," someone said, passing one of the circulating joints to me.

"Yeah, yeah," he said, lighting the cigarette that dangled from his lips as he nodded off again.

Sharon and I became frequent visitors. The Tree House was full of radicals, therefore famous names from the '60s would drop in at parties and wow us with stories. Saturday nights there was always a giant potluck. I began doing dishes and cleaning the huge kitchen while there and that, it turns out, was a rare contribution that made me a sought-after houseguest.

"I wish I had a dreadlock wig," my friend Peter said. "I spend all day testifying in Congress for NORML[†] and then no one will pass me a joint when I'm here. They think I'm a narc."

He lived at the Tree House, and like everyone there he was a serious activist. A towhead from the heartland with pallid blue eyes, ashen skin, and a conservative haircut, he spent his days in a suit, yet he was surely as radical as the black-beret-wearing roommates in this house.

There seemed to be a few drug addicts living there. When I asked about them my friend Jessie said, "We minister to heroin addicts."

"How do you help people on heroin?"

"We try to get them in rehab or we let them quit and be sick here. Sometimes we raise money to send them to Holland. There's a cure there, it's an herb called ibogaine."

"I never heard about it," I said.

"Yeah," she said, "it's from West Africa and it's a miracle for people that are physically addicted. We have a video on it if you want to watch it."

I didn't know any heroin users. After my short stint in drug dealing involving cocaine, I'd never seen a hard drug again.

"Hey, look at this!" Sharon said, pointing to a group of men running up the sidewalk in front of the White House. Across the street, a group of us were sitting on the curb, playing guitar. We stood to watch, and the men began leaping, one after another, over the wrought iron fence. They ran across the lawn towards that famous fountain. In seconds, the fountain's spray changed to red as they tossed vials of blood into the water.

[†] National Organization for the Reform of Marijuana Laws

Men in uniforms came running from all directions, tackling the group.

We ran across the street, and saw the men being marched away in handcuffs.

Later, we learned it was their own blood they tossed into the water to remind people of the bloodshed toll of war.

Within hours, armed men were sprinkled along the immaculate grounds of the White House. They stood silent with guns ready, black ball cap rims hiding their faces.

No one else was going over that fence.

FIVE

December 1990
Lafayette Park aka Peace Park
Washington, DC

You rows of houses! you window-pierc'd façades! you roofs!
You porches and entrances! you copings and iron guards!
You windows whose transparent shells might expose so much!
You doors and ascending steps! you arches!
You gray stones of interminable pavement! You trodden crossings!

From all that has touch'd you I believe you have imparted
to yourselves, and now would impart the same secretly to me,
From the living and the dead you have peopled your
impassive surfaces, and the spirits thereof would be evident
and amicable with me.

***

"Thanks guys! Thank you for being here!"

After they delivered their nightly report live in front of the White House the CNN guys would jog by and call out to us; the reporter in his suit, and the crewmen carrying camera and boom. I loved them for that.

In the evenings, I would often climb on a streetlamp directly across from the White House. The iron lamppost had a decorative circlet near the base. I perched on it, my arms encircling the post as I leaned back.

"President Bush," I would holler, "we don't want war! No more war! Don't send our troops to war!"

I did this until I was hoarse then I would retreat back to the shadows of the park and bury myself deep inside my sleeping bag.

Light snow fell some nights and the cops were directed to wake us hourly to make sure we were not frozen to death. Some apologized, some seemed annoyed, while one kicked us, and growled. I dubbed him Mean-cop.

"Get up you ingrates, get on your feet right now!" Mean-cop said.

"Come on, it's freezing," I said, pulling the sleeping bag over my head.

Then he kicked me and I scrambled to my feet.

Dawn was just breaking over the sleeping city and the chill of the night still lingered in the air.

"Go to a shelter then! Sleeping in public places is illegal."

"But we are here on a prayer vigil—"

"Shut up and move! Get the fuck out of my face, and take your stuff with you."

Sharon and I tossed our sleeping gear in the van, locked it, and headed to Hardees for hot tea. As we waited in line, we saw Mean-cop come through the door.

"Uh-oh," Sharon said under her breath.

He spotted us and smirked, clearly relishing the added opportunity to fuck with us.

"You need to get the hell out of my city and if you don't like it, get out of my country too. You people are disgusting."

Neither Sharon nor I replied. His face was filled with fury. I wanted to talk to him but I didn't think it was safe. He was the law, and he was super pissed.

Mid-month there was a great influx of people; boys and girls on respite from (Grateful) Dead tour, distant Rainbow Family, and college kids on winter break.

A young man with messy dreadlocks and a bushy beard approached me on a sunny afternoon, guitar in hand, wearing gloves that were cut so bare fingertips touched the strings.

"Sister, do you want to go play some music with me over by the capitol? Do you know John Lennon lyrics?"

"I do. I also love George Harrison."

He started to croon my favorite song, "Give Me Love," over light strums on the guitar. He smiled at me, and I smiled back.

We strolled towards the capitol building. He told me to take his arm and I did, and we stood in front of those grand marble steps and sang songs of peace until the feds shoed us away.

Harmony was his name. We walked to the National Mall and set our ponchos on the lawn to insulate against the cold ground. We sat down and he dug in his canvas rucksack and pulled out a blue and white book.

"Have you read the Aquarian Gospel?" he asked.

"No, I never heard of it." He handed me the dog-eared book.

"You can borrow mine for a while."

I read that book feverishly, till finally I went and bought my own copy.

In it, Jesus travels the world teaching and learning from Persia to India. The lessons mirrored much of what I read from Paramahansa Yogananda, my favorite teacher.

Since a young age I had great curiosity about the spiritual world. Once Seely died, I developed a near obsession with the afterlife and contemplation became my main interest.

Sitting on the sidewalk near the White House, I wore a long pink and red scarf like a loose hijab as I read passages from the Aquarian Gospel into a microphone plugged into an amp. Harmony strummed quietly on the guitar beside me.

"He said: if you would live the perfect life, give forth your life in service for your kind, and for the forms of life that men esteem the lower forms of life," I read, holding the tattered blue book in my lap.

People gathered around us to listen and I hoped the passages would stir something in them, as they did in me.

"Hey, you're that girl that reads the Aquarian Gospel down at the park, right?" People would ask when they saw me at the Tree House shindigs.

It was not anything I had expected to become known for doing, especially with my past. But no one knew I was a one-time drug lord. I never spoke of those days.

I was never tough or dangerous. I was soft, unwitting, and thoroughly unfit to reign in a dog-eat-dog world of violence, backstabbing, and bullying.

"*Boozhoo*, greetings, we have come to pray for peace with you," an aged man with silky white hair flowing over woolen robes spoke to us. "We are Ojibwa elders, and we have brought a peace drum here from our Nation in Canada."

Two grandmothers and two grandfathers nearby placed the large drum on the ground between them and began to tap with heavily padded sticks. It made a thumping sound, muffled and soft but you could still feel it pass through your body. The beat was slow and it went on for hours and then, around the clock.

Demonstrators joined in, and people took shifts drumming and it never stopped until the day George Bush declared, "Those damn drums are keeping me up at night!"

After that, the police came and wrested the peace drum from the Ojibwas' hands.

I went with some people to a nearby music store. We told them of our plight, and they promptly donated drums and sticks. Only a few hours later those drums were taken from us too.

By the next day, we were getting discarded five-gallon white buckets from bakeries and delis and beating on them with pieces of wood scraps we found in alleyways. The cops took those too.

Garry Trudeau, who wrote the comic strip *Doonesbury*, started making visits to the park and writing strips about the protestors and the drums.

I befriended the police stationed around the White House and the park. The officers I came to know by name were inquisitive, helpful, and a bit strict in the way that you would expect a federal cop to be.

"We're going to do an Om circle tonight," I told Jack when he arrived to do his evening shift policing the park.

"What's an Om circle?" he asked.

"It's a meditation where we make a simple sound. It's basically a prayer for peace."

"So there's not gonna be any problems, right? Right? I'm counting on you, Sena."

"I promise. We're going to stand in a circle right here in front of the fountain and join hands and pray."

"Okay, but if you have any drums were going to take them away. You can't be disturbing the President of the United States."

"I understand but I just want to say that we want him to hear us, that we want him to know that we are here and we are opposed to sending troops to the Persian Gulf."

He sighed. "I wish you guys could just send letters."

Chief was planning to lead the Om. As the sun went down a dozen of us gathered in front of the White House. Standing in a circle, we joined hands. CNN asked to film us and we agreed. We closed our eyes and started our chant while the bright lights of the TV cameras shined on us.

"Oooooooooommmmmmmmmmmmmm," we chanted. This went on for some time until the Om was all I could hear, my eyes shut to the city around me.

At Peace Park, so many people arrived that actions were now happening daily. When we heard there was a gathering for prayer at the Lincoln Memorial, Harmony and I decided to go.

Once there we joined a large circle of people holding hands. Harmony walked into the center of the circle with his guitar and began to play "Give Peace a Chance."

We joined in and sang the chorus on a loop.

A small band of people dressed completely in black with their faces covered arrived. They wore black ski masks and carried a large American flag on a pole. In moments, they lit the flag on fire and continued to carry it while flaming.

"Agent Provocateurs!" Someone cried out.

The circle broke and Harmony stopped playing. I walked over to him.

"Who are they?"

"I don't know, but here comes the cops."

The police were now descending on horseback from the small hill they watched us from.

"Don't group us in with them, we don't burn flags!" I cried in protest as the police chased us away, directing us with black batons.

Back outside the White House, I went to talk to one of the Park Police I knew named Steve. The Park Police governed the parks, the monuments, and gave permits for demonstrations.

"Steve," I said, "you know that was not us, right? We would not burn a flag; we would never burn anything. We pray for peace and we sing for peace."

"Who do you think it was then?" he asked.

"Not anyone we know. They were wearing masks and all in black."

I didn't mention the Agent Provocateurs, the much whispered-about secret government agents rumored to go to peaceful rallies and try to provoke the police into using violence against demonstrators.

Each day, Harmony strummed a selection of peace-themed songs.

"Come on, Harmony, we gotta play 'Give Me Love' again," I'd say, tugging on his arm until he tossed the colorful strap of his guitar over his shoulder.

A small group surrounded him and sang along. I said the lyrics like a prayer, hands folded, pleading for peace on earth and connection with God that would make this world somehow bearable.

A beautiful pixie named Deb with a sweet smile took my hand while we stood singing.

"Are you camped here?" she asked.

"Yes, we have been for a bit."

"My boyfriend and I want to invite demonstrators over for dinner. Would you want to come?"

Soon a small group of us were having dinner a couple of nights a week at Deb's. We brought food and we cooked and sometimes slept there, on couches and on the floor.

Emmanuel always led the prayer circle before dinner. Stern and sincere, he showed confidence and reverence for God. He had a solemn face, with large, reflective eyes.

"Let us see God in the faces of all those we share the earth with, let us remember him always, and let us give thanks for all we receive from him."

We bowed our heads while he spoke and ended prayers always with an Om in the Rainbow tradition.

Cops on horses are a common sight in DC but as the size of our group of demonstrators grew, the number of Park Police grew also. Their specialty is crowd control and now, they surrounded the park.

One night there was obvious tension. The horses stepped back and forth nervously, their iron shoes dinging the concrete walkways streaming through the park. The horses moved a step closer, the police sitting high atop them with gear and helmets. We took a step back.

"You need to clear this area now; we're clearing this area!" One of the cops said through a bullhorn.

A few people wandered away but most of us stayed in place. There was a period of still. Ironically, someone had brought a bucket of discarded carnations to the park that afternoon and I was holding a small handful of flowers. Thinking of the iconic photo of a man putting a flower into the barrel of an M16 during the '60s, I walked along the line of horses.

"Can I offer you a flower?" I asked each cop, holding a flower up towards them.

"No," most said, or simply shook their head. Many never looked at me.

High on the back of a huge brown horse a cop looked down at me with a warm grin.

"Good evening officer," I said, holding out a flower. "How are you doing?"

"Hi there, I'm good, thanks," he said, taking the red carnation from me and putting it through the buttonhole of his breast pocket.

The cop to his right looked at him with disdain. "The captain's not gonna like this. You're not allowed to put that on your uniform," he said.

The cop with the flower ignored him and continued looking at me with that relaxed smile.

"My name is Bill. I just got here from San Francisco," he said.

"Really? Did you transfer here?"

"No, they sent for extra reinforcements. They expect these demonstrations to get pretty big."

"Really? I hope so, I mean, we're trying to save lives is all."

Having a candid conversation with a mounted cop was unusual. I hoped the flower gesture had somehow worked.

Then, the moment passed.

"You need to immediately disband and clear this area!" a cop thundered through a bullhorn.

Then, the towering horses were slowly stepping towards us, closing in on us; the fear of being trampled was palpable.

Next, they smashed into us, the police kicking and hitting us with clubs from above. Darkness fell, and the clamor of the crowd engulfed us.

Sharon grabbed my hand and we scurried towards the edge of the crowd, trying to escape those approaching hooves.

SIX

January 1991
Lafayette Park aka Peace Park
Washington, DC

"What is wrong with you? You look ridiculous, why are you dressed like that! Why do you hate America?"

A burly young woman with blond hair pulled into a ponytail approached me, spitting questions rapidly.

Some of her friends joined her and now, just a few feet from the White House, two sets of women faced off. They had taken a bus from the Midwest to support the war. We had been living here six weeks protesting the war.

"Your sign says 'Nuke Iraq'! Do you even know what that means? You're talking about innocent women and children, elderly people, babies! They don't have anything to do with Saddam Hussein, he's a dictator!" I was yelling now.

"Screw them," her friend screamed at me. Her sign simply said: 'Fuck Iraq'.

"I think we should free Kuwait, just because you're selfish and lazy doesn't mean we shouldn't help them!" Another girl chimed in, her sign said 'Free Kuwait'.

"You can't free a place that isn't free!" I argued back. "In Kuwait women can't even drive, a bunch of women protested the war by driving and getting arrested!"

"Just tell us why you are so dirty and disgusting?"

"What are you even talking about? We are out here trying to save lives; we are out here feeding the homeless!"

"You're nothing but a bunch of losers!" The first girl said. "You're a cruel and hateful person and in no way can you call yourself a Christian! A Christian would never say, "fuck" an entire country full of *people*!"

I can't tell you what my friends said because I couldn't hear them over my shouting. There were about seven girls arguing loudly when cops appeared and stepped between us, pushing us apart, forming a blockade with their bodies.

"Let's not get into trouble here ladies, move along ... go back with your own group."

"They came over to us," I said

"Well, ignore them, then," the cop said.

We dispersed but I never forgot the argument or the signs they carried. I could not fathom what had driven them to such hatred.

Working with the homeless, I met a profusion of Vietnam vets. Plagued by nightmares, easily agitated, and broken inside, the men I met had scars—deep emotional wounds. Some had wheelchairs, some had canes, and some spent their days high on alcohol or drugs, straining to keep the anguish at bay. To add insult, they were now pariahs.

Society abandoned them to their decay.

Now, a generation of young people faced a future like the vets I knew. To not try to prevent that was to be complicit.

I walked to the bakery to pick up day-old bread with a Brother named James from the park. After, he dragged a clear trash bag full of croissants, hard rolls, and slices of bread down the freezing streets. I carried a paper bag with long loaves of French bread sticking out. This was food for hungry demonstrators. Now that there were dozens of people sleeping in the park, gathering supplies took more work each day.

We turned a corner, and bumped right into a group of pro-war demonstrators marching in the street. The yelled at us:

"Hey hippies, fuck you!"

"Go live in Iraq!"

"Free Kuwait!"

A line of police formed in order to keep them from us. They continued yelling insults as the cops held them back and I silently prayed that blue line would hold.

Our hearts racing, we walked faster until I heard a journalist on a payphone hollering in rapid French. I stopped and saw that the whole bank of phones had journalists on them, some quickly writing in notebooks while talking. Time slowed as I stood trying to make sense of the scene.

I looked toward James and asked, "What is going on?" "I don't know ... something ... "

The French journalist dropped the phone and stepped directly in front of me. He was so riled he simply left the black receiver dangling on its metal cord. "You selfish, greedy Americans! You want all the oil for yourselves, you just want everything for yourselves!"

I was silent in disbelief. I was wearing army blankets, living outside in the cold, and carrying discarded bread.

Before I could reply a group of people from the park ran up.

"We've been looking for you guys, Saddam just bombed Israel! They're bombing Israel! The war is starting!" they said. "Oh no! No! We've got to pray," I said.

We joined hands and kneeled down on the sidewalk, bowing our heads.

"Heavenly God, please help the people of Israel, and of Iraq, protect them from the horrors of war, protect us all," I said.

Some people thought I joined a cult but Rainbow had no charismatic leader, no indoctrination or treatise, and no requirements. It was a subculture and I long ago adapted to living in subcultures; first as a juvenile delinquent amid dissolute teens, then as a teen drug dealer among prostitutes and criminals, and now as an activist camping with hippies.

Om Tea Home. That's what Sharon and I named our kitchen. When we started our journeys Sharon had drawn a large Om symbol with white chalk on the black tire cover mounted on the front of our van, signifying peace.

"We are starting a free herbal tea dispensary. We will be traveling across the country, setting up camp and serving hot tea in addition to volunteering locally," I told the members of the co-op where we worked.

They donated a huge steel pot and mesh strainer to our kitchen, and we cashed in our hours for brown paper bags filled with chamomile, valerian root, and raspberry leaf.

It was time to leave this village of monuments.

I could barely face the black wall of names that made up the Vietnam Veterans Memorial. All those names! It hurt to read them.

I often peered at Arlington from the other side of the Potomac, while I sang songs at the Lincoln Memorial. The endless white tombstones broke my heart.

The blinking light on the Washington Monument was often in my field of vision as I lay down to sleep. Why was it an obelisk? I often wondered as I drifted off.

We had our last dinner with Deb, and she hugged me tightly while she sniffled.

"Sweetie, Debbie, please come with us. You know you can."

She confided in me her unhappiness with her relationship over these past weeks.

"I can't, I just can't," she said, and she slipped a handmade silver filigree ring off her finger and put it on mine.

I never saw her again, but I still wear the ring today.

"Sharon and I are going to the Gathering in Florida. If anyone wants to come with us, we have room," I announced at Peace Park.

We got a few riders; Tennessee, a quiet girl with messy red dreadlocks, an adorable girl from Wyoming named Prairie with a Holly Hobbie dress and chestnut braids, and Jai, a preening, handsome Buddhist boy who had just shaved his head.

The last two weeks Sharon and I had been sleeping at the home of two Brothers named Peter and Joe. The park had gotten crowded and rather dangerous. Counter protesters would show up drunk late at night and want to fight us!

I liked Joe but I couldn't figure out how we could be together since he had a job and a house in DC. Still, I spent a lot of time talking to him and getting close to him. In general, I was always looking for a boyfriend.

"This is Prairie, she just got here from Wyoming and she's going to be part of our kitchen," I said, introducing her to Joe and Pete.

We ate dinner together and later we played a game of Scrabble. We all took our places to sleep, which were mostly on the floor in our sleeping bags.

In the morning, I made oatmeal and when I called for people to come eat, Prairie came out of Joe's bedroom. I was instantly hurt, and a little stunned. After that, I no longer wondered about him and I.

"Goodbye, we love you," Harmony gave me a tight hug and brushed away a tear.

As we were hugging family goodbye, a young Brother approached and asked if I could help with a runaway girl. She was sixteen and looking for a ride to Florida to go to the Gathering. He took my hand and led me across the park to her.

"My name is Sparrow," she said, weeping and falling into my arms, "Singing Sparrow. I'm looking for a ride to the Rainbow Gathering, I have to get away from my mother; she won't stop hitting me and screaming at me. I can't live with her anymore." Her dark eyes brimmed with fear.

I embraced her. "It's okay, we're gonna help you."

I wanted to smooth her raven hair, but she was much taller than me.

"I'm from New York, you're allowed to be on your own at sixteen." Fresh tears streamed down her fawny cheeks.

"I understand, Sparrow. I've been through that, my mother was the same way. You can come be part of our kitchen."

There wasn't a lost girl I turned away from, and there wasn't one I met who didn't remind me of myself. I didn't even think about harboring a runaway or a minor.

Shortly after I turned sixteen, I was walking down the street in Spanish Town, where I had an apartment. A cop stopped his car and hopped out.

"Are you a runaway?" he asked.

"What?" I said. "No, I'm not."

"Well, we've been looking for you. You need to come with me, there's a report on you."

"No, I'm not coming with you," I said, "The law in New York State says I can live on my own at sixteen years old and I'm not going anywhere. I am legally allowed to live on my own."

He looked exasperated.

"Let me see your driver's license," he said.

I handed him my learner's permit.

"Okay," he said, and handed the paper back to me.

He walked towards his car and then slid in, slamming his door shut in frustration.

The guy walking with me was amazed.

"Chica! You're so fucking crazy! I can't believe the cop just walked away!"

"I know my rights and I'm not going to a group home!" I said.

The officer had been in the car talking on his radio. He rolled down the window as he drove off. "Call your mother, she's looking for you!" he said.

Then, he was gone.

Now, I was sure I could protect Sparrow the same way I had protected myself.

PART TWO
THE GATHERINGS

When the earth is ravaged and the animals are dying, a new tribe of people shall come unto the earth from many colors, classes, and creeds, and by their actions and deeds they shall make the earth green again. They will be known as the warriors of the Rainbow.

Old Native American Prophecy

SEVEN

Jan 1991
Driving South from DC
Northern Florida

I think heroic deeds were all conceiv'd in the open air,

...

I think I could stop here myself and do miracles;
I think whatever I shall meet on the road I shall like, and whoever beholds me shall like me;
I think whoever I see must be happy.

***

"Come on over here little lady," a guy called to me from the window of his Camaro. We pulled off the expressway in South Carolina for French fries and now, we occupied a nearby meadow, rolling down hills like kids, praising the sunshine and warmth.

I walked towards his car assuming he wanted to ask about where we were from.

"Hello." I smiled and put my hand on his door.

"I just wanted to give you this," he said, handing me a business card. "You should be on your way now, because we hate hippies, too."

Before I could respond he gunned the sports car and took off. I was confused until I read his card: *Knight of the Imperial Wizard of the Ku Klux Klan*, then his name.

"Oh my God, you guys! That was the Klan! They want us to leave!"

Everyone crowded around me to read the card.

"I say let's get moving," said Sharon.

"I agree, let's keep driving." I said.

We piled into the van and departed, crossing into the state of Florida late that night.

The next morning, using a map, I picked a small town on the east coast north of Ocala, where the Gathering was happening. We still had a few days to play and the ocean beckoned.

We parked in the center of town adjacent to a large park. Jai opened the side door of the van and Sharon sat on the doorsill and rolled cigarettes from loose tobacco.

I crossed the street to visit the park. I wore a long purple floral dress, beaded earrings, and bare feet.

A man called out to me.

"Hey Sister, is the show in town?"

"I don't know," I called back, continuing my amble.

People were always mistaking me for a Deadhead but the Grateful Dead was my father's favorite band, not mine.

When I moved back to my hometown my father insisted on taking me to a Grateful Dead show. I resisted. Though I idolized him as a child, I altogether rejected his lifestyle as a teen.

Both my parents abandoned me to indulge their addictions. Because of the demons they wrestled, my profound suffering was invisible. Now, I was on a mission to be nothing like them. To be the antithesis of everything they were.

Still, I finally agreed to go to Madison Square Garden with my father to see the Dead.

Music blared from a distant stage while a silvery voice sang "Black Muddy River" to a crowd of undulant fans.

We walked along the corridors towards our seats.

"It's a beautiful time," a young woman said to us in a singsong voice as we passed.

A garland of tiny blue flowers crowned her head. Her wavy blond hair fell nearly to her waist. She sat on the floor with her legs extended. A long turquoise skirt skimmed the tops of her bare feet.

Standing around her were folks who looked as if they time-traveled here from 1969. They wore colored glass beads, strings of tiny bells, leather bracelets, and long dresses with flowered print. The men wore tie-dyes aplenty.

"Hippies, Daddy, did you see that? Those were hippies! I didn't know there were hippies anymore."

"Oh yeah," he said, "There've always been hippies here, it's kind of timeless."

Now, I looked indistinguishable from those I admired that night.

We spent the next two days hanging out at the town square, where a five-minute walk brought you to the beach.

One night Sharon and I slept on benches along the boardwalk. The waves rhythmically hitting the shore lulled us to sleep. In the morning, a middle-aged man in a short-sleeve dress shirt walked up to us while humming to himself.

"Good morning ladies!" he said, offering us a large white bag. Sharon took it and he was off, continuing his stroll along the wooden planks. We opened the folded bag to find coffees and Danish pastries.

"Thank you!" we called after him.

He was smitten with the joy of surprising strangers with gifts.

I took a walk alone along the sea. I prayed daily for things big and small, but mostly small. I closed my eyes and pictured pineapple juice, my favorite. Then I gave prayers of thanks for having received the juice.

Later I told Sharon, "Today, I asked for pineapple juice."

"Hey family!" A tall Brother in faded jeans approached us with hugs. "You here for the Gathering? There is an amazing free lunch at a local church, why don't you come with me?"

The seven of us piled in the VW and drove over.

"Pineapple juice?"

A tiny white-haired lady wearing an apron was holding out a pink plastic cup filled with the juice.

I squealed and got down on my knees in an instant.

"Thank you God! Thank you!" I raised my clasped hands skyward, then put my face to the floor. She turned to Sharon. "Oh my, is she alright?"

Before she could answer I got up. "I prayed for pineapple juice just this morning. This juice came to me straight from God!"

"Well then, my dear, please take some," she said, smiling.

"I don't even need it now," I said, taking it anyway. It was the best pineapple juice I'd ever drank.

Later that day, back alongside the park, two policemen approached us.

"We are gonna need to see some ID from everyone here, please."

The side door of our van was open while we lounged inside our tiny parlor. Sharon passed hand-rolled cigarettes to Prairie and Jai and all three were smoking.

"What is that?" the cop asked, gesturing towards Sharon with one finger. "Marijuana?"

"No, it's tobacco," said Sharon, handing him her embossed package of Drum.

They told us a local storeowner called the police thinking we were smoking joints.

"Well, we are still gonna need to see some IDs," the cops said.

They collected our various IDs and took them to their patrol car to run them.

Sparrow was sitting in the van crying. "They're going to make me go back home, they're going to make me go back to my mother's, I know it."

I sat next to her and held her.

"Why did you give them your ID? You could've said you lost it … I guess we should've made a plan, shit. It's going to be alright Sparrow, I promise."

A few minutes later, the police handed IDs back to everyone except for Sparrow. The older cop asked her to step outside the van and I went with her, holding her hand.

"Young lady, you're a runaway and your mother has reported you missing. We're going to need to take you into the station to get you back home."

Sparrow burst into tears and grabbed onto me. "Sena, Sena, don't let them take me, I don't want to go, I don't want to go home!" "Look, officer, she's from New York State and they allow girls to be on their own at sixteen. I lived on my own at the same age because my mother abandoned me. I know what she's going through, she's from an abusive home and I want her to stay with me. I'm taking care of her."

"I'm sorry, I just can't do that," the officer said, putting his hand on Sparrow's upper arm and giving her a gentle tug.

"No, no, no, I don't want to go, I don't want to go." She was crying hard now.

"Sparrow," I said, "just go with him and we will figure something out. We will get you back."

She looked at me with huge frightened eyes, not knowing whether to believe me or not.

"I promise," I said, "we will come and get you. You're not alone, we're family. We will be right behind you."

"Okay," she said, tears still rolling down her face.

The officer apologized to me again and led her away to his car. I sat down on the curb and started crying. Jai came over and crouched down behind me, putting his hands on my shoulders.

"Sister, don't cry. We're going to get her back, you said so."

"Yeah but what if I can't? I don't know if I can," I said.

"You can, with God you can do it, we believe in you. Let's go get our Sparrow back."

We all jumped into the van and drove across town looking for the police station. As we drove we sang a song Sparrow wrote and often sang for us. All of us were chanting:

Love in and out our selves,

Freedom in and out our minds,
Peace in and out the world.

We burst into the police station—all of us—singing and chanting. The officer who took Sparrow rushed into the waiting room.

"You can't all be in here, I get that you're upset, but you're too loud. I can't have you singing in here ... look, I'm sorry, but you just gotta wait outside."

"You," he said to me, "you can stay here but everyone else needs to go."

"Thank you officer," I said, sitting down on the gray sofa in the waiting area.

Outside, they continued singing Sparrow's song. I could see them through the tall glass windows framing the door and I mouthed the lyrics under my breath with them. Jai approached the glass and used his hands to sign the music: putting his hands over his heart, placing his fingers on his temples, and then tracing a circle.

One of my favorite stories in the Aquarian Gospel was when Jesus went to Greece and saw a ship sinking, not far offshore, as he walked along the beach. Many people on the beach were on their knees praying for the drowning people. Jesus jumped into the water and started saving as many people as he could.

Later, Jesus lectures the people on the beach and says there is no benefit in an idle prayer.

"When human hands can do no more, thus God helps," he said, explaining that God will give you strength to rescue many more people than you can on your own, but prayer without action will not work.

'When human hands can do no more, thus God helps!' I began saying to myself in a whisper while I paced the waiting room. I repeated the phrase over and over and over.

The police officer came out to see me.

"I'm sorry, but her mother wants her back home. I'm going to need to send her up north."

"I understand," I said. "I can't thank you enough, you've been wonderful." Somehow, I was still undaunted. I felt sure she was coming with me.

"Do you want to come in back and see her?" he asked.

"Yes, please." I said.

He led me down a long hall to an office with a large conference table where Sparrow sat. I sat down next to her and hugged her tight.

"I'm so sorry honey, but please don't lose faith. Wherever you're meant to be God will bring you. Let's pray together. Everyone is outside singing your beautiful song."

We quietly started repeating the lyrics to her song together. A woman came to the office door to fetch the officer and he left, excusing himself from the room.

In a bit, he came through the door breathless, almost excited.

"I can barely believe this," the officer said, "but her mother called back and you can take her."

"Wait, what? I can take her!"

"Yes, I have your ID, I know who she's with, and I told her mother that you are a wonderful person."

"Oh my God, officer, how can I ever thank you enough?"

Sparrow was crying again and I was holding her hand. We walked out into the lobby and the cop held open the front door.

We walked over that threshold, out of the police station, and into the sunshine feeling she'd been freed by a miracle. The officer walked out with us.

"Honestly," the cop said to me, "I never met a person with faith like yours and it has moved me." He turned to Jai and Sharon.

"You people are all so beautiful, really, I never met people like you! I wish I had your faith."

A tear rolled down his cheek. I took a small crystal out of a hemp cloth bag I kept in the pocket of my dress. I handed him the piece of quartz.

"Oh thank you, thank you, I will always keep this with me!"

"Keep it with you while you're at work. Ask God for protection every day. I ask God for everything I need and I am always answered."

"You all have changed my life. I can't believe what I witnessed here today… it is an inspiration."

And then he hugged me. A middle-aged Florida cop embraced me and sniffled.

We celebrated that night, eating pizza and smoking herb while parked on the outskirts of town near the ocean; we watched the crashing waves while Baaba Maal played quietly in the background.

Sharon and I put our sleeping bags in the sand. It was our last night in this beach town before we headed to the Gathering. The girls followed us but Jai slept in the van.

In the morning Jai told us a cop came by and said we needed to move along. Then he spied the bowl and baggie of pot we left lying on top of the sink.

"I'll just get rid of this oregano for ya," the cop said, tossing the bag of herb and pipe into some scrub.

"He never came back either," Jai said, "so I just went back to sleep."

"I found it!" Sharon called out from behind the van. She came around to us holding the pipe and intact bag of weed.

"Holy shit, these cops are so cool and chill, I can't believe it." Jai said. "He left that there for us!"

"We've got good cop karma," I said.

Later that night we arrived at the regional Gathering in Ocala National Forest. It was too late to carry-in our gear so we camped in the parking lot. I slept in the hammock that emerged overhead when the camper van was popped up, treasuring the tiny sliver of aloneness.

I knew that by morning, I'd be back in the fray.

EIGHT

Feb 1991
Ocala National Forest
Florida

The first few nights I continued to sleep in the van, trying to get some deep rest. One night Jai offered to walk with me to the parking lot.

"So, would you be okay if I stayed with you tonight?" he said as we arrived at the van.

"Yeah, sure," I said.

We folded the couch down into a bed and spread blankets on top.

"Let's cuddle," he said as we climbed underneath the pile of bedding.

Then, he kissed me.

"Wait," I said, softly pushing him back with my hand on his chest. "I didn't know you felt that way."

"I'm crazy about you," he said. "You're a warrior woman. You didn't know?"

"No, I didn't know."

I was drawn to Jai. He had a sweet face, though he rarely smiled. He always looked uneasy and bleary-eyed. I thought it was part of his depth, plus I was attracted to troubled people.

I spent the next day cautious and confused around Jai. He wasn't pursuing me; he still seemed aloof and distant. I shrugged it off, attributing it to his beautiful mind.

A few nights later, he and Prairie walked into camp hand-in-hand. They sat down next to me on the log I was crouched on as I stoked the fire.

"Listen, Sister, Jai and I are now a couple," Prairie said.

I didn't say anything but tears filled my eyes.

"I'm sorry," Jai said.

"I'm sorry too," Prairie said, "you know I love you! We're gonna leave the Gathering, it'll be easier that way. We're gonna go to Tennessee and see some friends there."

With that they hugged and kissed us goodbye, retrieved their stuff, and were gone.

Jai and Prairie's dramatic nighttime exit left me keenly aware that my taste in men remained terrible.

"Hey Sister, I'm Sunshine."

A beautiful girl with long black dreadlocks and dark blue eyes sat down next to me on a bench we'd fashioned from a fallen tree.

Sipping on a cup of herbal tea from the brewing cauldron Sharon manned, she sat looking into my eyes for a time.

"Sena's eyes look like rainforests," she said, "they're green and gold and amber."

We became inseparable from then on, spending every day together until the Gathering was over.

Sunshine gave me a silver hoop nose ring with colored beads and soon we traded dresses, taking them off and handing them over to the other to wear. She was bossy and demanding and I did whatever she wanted, following her down the white sand trails that wound through the pine scrub.

Guys came in droves to the Gatherings, way more than women, and we ran into small clutches of them on our way to various camps.

"Hey, Sisters, can I have a hug?" They'd ask.

We'd say yes to obvious Brothers, guys with long hair and months of road dirt on their clothes. We were more wary of the college guys; although they wore tie-dye T-shirts and used the lingo, they sometimes had a party vibe.

Some of them surprised me when they expressed interest in spirituality and a genuine desire to connect with nature.

When I met someone I was drawn to, I'd catch Sunshine's eyes on me.

"Come on Sister, we've gotta go," she'd say, linking her arm with mine and pulling me away, usually while I was mid-sentence.

Then she'd laugh and clasp my waist saying, "I just want you all to myself."

Sharon painted a white sheet with a large rainbow and beautiful script that said OM TEA HOME. We hung it from tree branches at the entrance to our camp as was as the custom here.

"I'm going to get water, Sis," she would say, walking past me each morning with a large bucket in hand.

During setup a length of flexible black pipe was set into a percolating spring for on-tap water. After the bucket was filled and she hauled it back, she poured it into a large steel pot and stoked the fire underneath. Dried chamomile flowers, valerian root, raspberry leaf, and others were sprinkled into the water. Then, all day into night Sharon ladled hot tea into visitors' cups.

Two older men walked into our camp one morning.

"I'm Water, and this is TC. We're from CALM, the first-aid camp in charge of medical emergencies, health, and sanitation. CALM stands for the Center for Alternative Living Medicine. We heard you have some herbal teas here?"

"Yes, we do," Sharon said.

We exchanged hugs and they sat down on our log bench. Sharon handed them cups of steaming tea.

Water had a long dark ponytail, shaded glasses, and a brown leather outback hat with the side brims rolled up.

TC looked like a member of ZZ Top, with his extra-long beard and cascading red hair. I later learned he was a mountain man from deep in the Ozarks.

"We were wondering if we might see what you have? Maybe you can help us treat folks? We could send them over with a prescription," Water said, his hands on his hips.

"I'd love that," Sharon said, gesturing for him to follow her to see her large herb collection.

Water began sending people to her with prescriptions he wrote, and she made custom brews in a smaller pot for people with ailments from headaches to insomnia.

Lemongrass walked into our kitchen one morning.

"Sister, I have missed you so much!" she cried when she saw me. We embraced for a long time.

"I have missed you too, Sister!" I said. "Where have you been? I was in DC at the peace vigil."

I grabbed a blue-specked tin mug and ladled tea into it for her.

"DC? Really? Did you go to the Tree House? Those are my dear friends, I live in DC, but I haven't been home in months."

"You live in DC? I had no idea," I said. "I spent a lot of time at the Tree House!"

Questions about a person's name or genesis were discouraged at Gatherings. The anonymity gave the opportunity to reinvent yourself, to break off the shackles of oppressive socialization, and to more closely express your essence.

"I love DC girls," I said. "brainy activists are my favorite people."

She smiled, and flipped her long blond hair over her shoulder while she sipped tea. "I was out west for a while, I haven't been home since summer. I'm gonna go back soon. I'm here with the Church of Bob. Do you know them?"

"No."

"Let's go over to their camp then," she said, quickly washing her cup in a bucket of soapy water, dipping it in the rinse bucket, and leaving it on our wooden drain-board, then taking my hand to lead me away.

We passed a hanging painted cloth with a 1950s-looking character smoking a pipe.

"That's Bob," she said, giggling.

We sat in their camp reading The Book of Bob, a parody religion. It was hilarious and kind of nerdy and it made me like her even more.

There was such joy encountering friends in different states with no plan. None of us were in contact; we were simply on the same circuit. When you caught sight of them at dinner circle, or in town at the Laundromat, or they simply appeared in your camp, it was a happy surprise.

I gathered followers. Sharon teased me about it, calling them "Senites," and if she hadn't I might not have even noticed. I long ago overcame the limitations of my introverted personality in order to survive in the world alone but still, I was often unobservant of the people around me.

I was walking on the trail alone when I bumped into a group of young Brothers just back from town. They were looking for me to gift me with a bottle of white grape juice.

"Oh my God! Grape juice? White? Give thanks and praise to the most high," I cried out, while sinking to my knees in the white sand and bowing my head.

They were delighted with my response, though a little surprised, so I explained the grape juice was not red, but white, which was *exactly* what I prayed for that morning while I sat with Sunshine by the swimming pond.

I was astounded whenever my prayers were answered with such precision.

They bowed their heads slightly in reverence. They were believers.

"And thank you for the gift, Brothers!" I said, hugging them in turn.

I knew them; they often came to Om Tea Home to listen to me read prayers from Paramahansa Yogananda, whom I was enchanted by. I carried numerous books of his in my van.

I often prayed for simple things like juice or candy. Since my little sister died in a car driven by my estranged boyfriend, I had little desire for anything material. I blamed myself for her death. I felt guilty for being alive, for laughing, for eating.

I had a strong relationship with God growing up, a lifeline in a family where cruelty, chaos, and violence ruled. But now, connection to God, and care of the soul, became my chief interest.

My sister's death turned me toward God in a way that eclipsed my entire life.

"We're getting married tonight so we're inviting everyone down to the beach to bless our union."

A doe-eyed couple, barefoot and fresh off Dead tour stood embracing near the fire, smiling and giddy with newfound love. Hugs were had all around.

"Who's gonna marry you?" I asked.

I had not seen a wedding at Rainbow yet, but I'd heard they were rather common.

"Golden Eagle, he's here from Tallahassee."

As if summoned, Golden Eagle appeared. He wore the shaved head, saffron robes, and tilaka[3] of a Hindu *pujari*.

They introduced him to me and his dark eyes filled with a look of recognition and softness.

"My Sister, my Sister, blessings to you." He folded his hands at his breast and bowed. "You are special. This is your last incarnation here on earth. Did you know that?"

"Yes," I said, not being sure of the afterlife but knowing what the Hindu scripture said: When copious adversity is upon you from birth and you are *faithful*, you are burning up loads of karma that can allow you to escape rebirth (birth here is considered a misfortune due to the inescapable suffering of life on earth).

No one knew about my past. Did he see the damage in my face? Could he see my brokenness somehow?

He took a cup of tea and sat down with me.

"I'd like to meditate or pray with you sometime. Do you chant Hare Krishna?"

"Oh yes, I do, and I'd love to do that together. I pray a lot and I do some readings here from Yogananda and the Aquarian Gospel."

"I love Yogananda!" he said. "Kriya Yoga, right?"

"Yes!"

"The Aquarian Gospel I haven't heard of but I'd like to hear you read sometime."

We became dear friends, and often meditated together.

---

[3] a vertical mark on the forehead, made with paste

A campfire set in the center of a circle of people was the only light. Golden Eagle and the bride and groom stood naked near its warmth.

Eagle stood between them, holding their hands as he led them to jump over a stick in an ancient marriage ceremony.

I was surprised the bride and groom were nude, and even more surprised the officiant was, but I was not shocked. Little was unthinkable here; Rainbow was filled with the way-out, including me.

After, we sang songs.

"The earth is our mother," a man shouted out in a singsong fashion.

"*The earth is our mother,*" we began signing, "*we must take care of her, the earth is our mother ... "*

And, "*We are one with the infinite sun, forever, and ever, and ever. We're in tune with our sister the moon, forever, and ever, and ever ... "*

There were a dozen or so ballads sung at Rainbow, simple chants with lyrics about inclusion, peace, love, and nature. Some were purported to be traditional Native American chants.

We sang them all that night, and we even sang Sparrow's sweet song.

Later everyone went to Lovin' Ovens for wedding cake, and to the drum circle for dancing afterwards. It was a magical night.

"Come to our cuddle pile today," Leprechaun said to us while Sunshine and I ate warm chocolate chip cookies at Lovin' Ovens kitchen one day. The smell of baking cookies in the air lured us from the main trail.

"What's a cuddle pile?" I said to Sunshine.

"You've never been to one? A puppy pile?"

"No, I don't know what it is ... there's not puppies here, right?"

She laughed and said, "No, silly, no puppies."

When we approached the camp the crackle of the campfire signaled people were near, but it looked empty. As we got closer, we saw that everyone was on the ground! Under a large tarp roof, people had spread out blankets and were lying on top of them cuddling.

"That's a puppy pile?"

I jumped in without hesitation.

This might've become my favorite part of Rainbow. I didn't even know it existed; I thought you had to be in a relationship to get cuddles.

As a teenager I cuddled with some of my girlfriends, but it seemed like it wasn't something people normally did. I'm sure they blamed drunkenness, but I simply craved hugs.

A crowd of regulars formed in our camp. Some brought their gear, moving in and joining our kitchen. There was a sweet skinny boy just back from India where he'd shaved off his waist-length hair while staying at a temple. He refused to say his name because he hadn't gotten a Rainbow name yet. He would get all the firewood for Om Tea Home and we'd refer to him simply as Brother.

One night as we slept in a ring around the campfire a coal jumped out of the fire and landed on Brother's sleeping bag, starting a small fire. We jumped up and stamped it out.

"We should call you Fire-Catcher," I said.

"Oh my God I love it, that's my name!" he said.

Granola showed up with equipment and supplies to make fresh granola but needed a fire. People did not make individual fires at Rainbow, all of the fires were kept at camp kitchens either cooking meals, baking, making tea, or brewing coffee.

Granola would tie his long wavy hair into a ponytail, then begin to spread oats, raisins, and nuts on a cookie sheet. Next, he poured oil and honey over the mass. Then he put the metal pan on top of the fire and stirred the mix rapidly with a large spoon while it toasted. It was the best granola I ever tasted! He also joined our kitchen, so now we offered granola as well as tea.

Next was an adorable man with bright turquoise eyes from south Florida who was attending his first Gathering. He waxed poetic about surfing in a thick soft-around-the-edges southern twang that made every word polite. Plus he always called me 'young lady.'

"I'd like to name you Ocean," I said.

"I love it!" he said.

I was now deemed a 'namer.'

When we packed up to leave we had Fire-Catcher, Granola, Sharon, and I. Ocean wanted to go home and liquidate his stuff then meet us in Georgia where we planned to visit a Rainbow farm we read about in a homemade booklet listing Rainbow Family all over the country.

Sparrow joined a group of teens and was headed for Dead Tour. I hugged her, kissed her, and made her promise to stay safe. She pushed me away, insisting she would be fine.

People were saying their goodbyes all over camp, not knowing when or where we'd see each other again.

"I love you, Sister," said Sunshine while placing a long white strand of Job's tears around my neck. "These beads are sacred to the Cherokee, who are my people."

She was wearing one of my flowing prairie dresses; it bent the tall grass as she walked across the field towards me. The dark purple fabric made her blue eyes look indigo.

"I'm gonna miss you so much!" I said, hugging her tightly.

"We'll see each other soon. I'm going home and then to Zimbabwe to see my mother," she said.

"Zimbabwe? I want to go to Africa! It's a dream of mine to go and travel there. Why is your mother there?"

"She lives there, she's a schoolteacher."

"So where is home for you?"

"DC," she said.

"God, I love you DC girls!" I said, laughing.

She kept my dress, and I put the beads around my neck twice and pulled, wearing them like a long strand of 1920s pearls; tight around the throat, then falling down to my waist.

We decided to attend seed camp in South Carolina, which meant we'd show up at the Gathering a week early. A Gathering lasts a week but takes a week to set up and a week to break down.

Sharon and I were traveling with three boys. I rejected Fire-Catcher's advances, and now Ocean wanted us to be together, but I wasn't sure. He was awfully cute, and sweet, and polite, and affable as hell. But I just didn't feel that spark and I was awful at rejecting people, so I hoped his feelings would simply dissipate when he went home.

Dating at Rainbow was confusing; it wasn't like going on a formally arranged date and then waiting for a phone call. These were people you already lived and worked with and said, "I love you" to regularly.

Regional Gatherings are small compared to the yearly National Gathering on July 4th, and they are about seventy percent men. My past choices led to such disaster, I was often frozen with fear, and though there were many good men around me, I continued to make bad choices, like Jai and Mud Bear. There was no doubt that romantic relationships were my Achilles' heel.

"Are we going to make our kitchen out of all your current and discarded boyfriends?" Sharon said, laughing.

"No!"

"We'll see," she said.

She was teasing me but it still smarted. I felt destined to be burdened by guilt no matter what I did.

NINE

March 1991
Rainbow Farm
Macon, Georgia

From this hour I ordain myself loos'd of limits and imaginary lines,
Going where I list, my own master total and absolute,
Listening to others, considering well what they say,
Pausing, searching, receiving, contemplating,
Gently, but with undeniable will, divesting myself of the holds that would hold me.
I inhale great draughts of space,
The east and the west are mine, and the north and the south are mine.

I am larger, better than I thought,
I did not know I held so much goodness.

***

We piled into the van, heading north towards Georgia. We stopped at one of the teeny towns along the highway to do laundry and gather supplies. At the Laundromat, friendly strangers told us about a Sunday dinner offered at a local church. So we drove there, following a crude map they drew for us.

Once there, we approached a group of weathered men standing outside the chapel.

"We're here for the dinner," I said. "Is this the line?"

"Yes," one of the men said, "the service is about to start."

"Oh, we're not here for the service, we were going to come to the dinner and then volunteer after," Granola said.

"The service is mandatory," he said.

"Mandatory?" I said. "I've never heard of that. We're of a different faith, so we're gonna skip the service."

We walked back over to the van, sliding open the side door and hanging out in our little living room. In the distance I saw a plump black man in flowing robes marching towards us, flanked by a small posse.

"You followers of Beelzebub! I will not feed you while you're worshiping false idols," he said, his voice booming.

It was the preacher himself. He was livid, nearly spitting while he hollered into my face.

"What are you talking about?" I said, "We are traveling and volunteering—."

"Don't try to fool me with your words! I know who you are and I know who you worship. You worship the devil!"

"No, we don't," Sharon jumped in, "and you don't even know us!"

"You wear the mark of the devil around your neck!" he shouted, pointing at me.

I touched my throat and remembered I was wearing a pentacle that Jai gave me. He made it himself as a silversmith apprentice. It's an innocent symbol in most of the world and throughout history.

"It's a five-pointed star, it's in the Bible, and it's one of the symbols used to create the Seal of Solomon. There's nothing bad about stars in the Bible," I said.

"You have dabbled in the sacred book and dare to challenge me with twisted knowledge and cherry picked passages." His voice boomed like thunder. The men standing around looked frightened.

"What would Jesus have done? Wouldn't he have fed anyone who asked for food?" I asked.

Abruptly, he walked away muttering that he didn't have time for this.

Defeated, we got in our van to leave and one of the men came up to the window.

"I agree with y'all, Jesus says feed people, so I'm gonna give y'all this ten dollars so you can get some supper."

"No, no, we can't take your money," we said.

"But I insist, please take it, please, pass it on if you need to but take it."

"I'm sorry we caused such a commotion. I didn't want to fight with your minister," I said.

"I know, it's okay. Just get yerself supper, then I'll feel alright. I don't like all this fussin', we are meant to be hospitable to visitors. That's what the good book says."

The streak of kindness continued when later we stopped at a farm stand on a lonely road. The elderly farmer who came out of his house to greet us told us he didn't grow much these days, but he had fruit and tomatoes for sale.

He overheard us talking about dinner.

"Are you kids hungry? Huh? Come on inside and have supper with me."

We followed him towards the weathered house, and he gestured to an old tractor near a barn.

"Can't really farm much these days, can't get up on that there tractor anymore."

In his kitchen he spread supplies on the Formica table and began making us peanut butter and jelly sandwiches. Sharon and I started to clean his kitchen.

"No, no, children, y'all don't need to bother yerselves with that," he said.

"We really want to help," I said.

"Well y'all are visitors and visitors are here to visit! Not to clean up after an old man. My wife is gone and I'm just so happy to have company. I don't get much company these days."

We stayed awhile and he told us how he sent all his money to the preacher Billy Graham.

"I'm a Christian, I believe in helping people that's why I send away all my money," he said. "Money won't do me no good in heaven, but a lots of people 'round here need help. Well, really, people all over need help."

When we left he wept and hugged us, making us promise to return.

We continued on to the fallow farm owned by a Brother, where we planned to spend our layover. There were four weeks between the Gatherings, leaving time for travel, visiting, working, and Gathering supplies.

On the farm we found a small band of hippies camped out on the ruddy clay fields (plus one young couple who told us they were Druids). We took over a tiny shanty with a working woodstove and I cooked evening meals on top of it in a cast iron kettle.

We made weekly trips to Macon, the nearest town, to visit the friendliest Salvation Army on earth.

"Here they come," the jolly man who managed the front desk would jump out of his seat and load his arms with fresh towels when our motley group walked through the glass doors of the shelter.

We took blissful hot showers, changed our clothes, and entered the large dining hall.

We were minorities in Macon; as white, as Northerners, and as vividly dressed hippies, but that did not hinder the fabled 'southern hospitality' we seemed to encounter most everywhere.

Once we sat down we were swiftly joined by curious locals, and peppered with questions asked in a drawl.

"Where y'all from?"

"Whatcha doin' in Georgia?"

"Why doncha get yourself some of this ham? It's real good."

After dinner was finished, we swept the large hall, and we asked some of the men cleaning up with us to direct us to the best Laundromat.

"I can take you there," one of the men said, "Name's Ernest."

Ernest ended up staying with us while we did laundry. He seemed fascinated with us. We played Bob Marley CDs in our van with the doors open and we danced in the parking lot.

"Y'all are just so interestin' ... so interestin' ... I didn't know people like you existed," Ernest said, his eyes wide with wonder. "Can I bring you back to my house to meet some of my friends?"

After our laundry was done, we drove Ernest to an aging flophouse with darksome walls. Older black men sat on shabby sofas lining the large room and watched television with yellowed shades drawn. The home seemed sound, but there was a gloomy atmosphere that saddened me.

"These here are my friends," he told them, stumbling over Fire-Catcher's name.

"Nice to meet you," they said.

If they were shocked by our appearance they did not let on. They offered us iced tea and asked how long we'd be in Macon.

"We are visiting a farm an hour away, we're staying in Georgia for a couple of weeks," Sharon said.

"How are y'all enjoying the South?" one man asked.

"We are always surprised how friendly people are, and how kind. In Jersey, where I'm from, strangers would never talk to you," Granola said.

"Or even look at you," I said.

On our next trip to the Macon Salvation Army, Ernest spotted us from across the room and came rushing over.

"Listen, I'd like to join y'all. I want to travel, see the United States, and talk to folks. I've been thinking about it all week and I know I want to go. I have a small social security check—should I give that to y'all?"

"No, no," I said, "it doesn't cost any money to come with us. You can chip in for gas sometimes if you want."

"Oh, okay. That's it? It's free to go to the farm? And stay there?"

"Yes, everything we do is free. We live outside mostly, we live off of the discards of the richest nation and the largest consumers on earth." I said.

"Now what now?"

"We live off trash," Fire-Catcher said.

"You're gonna scare him!" I said.

"Scare me how?" Ernest said.

"Listen," I said, "you'll understand more when you are with us at the Gatherings. There's no money allowed. Everything is either free, or traded at the Trading Circle. Sometimes we stop and work a little, for cash for gas and stuff."

We drove him to his house where he packed up a small suitcase, said his goodbyes, and gleefully jumped in our van. On the drive we chatted about politics and the Gathering coming up in South Carolina.

Suddenly Ernest cried out, "Oh my God, y'all are going to eat me aren't ya? Y'all are going to kill me? Oh my God y'all going to kill me ... I know it!"

"Oh no, Ernest, never! We're vegetarians," I said, "we don't believe in killing, we don't kill anything, we would never kill a person."

He nodded silently, but his face was pure fright.

A pall fell over us, and we rode in silence the rest of the way. When we got to the farm, Ernest slunk off into the dark.

"Hey, Ernest," I called, "don't you want to come with us to the cabin?"

"No, no, I want to sleep outside, you know, see the stars."

"Do you want a sleeping bag?"

"No, I've got my blanket, I'm fine."

"Well why don't you sleep on our porch then?"

He settled on the rickety porch of the little cabin but refused to come inside.

The next morning as I walked with two buckets to haul water from the spring I bumped into him. The alarmed look on his face had not left.

"What's up Ernest?"

He was wearing a blanket poncho someone must've given him, and holding a walking stick. He muttered that he was good, but it truly seemed like he'd seen a ghost.

The next day he vanished along with his suitcase. We figured he went back to Macon.

I was streetwise in that I was good at surviving and resourceful, but I was still naïve; I thought that if you were kind to people they would trust your intentions. I wanted everyone to find the peace and the joy that I felt living with the Rainbow Family. I had no comprehension of the cultural barriers to this lifestyle and I didn't know that people needed to change their view of the world from the core to live this way.

I'd been raised without any particular ties to tradition, or religion, in a shifting landscape of schools, homes, and stepparents. I was an outcast child, then a teen delinquent, and later a detested felon.

Politics were big; my father and his family were incensed about injustice and full of opinions, and *always* for the underdog. The suffering of the hungry, discrimination of homosexuals, and the treatment of minorities topped the list of grievances.

That upbringing primed me to slip easily into an unconventional lifestyle.

"You know, I love hanging out with you so much," Granola said as we walked across a dusty field carrying large white buckets to the spring.

"Me too," I said. "I've been loving cooking with you the past few weeks."

"And you always turn me on to the most amazing music! I love it."

"Yeah, music is my life, it totally saved me as a kid."

We placed the first bucket under the jutting pipe. As we waited for it to fill, Granola pulled me close and kissed me.

After washing dishes that night in creek water we heated on the woodstove, I told Sharon we were going to sleep in the van.

"I knew it," she said. "Sister, what about Ocean?"

"I don't know, he's gone, maybe I'll never see him again. And we weren't actually together yet, I mean we talked but—."

"Right," she said, "I know. I've seen it before. You're a heartbreaker."

"I hate when you say that," I said, "I don't mean it, I don't mean to do it, it's just, I don't know what happens. I'm so fucked up, I mean, I think I want to be with somebody but when I get close I just want to get away and I don't even know why."

She gave me a bear hug and said, "I know, Sis, I know."

"Hey, can you come with me to town to collect dandelion greens?" the owner of the Rainbow farm asked while I walked past his camper one hazy afternoon.

"Of course," I said, "I'd love to."

He was a scrappy middle-aged man, who spent time both gardening and collecting wild edibles. Mornings he made scrambled eggs mixed with dandelion greens and often invited us to breakfast.

We went to town in his old pickup and he spotted a cache of the yellow flowers.

"Look, up on that hill, that's where I get 'em."

"At the police station?" I asked.

"I like to get them there, show the town that these are not weeds—they are food! It's not illegal to gather food!"

So we crawled about the hillside lawn outside the tiny brick police station, pulling up dandelions to take back to the farm.

A few days later, alone, and walking on the path towards the parking lot I ran smack into Ocean. I can still see the look on his face of surprise, then excitement.

"Good morning my lady!" he cried out, dropping his staff on the ground and rushing towards me with open arms draped with a bright woven serape.

"I just got here! I am so happy to see you first!" he said, hugging me tightly.

"I'm sorry, Ocean," I said, pulling away, "please, please don't hate me but I'm with Granola now."

"Oh," he said, the smile leaving his face.

"I wanted to call you, I wanted to reach you, but I didn't know how … "

"It's okay," he said, looking down at the ground.

"You're a great guy, an awesome Brother. I want you to stay with our kitchen."

I felt terrible, but the tension seemed to clear quickly, and he stayed with us a few more months.

We left the farm and headed north to Athens, Georgia where we heard there was a cool scene. We found ourselves in a colorful college town. We hung out a few days and listened to music played on the campus lawn.

Granola and I were in our honeymoon phase. One morning while we were cuddling he said, "Let's get married!"

"Married!" I said, "Are you serious? We can't get married!"

"Yes, we can get married at the Gathering ... in the National Forest, in the woods. It will be so spiritual and beautiful!"

"Okay," I said, not taking it too seriously because I knew it wouldn't be legal. Although I wanted a partner I never thought of marriage; I assumed I would never get married. One of my biggest fears was divorce; I watched my parents go through two brutal divorces *each* by age fifteen.

Before leaving town for the Gathering we went to phone booths in town. Granola called his parents and told his father, "I'm getting married to a nice Jewish girl from New York."

We were all laughing and I wondered if I should tell my father?

So I did.

"Are you kidding? Are you really getting married?" he said.

"Well, yeah, people do it all the time here, they have a little ceremony in the woods around a fire."

"How long have you been together?" he asked.

"A couple weeks," I said

He chuckled, not taking me seriously.

"You're a heartbreaker," he said, "and if you were getting married I would think you were going to marry a foreigner."

"Wait, why do you think that?"

"It's just a feeling I have. I think it will be a black man, too."

My father had long believed in his ability to predict the future.

"You're just saying that because my last two boyfriends were from African countries. No, I mean why does everyone think I'm a heartbreaker? My heart is the one that's broken!"

No one seemed to know how much pain I carried inside—not even the people closest to me. Not even my father. I felt like it was always showing.

But in fact, I went out of my way to cover it up.

Inside I was filled with unrest and regret, and distracted always by grief. I thought about dying every single day. How could I even talk about my life to others? It frightened and confused them.

Granola didn't know about my background or my family, or the closet full of coke, or my little sister's broken body at the town cemetery.

TEN

Late March 1991
Sumter National Forest
South Carolina

O highway I travel, do you say to me Do not leave me?
Do you say Venture not—if you leave me you are lost?
...

O public road, I say back I am not afraid to leave you—yet I love you;
You express me better than I can express myself,
You shall be more to me than my poem.

***

Shortly after we arrived at setup camp, I canceled the wedding with Granola. "I'm sorry," I said, "I'm terrified of marriage, I said yes on a whim. I'm so sorry, I'm just too scared. It's all too fast."

"You can't do this to me! I told my parents, why are you doing this?"

I started crying and he did too, but the fight only escalated until he went and found a mediator to sit with us.

"I'm sorry, I just lost my nerve and I can't get married," I said. "My parents were married three times *each* by the time I was fifteen. I swore I'd never go through that."

Two hours later Granola was leaving our kitchen. I never saw him again, and I never got as close to marriage again.

"I'm sorry, Sis," Sharon said, sitting down next to me, extending an arm and placing it around my shoulders. She gave me a squeeze.

"You understand, right Sharon? You know how fucked up I am." I was hunched over by the fire, holding my knees, my eyes swollen from crying.

"You're alright, Sena Bear."

"All I ever want is to be with someone, but then I can't, I don't know why. And I can't tell him things ... there are so many things."

"I know," she said, "I know."

"Have you ever had your palm read?" A Native American man wearing a green forest ranger uniform asked me as I stirred the simmering tea. "No, but I've had tarot readings."

"I'm Cherokee," he said, "I work with the Forest Service so I can protect the lands of my ancestors but my grandmother taught me how to read palms and I want to read yours."

"Okay," I said.

He seemed interested in me ever since I arrived. When he first spotted me, he broke away from the group of rangers he was walking with to talk to me, peppering me with questions.

"You're part Native American? he asked.

"I have no idea," I said. "Some of my ancestry is unknown. I'm Black Irish, and Ashkenazi, as far as I know."

"Well, where were you born?"

"Upstate New York."

People often asked my ethnicity. I was regularly mistaken for Greek, Italian, Spanish, East Indian, and Native American. My mother insisted Gypsies switched me at the hospital and I was not hers. (Every one of those ethnicities showed up in a DNA test I took years later.)

"Let me have your hand," the ranger said. He sat across from me in the tiny parlor of my van, examining my hand.

"Now, close your eyes. I want you to visualize a meadow."

I did and, in my mind, as I gazed at the meadow, I saw a white horse walk into the scene and begin grazing.

"Okay, he said, "You can open your eyes now. What did you see?"

"I saw the meadow you described."

"You should have seen a white horse."

"Oh my god, I *did* see a white horse, I totally did! How did you do that?"

"That's your fortune," he said. "You have a huge blessing coming into your life."

"Really?"

"Yes, let me ask you something. Are you a lesbian?"

"I, um, well ... "

"But you have been with women? Or you have felt things for a girl?"

"Yes," I said.

"This fortune has to do with a girl, it will be a big thing. You'll know it when you see it, you'll know. The white horse represents a woman. I see her as a soul mate, and I see you happier than you've ever been in your entire life. I see healing for you. You've had heartbreak, troubles, loss."

"Yes," I said, and then the tears I spent my days keeping back were falling.

The most peaceful times I recall were at my father's house on the weekends in the seventies, when he was in full-fledged hippie mode. There was no TV. There was a marijuana grow room in the basement. Us kids played outside in nature all day; we caught bullfrogs in ponds, climbed trees, swam in the creek, and sat reading near the red brick fireplace in the evenings.

Now, I live in the woods. I sleep in the forest each night and I sit by a fire every day. I swim in ponds and creeks and take solar showers. Every meal I eat is cooked on an open fire.

I prayed nature would be my panacea; I desperately needed one.

"Good morning Sister, come have some pancakes!" a guy called out to me.

The smell of cooking wafted through the air mixed with campfire smoke. I walked alone through the woods that morning, then landed at Breakfast Bear's camp.

It's hard to describe the freedom I felt waking up every morning; the events of the day unfolding rather than scheduled, no calls to return, no bills to open. I embraced feeling carefree.

I took a cooled pancake and ate it while standing near the kitchen fire.

A sloping muddy path led down into the valley to where the kitchen stood. A group of young Deadheads just off tour came down it hand-in-hand, forming a color-filled chain of handmade patchwork dresses and Guatemalan pants.

Deadheads have a playful exuberance that rattled some of the older Rainbows, but I was attracted to that vibe.

As I stood watching them descend, one girl caught my eye. She had short golden-blond dreadlocks and a bright smile. I went to talk to her.

"I'm Helena (helen-nah)," she said.

A distinctly non-Rainbow name, I thought. "Where'd you come in from?"

"Tour, we all just came from the shows in Atlanta."

She reminded me of a painting of the smiling sun I'd seen and she was like the sun: yellow-gold, radiant, warm, and serene. She seemed to rest in her smile.

"What made you dread your hair?" I asked.

"It just gets you away from Babylon. When you're living on the road you can't be doing your hair. This hair is no work at all; you never have to brush it. Yours would make gorgeous dreads, you could probably have dreads in a day!"

"Yeah, I think I could. You just stop brushing it right?"

"Yeah and you kind of separate them—you pull them apart so it's not just one big knot."

Helena came by my kitchen often and we would have long conversations about life. She was just eighteen but she'd been touring with the Dead a couple of years already.

"I want to travel with you, Sena! Wouldn't that be great? To travel together?"

"Yes, I'd love it!" I said.

"Someday," she said, "someday we will!"

Jai appeared at our kitchen one morning with a girl he was traveling with named Butterfly. Prairie seemed long-gone.

"Look at you, Mama Sena, sending your boys off to peace!" he said, standing with hands on hips, surveying our kitchen.

"Mama Sena is so perfect for her!" Sharon said, foretelling the new name would stick—and it did. The camp was overflowing with teenagers and soon all of them referred to me as Mama Sena. It was ironic I made such an appealing mother figure considering how I was *not* mothered myself.

Early one morning, as I lay sleeping on the ground of our tarp house, a teenaged girl I knew came running into our camp.

"Mama Sena, Mama Sena!" she called.

She was naked and crying. She lay down beside me, on top of my sleeping bag. I covered her with a blanket. Now she was sobbing.

"What happened, Autumn?" I asked. "Are you hurt?"

"No, no," she said. "I was in a sweat lodge thing but the energy just got weird … so weird … so creepy."

"What do you mean?"

"I don't know, it was run by Crow and I just got really scared."

She started crying harder.

I held her tight in my arms.

"Did he say anything? Or do anything?" I asked.

"No, no, he didn't touch me. He just scared me, he just … his energy was dark. It was so dark, like he was the devil. I don't know what happened, it was just so scary!"

Then she sank into deep sobs.

I knew what she meant. River Crow had blown into seed camp one afternoon in a two-seat sports car, a most unusual choice here. He set up camp next to our kitchen, and he told me I was a medicine woman, and I should meet his tribe in Montana. He showered me with an excess of gifts that made him seem suspicious to some. Mostly he gave me Snickers bars; candy was one of the most treasured items at Gatherings, but he also gave me herbs for tea-making, orange juice, and weed.

"Crow, you are spoiling me," I said, "but I also feel, I don't know ... hunted? Why are you like a cat?"

"I'm a Leo," he said, glancing up at me from underneath a black Stetson. "But you don't have to be afraid of me, I'm just drawn to your light."

Still, I did not trust him. Rumors spread that he was an undercover Agent Provocateur. I argued that he was too obvious to be undercover so I just didn't think he was.

"He's a *federale*, I know it," said Fire-Catcher.

I continued to study Yogananda, and people came around to hear me read passages like:

"The purpose of life is the evolution, through self-effort, of man's limited mortal consciousness into God Consciousness. We must overcome evil by good, sorrow by joy, cruelty by kindness, and ignorance by wisdom."

After one of my readings a man named Ananda approached and said he was a follower of Osho, also known as Rashneesh. I'd never heard of him. Ananda invited us to come visit him in Charleston after the Gathering. We wrote his info down and told him we might come.

We continued to do regular runs to town to gather more discarded supplies. 'Dumpster diving' we called it, when we went behind the stores to look for discarded food. Once, we found boxes of perfect cantaloupes and celebrated our fortune, eating them for days before we heard there was a salmonella scare that sent them to the trash.

Behind a chain drugstore in town we found cases of candy being thrown out. Cases! Easter was over and dozens of boxes of M&Ms in pastel colors, Cadbury eggs, and solid milk chocolate bunnies were stacked outside the back door.

We arrived back at camp with a cache of candy and thrilled everyone there. But we would soon learn that in some places, taking food from the trash is illegal.

"Stay right there," a voice behind us said.

We turned to see two policemen. Ocean froze, bag of potatoes in hand, as he stood inside a mammoth dumpster behind Piggly Wiggly.

"Y'all cannot climb inside that dumpster. You're breaking the law and that's stealing too," said the cop.

"Officers, we are repurposing food that is in the garbage—"

The cop cut me off. "All of you can go to jail if you'd like, so one more word and you're next."

Jail? I thought, for a violation? How is that possible?

Then I was watching Ocean being handcuffed and put into a cop car.

I turned to Sharon. "This can't be happening," I said.

"Come on Sis," she said, "let's follow them to the police station so we can get Ocean back."

At the station we approached the counter. The cop looked through some papers and told us they'd be keeping Ocean.

"Officer, wait, I'm sorry, you're keeping him? In jail? For taking garbage?" I said.

"Yes, we're going to keep him here and he'll see the judge tomorrow."

"But is there bail?"

"No bail."

"No bail? I'm sorry, I'm from New York, and I never heard of that before, I'm just trying to understand … "

"Since you're from New York you should be respecting the laws we have here. Apparently, your friend didn't and that's why he will be seeing the judge in the morning. We can't let him go until he sees the judge."

"What time does he go before the judge?"

"9 a.m."

We left the police station.

"Where the hell are we, are we still in America? I can't even grok this shit!" I said, "I can't even get my head around it!"

"Listen, Ocean is going to be okay. We will come back tomorrow and the judge will let him go. I don't know what else we can do except get ourselves locked up," Sharon said.

She was always the voice of calm reason.

The next day we went to the hearing. We assumed he'd be released with a dismissal or a fine. We prayed there wouldn't be a fine but we didn't prepare ourselves for what would happen.

"Sir, come forward and explain yourself," the judge commanded Ocean.

"Your Honor, I follow the teachings of Jesus and therefore I feed people. My friends and I have fed people all across the country and that's all we were doing, feeding the hungry and the homeless."

The judge frowned deeply and rubbed his eyes.

"I do God's work, Your Honor. That's all I was doing and that can't be wrong," Ocean continued.

"Okay, I've heard enough now. I'm sentencing you to ten days in jail."

"What!" I cried out and Ocean looked back at us sitting in the gallery.

He smiled and said, "Don't worry, I'm doing God's work here too."

As he spoke, the sheriffs began leading him back to jail.

We stood outside our van in the warm sun.

"This cannot be happening, you can't get ten days in jail for being in a garbage can, this can't be real," I said.

But it was real and we drove back to the Gathering in stunned silence without Ocean.

A few days later, we went to town on another supply run and we saw an open-back pickup truck with two benches running along the length of the bed. A group of men sat on the benches, each holding a shovel. They wore orange reflecting vests on over prison jumpsuits. It was a roadwork crew of prisoners.

Then we saw that Ocean was in there!

"Ocean! Ocean! We love you!" we called from the van as we passed the truck.

He saw us, blew kisses, waved, and laughed at the absurdity of the situation.

"Oh my God, they're using him as fucking road labor! I need to get back to New York. This is insane," I said.

Ocean served his time and did the daily roadwork, and when the ten days were over we excitedly brought him back to the Gathering, now in cleanup mode.

People were saying goodbye. Helena came by to see me when her ride was leaving.

"Mama Sena, we will see each other again soon. And I definitely want to travel with you one day!"

"Me too!" I said. "Are you coming to Kentucky?"

"I don't think so," she said. "I'm going to be on tour but I hope to make it to the National in Vermont this summer."

The National Rainbow Gathering happened once a year during the first week of July on the anniversary of the original Gathering in 1972. It was huge compared to the regionals, usually around 10,000 people.

"I hope I can find you there, Sister." I said.

"You'll find me! We will definitely see each other again. We're going to travel together someday, I know we will."

She was beaming her infectious smile, and I had to smile too.

As the Gathering wound down the rain began. It poured down for days until we were living in mud. There was not a dry spot in the camp. We broke our kitchen down and decided to go to a hotel for one night where we could shower and get dry.

Sharon and I created a savings account before we traveled, adding money from our jobs as well as proceeds from the stuff we sold: our cars, furniture, and appliances.

We used our money mostly to pay for gasoline. Tonight was a splurge.

Ocean, Fire-Catcher, Sharon, and I sat on the beds and spread out maps to plan the next part of our journey.

"Ananda invited us to visit him in Charleston. He lives on a houseboat. We could go see the ocean and hang out with some family?" I said. "Plus, I really want to see Charleston."

"Yes let's do it," Fire-Catcher said.

"We might even be able to get a little work there. There has to be a co-op, it's a pretty big city," Ocean said.

It was decided that in the morning we would head to Charleston. After that, to Kentucky and seed camp to help set up the next Gathering.

ELEVEN

April 1991
The Daniel Boone National Forest
Kentucky

All seems beautiful to me,
I can repeat over to men and women, You have done such good to me, I would do the same to you.
I will recruit for myself and you as I go;
I will scatter myself among men and women as I go;
I will toss a new gladness and roughness among them;
Whoever denies me, it shall not trouble me;
Whoever accepts me he or she shall be blessed, and shall bless me.

***

"This book is totally wack!" I told Sharon as we lounged on neighboring porch swings near the Charleston Harbor, relishing the breezes that blew in from the sea.

After meeting Ananda on his boat, he brought us here to a party, and the owner of this huge, beautiful house invited us to stay. And, he gave me *The Orange Book* by Rajneesh.

"What does it say?" she asked.

"He's discussing the benefits of eugenics. Fucking eugenics!"

"Oh, shit, like breeding people?"

"Yeah."

"I read spiritual books all the time and I can always understand what they're talking about but he just doesn't make sense to me. His language and his phrasing are odd, usually these books reference each other's language. It's like he made his own language. It kinda reminds me of *Dianetics*."

"You read that book?" she laughed.

"Yeah in the '80s, it was everywhere. It never interested me though, not like books by Thich Nhat Hanh or Krishnamurti. Those books are so inspirational."

The next day, I questioned Ananda when he came to visit.

"Tell me more about Rajneesh. Did you go to his temple in India?"

"I did. I spent some time there and he gave me my name. He was doing these encounters where he orchestrated orgies; he told you who your partner was going to be."

"In the orgy?"

"Yes, but also sometimes who your partner was going to be in general. He paired me with this beautiful German woman and I had a really nice time sleeping with her."

"That sounds bizarre to me," I said, "and how does that get you to spiritual enlightenment?"

"The energy in that room was so high it was like a drug—no, better than drugs—it was one of the best natural highs of my life. You know ... you follow your bliss to awaken."

I understood the highs that came from sexual encounters, but I could not get my head around being "paired."

"The path I'm on is about direct connection with God, internally. You know, talking to God directly," I said.

"Yeah, I get it," he said, "but a guru shows you how to do that."

I just smiled. I had zero interest in gurus; I was on a self-determined spiritual path. I loved to learn about all faiths, but I often said the only religion I follow is Sena-ism.

Later that evening we talked to the guys.

"Sharon and I were thinking about going to Ohio to visit Joann and Bear. What do you guys think? And also, we are going to take Cat with us to look for River in Kentucky, is that cool?" Everyone agreed.

We met Cat, a willowy blonde with a deep-south accent, in town and she asked us for a ride to the next Gathering.

"Hey family! she said, rushing up to us and hugging each of us in turn. (People often recognized us as Rainbow family). "I'm looking for someone," she said, "A Brother named River. He's from North Dakota. Were you guys in Florida?"

"Yes," we said.

"I met him there, then we both left with our friends. But now I found out I am pregnant, and I really need to see him again and tell him."

The next day the five of us left for Ohio to visit a cool couple that spent a lot of time in our camp in South Carolina.

Cat and I were lying on the bed in the back of the van exchanging stories from our lives, while Sharon drove with Fire-Catcher in the copilot seat and Ocean in the seat behind hers. It was a stormy night and rain was falling hard. We were on the outskirts of Columbus.

"I was a prostitute, she told me, "I was living on the streets, I had no choice."

"Oh my God," I said.

"You don't hate me, do you?"

"No, Sister, no way! I knew a lot of prostitutes when I was a teenager. I understand. I was dealing drugs myself."

She hugged me tightly, her eyes filling with tears. "I got out after a horrible rape. Three men, it was so bad ... I knew them, I thought they were cool. I got into a van with them to snort some coke and they turned so violent, out of nowhere. 'How can you do this to me?' I asked one of 'em while he was raping me, I was crying so hard. 'Shut up,' he said, 'and stop looking at me!'

"I was injured, bad, I went to tell some cops standing near the corner—this was in Miami—and they just laughed at me. 'Sorry you didn't get paid,' one said. They didn't believe me."

Suddenly the van lurched sharply to the right, and then the left, as Sharon tried to get us back on the road.

"What happened?" I called.

"Oh shit, I think its Skinheads! That truck ahead tried to run us off the road," she said.

I rushed up to the front of the van to look at the truck. It was a souped-up Chevy with a sticker of a Confederate flag on the back window. It had been behind us before passing and the back of our van was covered with stickers that said things like 'kill your television,' and 'love your mother' on a photo of planet earth.

I saw an arm come out the window of the truck and in seconds, the van lurched again.

"Oh my God! What was that?" I said.

"They're throwing things. I think I have a flat tire," Sharon said, still driving, still trying to control the van. And then arms were out the window again, followed by more frantic steering of the van until we had to pull over.

Sharon and Fire-Catcher jumped out to inspect the damage.

"Holy shit I can't believe this," I said, "I've never seen a Confederate flag sticker on a car!"

"Oh, I've seen plenty," Ocean said, and Cat agreed.

They came back in the van to give us the news. All four tires were flat from spikes they were throwing out the window at us! Sharon held one in her hand. It was nails fused together and bent; it reminded me of jacks.

"Welcome to fucking Ohio," Cat said.

We managed to drive to a garage and call Joann, and Bear came to pick us up shortly afterwards.

"You could've been killed," he said, alarmed when he saw the spikes that flattened our tires. "You must be an amazing driver not to have crashed!"

"She is, she's the best," I said.

We had to buy new tires for our van. We stayed for a week or so then we packed up and headed south to Kentucky.

Kentucky might be the most beautiful state in the US. The weather is near perfect, and soft curving mountains surround verdant valleys. Lush green forests dominate the landscape. The remoteness is uncanny; people live miles from each other. Wild hemp grows along the roadside looking like its cousin marijuana.

The ride was glorious; we opened the windows and blasted CSNY, singing along as the hours passed. Sharon said we were getting closer to the Gathering, so we started to look for a grocery store to bring in supplies.

We pulled into the parking lot of a small country market. Ocean and Fire-Catcher went into the store.

We saw some family come out of the store being followed by an older woman who was shouting.

"I know you stole somethin', I seen you do it! I called the police."

The Rainbow Brother continued to walk towards his car, ignoring her. Two girls trailed behind him.

"I already told ya, I didn't steal anything. This is ridiculous," he said.

"He didn't steal nothin'," one of the girls said, "we just were gonna buy some groceries, that's all."

He tried to leave but the woman stepped firmly between him and his car, crossing her arms.

"Y'all are stayin' here till the cops come!"

Sharon and I looked at each other and in silence agreed to get involved. We hopped out of the van and walked towards the melee.

We tried to talk to the woman, who turned out to be the storeowner; a rural countrywoman frightened by outsiders.

Now Fire-Catcher stood beside us, and two women emerged from the store and came over to us.

"Now git, young'uns, git," they said to us as they came to support their boss.

"We're just trying to help. What happened?" I asked.

"This dern boy here, he was stealing, I seen him myself," said the storeowner.

"Yes, I seen him too!" said one of the cashiers.

We weren't doin' nothin' and she just started accusin' us!" one of the girls said, pointing at the owner.

"Brother, what's your name?" Sharon asked.

"Ben," he said, "and I swear, Sisters, I didn't take anything!"

"Ma'am, what is your name?" I asked the storeowner.

"Janice," she said, "and I called the police and they're comin'."

"Well, Janice, we're about to have a big Gathering near here and there will be a lot of people coming to get supplies—including us. We have money, we're not going to be stealing."

"Well, I don't want you'uns comin' into my market! We are simple people here and we don't want strangers comin' and thieving. Y'all gotta find somewheres else to go," she said.

The State Police arrived in gray uniforms with brimmed hats. Before I could even begin to step into Cop Council role the police put Ben into the back of their car, arresting him for stealing based on the word of the shopkeeper.

"You can come and see him at the town hall, that's where we'll be bringing him," the trooper told us.

Ben looked out the back window in desperation as the police drove away.

The girls agreed to take his car to the Gathering and we went to ask what was next for Ben.

"Here we go again," Sharon said, shaking her head as we walked towards the van.

She fired up the noisy engine of the van and Cat sat up sleepily. She'd been napping for the past hour. She gave a big yawn with outstretched arms, her golden hair falling down her back. "What the hell people! Were the cops here?"

There was a small jailhouse attached to the town hall. Sharon and I went inside and found a desk manned by a state trooper.

"Your friend will have a trial. He'll be able to see the judge in a couple of days."

"A couple of days?" I said, "So we can get him now and bring him back for court?"

"No, we're not gonna let him out because he'll just run away. He's got nothing to hold him here."

"What about bail?" Sharon said.

"No, we're just going to keep him here, y'all should come back in a few days, judge should be here on Friday."

Once again, we watched a person being held for no significant crime and bail not available. I thought bail was some kind of human right but apparently, it is not.

As a teenager, I was held without bail, but I was facing multiple life sentences. By law, I had to be given a bail hearing within seven days, and then I did receive bail. I had never heard of violations or misdemeanors having no bail.

I got in the van and said to Fire-Catcher, "They're keeping him. They said in a few days he'd get a trial. What kind of kangaroo court shit is this?"

"This is terrible ... we're going to have to find another grocery store too," he said. "That lady is just gonna call the cops again if she sees family. We should warn people."

"Let's go to the Gathering and find out what the Focalizers there know. And we can consult with the elders about Ben's situation," Sharon said.

We all agreed and headed towards the Gathering, but this was not to be our only encounter that day with the police.

The deeper into the forest we went the slower we drove. The dirt roads were riddled with holes. Often this last part of our journey took hours and was the hardest bit.

Driving deep into a national forest on a pitted, muddy road while following a hand-drawn map was typical for us; coming upon a barricade of State Police was not.

They stood in a line, rifles in hand. Two stepped forward and ordered us to evacuate our van. A small group of troopers searched it thoroughly, finding exactly nothing. After, we returned to our van to clean up the mess.

"Seriously, I don't know how I'm going to do Cop Council here, these troopers do not seem friendly at all," I said. "And I can't believe they drove all the way back here! Is this so we can't get away?"

They had stopped other family and we guess found things since some people were being handcuffed and escorted away.

A Brother with a colorful striped vest walked up to us.

"They're seizing herb, basically. I'm going to go warn the cars coming behind you."

"So, what, are they going to get ten years now?" I asked Sharon.

She shook her head, frowning.

We set up camp in a hollow next to a river where tiny scorpions sunned themselves on the rocks. I built a shelf between two trees and set up a small lending library with some of my books. Sharon built us a tarp house with blue and green tarps tied high in the trees as a roof. Some tarps hung horizontally, making a wall, and inside was a large communal sleeping space.

There was a strange element in the alcohol camp. It was the usual bunch of veterans and old-school hippies—the people I knew, but the locals were different in the way I couldn't quite put my finger on. They looked a bit like bikers with long beards, denim vests with patches, and leather belts and boots. But they did not have bikes.

River Crow showed up for seed camp. We were in a narrow valley; there was no way to camp next to us, so he set up in a small field off the main trail.

"My Sister," he said, bowing then presenting me with an entire box of Snickers bars.

"Thanks Crow, I'll share this around."

"Great, now how can I help?"

"You should talk to A-camp, they've been here the longest. And if you see any kitchens loading in you can help them haul in their gear."

Some people still suspected Crow of being a government plant. I did not, but he was unusually flashy for a man pursuing a life of camping. Then, there was how Autumn cried that morning. These things made me pause but still, he was family, and he'd done nothing wrong I could name. As far as I'd seen he was helpful and generous so I figured we'd be neighbors again over the next few weeks.

"Listen here, Sena Bear, that man, that River Crow, he says he's friends with y'all."

"Yeah, kind of," I said, "we met him at the last Gathering. Why? What's up?"

Charlie, a vet I knew from A-camp, looked nervous. He stood wringing his hands. He'd walked up from A-camp to find me at Om Tea Home.

"Well darlin', you know them there people I've been visitin' with in town? You know, Van and Chris and them?"

"Um, yeah ... "

"Well, they are saying that he ... that the black guy has got to go. They are just trying to help us, they say the KKK is around here and it ain't safe if he stays."

"What are you talking about? And why are you hanging out with the Klan?!"

"The guy with the little fancy car? Came in yesterday?"

"He's Native American. What are you talking about?"

"Okay, so, when I went to their house, they had somethin' hanging by the front door, and I tried to see it and it was a noose with a doll of a black man in it. Now, I don't like that kind of stuff, I've been in the military with all kinds of people and I've traveled all over—but I didn't say nothin'. They had moonshine, and guns. I just like to drink with them. This here's a dry county, Sister!"

"You like to drink with the Ku Klux Klan? What the hell are you even talking about? They chased us away in South Carolina and said they hate hippies too!"

"Well, these guys don't hate hippies but they are not gonna tolerate a black man—"

"Fuck them! Tell them too bad! He's family! He's done nothing wrong. This is bullshit, Charlie!"

"Just tell the guy I am sorry, but he's got to go."

"Why should I just give in to the Klan? So you can get moonshine? You're going to sell out a Brother for a drink? I thought you were a military man!"

"Look, I'm sorry, you know we're here to keep the peace. That's all we're trying to do. We're not against him at the Gatherin,' we're just trying to protect him and everyone here."

"Well, I'm gonna call a council because I don't agree with this and I don't think those guys should be hanging out at A-camp. I'm not going there if there're Klansmen there!"

I brought the news back to River Crow and just like that he decided to leave.

"I can't tell you not to leave. I guess it's better for you, I don't know. I don't know anything about dealing with the Klan," I said.

"Yeah, it's just better if I go," he said. His eyes showed unmistakable fright, and I silently questioned, once again, if I was still in the United States.

Crow left the Gathering, chased away by the Ku Klux Klan, and I was furious. A lot of the Brothers there were southerners; maybe they were used to shit like this?

I was not. "Why aren't we standing up to the Klan and protecting Crow? He's family!" I argued, "Why isn't anyone upset except me?"

"We're upset too," TC told me, "but we're from the Deep South and we all know you don't challenge the Klan. They will come here at night and burn us out! They're gangsters, and they're locals; we need to keep the peace with them. We hate them as much as you do!"

"I don't know," I said. "There's no 'keeping the peace' with racists, they're pure evil. And they shouldn't be hanging out in A-camp just because they have moonshine!"

I avoided A-camp the rest of the Gathering, and I stated my case angrily to anyone that would listen.

The Gathering has a lot of muckety-mucks but maybe none higher than Plunker, one of the founders of the Rainbow Gathering. I asked him to go with me plead the case of Ben, who was still locked up at the local jail.

"He sees the judge today," I said. "Can you come with us to court?"

"Okay, Gal, I'll go with you," he said.

Gal? I never heard that before. Turns out Plunker is from Montana.

On the ride to town hall he sat next to me on the red vinyl couch. Sharon and Fire-Catcher sat up front. Ocean stayed behind to man Om Tea Home.

"Did you say your name is Sena?" he asked.

"Yup."

"Like Shantisena, that's what I named Rainbow's peace-keeping force. Shanti means peace and Sena means keeper."

"Sena means army, actually."

"You don't say? Hmmm. Well, don't you worry Gal, I'll go in and have a talk with the judge before court."

And sure enough, Plunker, looking like a western frontier man with two long braids and a brown leather outfit; pants, vest, coat and all, topped with a bullhide slouch hat, got us in to see the judge in his chambers.

"Look your honor, you can release the boy into my care, I will vouch for him and if he is to return to court, I will personally bring him," Plunker said.

"I can't do that," he said. "If the boy pleads not guilty, he'll stay here till trial and if he pleads guilty, he'll be staying here with us a spell."

"He's not guilty," I said. "He's going to plead not guilty."

"Well, then, the trial 'ill be next Friday," he said.

"But the State Police told me it would be today," I said.

"Well, if he's gonna plead not guilty we got to get him a lawyer from the county. There ain't anyone here now to represent him."

"Sorry Gal, he's guilty, sounds like," Plunker said when we left the judge's chamber.

"You weren't in the store, you didn't see what happened ... this is the word of the store owner, there is no evidence."

Everyone went to the van except for Sharon and me. We went to visit Ben.

"You should plead not guilty today," I said, "then they're going to get you a lawyer but your trial won't be till next Friday."

"Alright, I'm gonna do that then," he said.

"Listen Brother, no judgment, I swear, but did you steal anything?" I asked.

"No, I swear, I didn't!"

"So they didn't find anything on you when they searched you?" Sharon asked.

"Nope, nothin'."

"Then yeah, you should definitely plead not guilty, and we'll be back next Friday for your trial." Sharon said.

"How are you doing in here?" I asked.

"It's okay, I mean it's just a few guys in here and we're at work all day and in church on Sunday."

"At work?" I said.

"Yeah, they take us out every day after breakfast to do lawn mowing and landscaping and shit. We mostly work on the roadside."

I jumped into the van, slamming my door. "I can't take this anymore Sharon! Even if he did steal how can he be in jail working on a road crew? He's not even sentenced! I feel like these towns just need free labor."

"The laws are different here. You from the Northeast? I'm bettin' New York?" Plunker said.

"New York, yes, they have to have bail set within seven days."

(People identified me as a New Yorker almost instantly. Though I was from upstate, that hallmark nasal accent had made its way north.)

Zeus was a crabby Greek man who ran a unique kitchen. He *only* made soup—earthy, utilitarian soup, and he had strict rules for his kitchen. He posted a handwritten cardboard sign on a tree that said: No bibles, No religion, No politics, No drugs, No smoking, and possibly more that I can't recall. I found his constant rants on said subjects amusing.

I dropped in one night to grab a bowl of hot soup and he confronted me.

"Listen, some people told me you were reading some kind of holy book ... the gospel something ... at your kitchen?

"The Aquarian Gospel?"

"Yes, well I can't approve of that and I can't have you at my kitchen."

"Zeus, I'm not reading the book here."

"I don't like religious people and I just don't want them around me," he said. "Please don't come here anymore."

I just laughed at his outlandishness.

I like to walk without a flashlight at night in the woods. When your eyes adjust you see more than you can in the narrow beam of a flashlight. A dim light radiates from the sky, even when the moon is dark. If there is a trail, you can follow the tree line framing it by looking skyward.

Passing noisy groups with flashlights would interrupt my quiet, but there were always hugs. "Welcome Home," I said to the newcomers.

One night as I headed home, a girl walking out said, "Sister, be careful, there's a couple making love in the middle of the trail."

"What! Why are they on the trail? That can't even be comfortable," I said, laughing.

I never saw the couple but the next day they showed up at our kitchen.

Star was tall and stunning, with thick, shiny black curls reminiscent of mine. She and Uncle John were swathed head to toe in bright tie-dyes.

"Was that you guys on the trail last night?" I asked.

"Yes, it was," Star said. "Sister, it was the most beautiful, magical night of my life! We were both tripping pretty hard ... I swear I saw God!"

"Really? My father took LSD when I was four and he didn't come down for weeks. He was taken away in a straitjacket. The girl he dropped it with, Judy, later hung herself. I've always been afraid of it plus I haven't taken drugs since I was a teenager."

"Holy shit Sister! I'd be scared too but your father definitely got bad shit. There were government plants spreading bad stuff in the '60s, trying to crush the movement. The stuff we took is not drugs—it's pure God; it's enlightenment."

Tripper, who was sitting nearby, nodded his head silently. He was doing a 'speech fast.' In fact, this was the third Gathering I saw him at and I'd never heard him speak. He did carry a small notebook and pen, though, for basic communication.

I was curious about him, as I knew silence was a practice of monks, seekers, and cloistered nuns.

I tried asking him about his practice and he wrote on the paper, "You should just try it."

I decided to do it for three days. To be among people and not speak, to listen more than I have ever listened in my life. Like everyone else, I would think about what I was going to say next, or how to respond. All of that falls away when there is no option to speak. The groups of people around me talking became like theater and I could see every dynamic. I saw people bullying, cutting others off, and not responding to what they said; and I could observe it all from a distance.

I sat Indian-style on the ground at different campfires and silently made beaded necklaces and earrings by sewing tiny colored beads together in patterns.

One of the first things I felt was the copious amount of energy I used to communicate with others. Reaching inside and forming thoughts into words was draining. Now, I could feel my energy increasing. This surplus of energy put me into an altered state and by the third day, it was hard *not* to smile. I was blissed out.

"Water, can I go with you on the next supply run?"

I had returned to speaking and I was curious about what the Magic Hat money bought, plus I wanted to get some supplies needed at Om Tea Home.

"Sure, I'm going tomorrow. Meet me in the parking lot after breakfast. You know, morning-thirty."

I walked through the store collecting things Sharon asked me to get, like fresh fruit and honey, two things not usually seen at the Gathering.

I found Water standing on the checkout line and I joined him. I looked down at his cart and was stunned. There were a dozen large bottles of Clorox bleach.

"What the hell is this?" I said.

"It's bleach."

"Right, I know it's bleach. It destroys the environment, I haven't used anything like this for years. How can this be good? All this bleach is going to be poured out in the woods?"

Water was annoyed. "Sena, you know it's a rule that all kitchens put bleach in the rinse water."

"I didn't know it was a rule. I certainly would never have bleach in my kitchen. I boycott this company, and all chemicals. I'm an environmentalist, and I thought you all were too."

"Well, there's environmentalism and then there's public health. I've seen outbreaks, especially at the large Gatherings. Have you?"

"No, but this disgusting bleach kills every living thing: frogs, fish, birds …"

"Look, Sister, I'm done with this lecture," he said, "and I don't want to find out that you're not using bleach in your rinse water or it's going to be a problem."

"What are you talking about?"

"Bleach in the water is not a suggestion, it's a rule, and I am in charge of the health of the people of this Gathering and I will close your kitchen."

"We only serve tea, so please chill, Water. I make my own cleaning products with vinegar, baking soda, and hydrogen peroxide. Hydrogen peroxide is an effective disinfectant and it's non-toxic."

"I'm sorry, but you can't use hydrogen peroxide and if you refuse to use bleach I will have to come and shut your kitchen down."

I still refused to use bleach. Now, I explained the horrors of bleach to people when they came to my kitchen. I knew there was bleach use in the camp, I didn't approve, and I didn't put my plate in those buckets. But when I saw a dozen bottles of bleach being carried into the woods, and knowing every drop of it would end up on the ground once the rinse water was dumped, I was horrified.

I felt tension growing between Sharon and me. I asked if she was upset with me but she insisted everything was fine. I kept feeling like she was silently mad at me.

"Well listen honey, is she gay?"

I confided in TC, who was a dear Brother to me. He was at every Gathering, camping nearby and running CALM with Water.

He sat in folding green camping chair near a low table fashioned from a board, smoking a cigarette. Like us, he had tarp house with a high roof. He lit a small lantern and sat back, smoothing his long bread with one hand.

"No, I mean, not that I know of. She's never said she is."

"Yeah, but have you ever seen her with a man? Or even interested in a man?"

"No."

"And yet you have boyfriends at every Gathering."

"No I don't!"

"Well, how long have you two been friends?"

"Two or three years."

"Has she ever told you she liked a man or ... I don't know, anyone?"

"No, she hasn't, but I don't know, I feel like she would've said something. She knows I had a girlfriend once."

"I'd like to hear about that!"

"TC, forget it."

"Come on Sena Bear you know I've been carrying a torch for you, honey you should be with me."

"You're crazy and I'm trying to talk to you about Sharon."

"Don't be such a bitch, Sena."

He laughed and took another deep drag off a cigarette. He often needled me, but there was something very soft about him.

"I feel like she's in love with you and I've always thought that since I met you both in Florida," he said.

"Oy vey TC, if that's true I am so screwed!"

The day of Ben's trial came.

I hopped out of my van in a long-sleeved turquoise gown with thick embroidered gold loops across the front, and on the sleeves and hems. It was long, brushing the top of my Birkenstocks.

I always wore a silver nose hoop and dangling beaded earrings. Sunshine's white Job's tears necklace fell to my waistline.

As we walked in, we were photographed and later written about in the local newspaper, my outfit in particular being described in great detail. Someone brought a copy of the article to my kitchen and we all read it and laughed at the descriptions of ourselves.

"'They're offering a plea deal. If he pleads guilty he gets time served and they will release him," said the young lawyer who had fetched me, saying, "Ben wants you to be part of the proceedings."

He continued, "I think it's the best deal for him, but he doesn't want to take it."

We three sat in a small room off the main courtroom.

"I don't want to plead guilty when I'm innocent," Ben said.

I squeezed his hand under the wooden conference table.

"If you go to trial they're going to keep you here for months. Listen, close-knit family runs this town; you don't want to make them angry. I would take their deal," said the lawyer.

"I agree, Brother, I wouldn't take a chance. We can get you out of here and back to the Gathering at least."

"Yeah, okay, I will, if you really think I should. But it's wrong and it's not fair. I didn't do anything."

I went up front with the lawyer and Ben was brought out. We all stood in front of the judge.

"How do you plead? The judge asked.

Ben hung his head and mumbled, "Guilty, Your Honor."

"I hereby sentence you to four months in jail." the judge said, slamming down the gavel.

I started to protest and the bailiff sternly told me not say another word or I'd be removed from the courtroom.

I looked at the public defender and he was ashen. He asked me to step outside and I followed him down the steps of the courthouse to the parking lot.

"I'm so sorry," he said in a timorous voice, "I didn't know that was going to happen."

"But that's illegal! It's against the Constitution or something, right?"

"Look, this town is run by one family and I'm scared of 'em. I was assigned here, I'm not from this part of Kentucky. I don't know what I'm gonna do, I'm scared to report 'em."

He wiped sweat from his brow with the sleeve of his jacket. His terror was obvious.

"But you're a lawyer! Shouldn't you call the FBI or the governor or someone? You have to report them!"

"I know, but we're up against serious corruption and thugs, maybe even the Klan … "

"This can't be happening. This is a kangaroo court! How can there be a kangaroo court in America in 1991?"

"I can't say I know," he said. "It's just how it is."

Sharon and I returned to camp defeated, my mind still reeling from what I witnessed.

The Gathering was winding down.

"Rainbow Bear loves you, honey!"

Bear held me tight against his expansive chest, his tie-dye shirt smelled of sweat.

"Rainbow Bear, we are going to DC for a Rainbow meet up and demonstration, why don't you guys come?" I said.

"We've got some other stops to make but we will definitely be in Vermont. You're going to be there right?"

"Of course!"

He kissed the top of my head. "Rainbow Bear will miss you, honey!"

Cat decided to ride with Plunker and I hugged her tightly. "Sister, I will miss you so much!

"Me too," she said, "but I'll be in Vermont by June. I'll come camp with you there. I still gotta friggin' find River! That's why I'm going with them; they're gonna go to a Rainbow council meeting and River might be there."

Fire-Catcher and Ocean made other plans to travel too, it was nearly two months between the end of Kentucky and the National Gathering in Vermont, but they promised to meet up with us there.

Sharon and I had adopted a stray, a guy named Crunch. He'd had a bad trip on acid and people brought him to us. We ended up taking care of him all night. His meltdowns came cyclically, and were mostly delusions of people after him.

"Does this mean there's bad acid going around?" I asked Sharon.

"I'm not sure. He could be mentally ill and then it's like a bad mix."

He towered over us, shirtless, with ripped abs and black Doc Martens. Conversely, he had the innocent face of a young boy.

The next morning he said he was sorry, though he still seemed disturbed.

"I'm a punk who hates hippies," he told us, "but you guys have been really good to me so I kinda trust you."

We told him he could come to DC with us. The problem was even without the drugs there was something seriously wrong with him. He was continuously agitated. I was afraid of him, but family was family so we packed him in the van and headed off to our old haunt.

We stopped at the jail on the way out to see Ben. It was a Sunday so he was there and they brought him out to visit with us.

"Ben, Brother, I'm so sorry," I said, starting to cry. "Brother, I can't believe what happened in that courtroom. I didn't know prosecutors were allowed to lie like that. I'm still shocked it happened."

"Don't worry about it. I'll be out of here soon, I'll see you in Vermont."

"But I feel so guilty leaving you here."

"Look, you have no choice so just go, and please don't feel bad, it's not your fault. Are you heading straight to Vermont?"

"No we're going to DC to demonstrate against the Persian Gulf War," Sharon said.

"Just remember me there, I'll be with you in spirit and I'll find you again. Thank you so much for everything you did for me."

"We didn't do anything, you're still jail and basically enslaved. I feel terrible I told you to take that deal," I said.

"There was no other choice and there's no way you could've known they were crooked. I'm okay."

I was so disheartened over the Klan, A-camp, the way no one stood up for River Crow, and the kangaroo court. We drove away from Kentucky and left Ben in jail. I felt so helpless. I knew how shitty jail was, and how the job of jailer attracted sadists.

I knew how crushing and demoralizing it was to lose not just your freedom, but also your humanity.

TWELVE

May 1991
Peace Park
Washington, DC

"You're a plant, a *federale*, aren't you? I know you are!"

"Crunch," I said, "you're going over the edge now, you're totally paranoid."

Timing is a weird thing. Seemingly on cue one of my favorite cops walked by. He stopped short, looking at us sitting on the bench under the flood of the streetlight. He bent his knees slightly, putting his hands on his thighs.

He was grinning now. "Sena, hey, Sena! You're back? Girl, it is so great to see you!"

Crunch jumped up and screamed at me, "You witch, I knew it, you ARE a *federale*!" And he ran off into the night of the city.

"What's that about?" the cop asked.

"Oh, nothing, you know, just trying to save another one. Save 'em all if I could."

He nodded and smiled. "When did you get here?"

"Just tonight, an hour ago. Listen, I was gonna sleep here, in the park." He was one of those cops I could not help being attracted to. He was handsome and warm and maybe twenty-five. But I couldn't even think about it, I didn't let myself. I could never live in his world.

"Well, I can look the other way but when I go off duty … you know how it can be."

It was warm, so I slept on the soft grass of the park with just an army blanket. The lights in the White House were dimmed. I listened to the fountain's endless splashing, and watched the blinking red light on the Washington Monument. It sort of felt like home.

People filtered in for the rally and Peace Park became a mini-gathering. I hadn't seen Crunch in days and suddenly he was in front of me, smiling the brightest smile I'd seen.

"Sister, Sister, I'm sorry, I'm so sorry." Tears ran down his face. "I was in the hospital; I had a goiter, and they removed it. It made me angry, crazy, I was sick."

"Crunch, it's okay." I hugged him, and the stubble of his shaved head brushed my cheek.

"I'm going home to Alabama to see my mama, to take a break. I called her from the hospital."

The next day he left town on a Greyhound bus.

Some of the people I knew from winter were still here; the die-hard demonstrators, the locals, and the homeless we often fed and socialized with.

I decided I did not want to wear shoes because they separate you from the earth. I walked all over Washington DC with bare feet. I got far away from the park once, and decided to jump on the subway to get back. As I sat studying the map tacked up beside me, a transit cop approached.

"What do you think you're doing? You can't be on the Metro with no shoes! Don't you know that? You have to get off at the next stop!"

"I'm sorry," I said, and he frowned.

At the next stop, he escorted me off the train. "You should go to a shelter or something and get yourself some shoes. Don't let me catch you here again like this!"

I walked barefoot the many blocks back to the park and when I got there, I saw a familiar figure: Sunshine!

We hugged and jumped and sang and skipped, holding hands.

"Sister, Sister, I'm so happy to see you! I just got back from Africa!"

"Wow, how was it? How is your mother doing?"

"It was so beautiful! I played music all day, and I brought back some stellar instruments. I walked all over Zimbabwe, Sister, it was gorgeous, the people are true *irie*. It's the Motherland. My mom is happy, she's running a small school."

"And I was here, stuck in racist Kentucky with the Klan!"

"The Klan? What the fuck?"

"It was a nightmare, they brought moonshine to A-camp because we were in a dry county, and then A-camp made a Native American Brother leave the Gathering because of his skin color."

"No fucking way!"

"I'm serious, and I'm ready to move to Africa, I just can't take it. Why is the Klan even legal? Hate groups aren't legal in Germany!"

"Girl that is so fucked up! I can't believe that happened at Rainbow. You should take it to council."

"Yeah, I should ... maybe at the National. Sun, are you going to be there?"

"I don't know yet, I might be going back to Africa. Also I really want to go to school."

"I miss you so much," I said to her, holding her around the waist, looking into her jewel-blue eyes. She took off a beaded bracelet and put it on my wrist.

"I miss you too my beautiful Sena! Listen do you want to go see some roots reggae with me tonight? I've got free tickets, I know the promoters."

"Oh my God, reggae is my all-time favorite! I used to go to in New York all the time to see live music. My favorite is Israel Vibration, they play that old roots style."

Later that night, we walked to the venue hand-in-hand; her in a royal Zimbabwean gown with swatches of bright red and gold, and me in a billowy lavender cotton dress trimmed with tiny tassels, layered underneath with a pale green skirt, and a dark green shawl draped over my shoulders.

"Good evening my Sistren," said the guy at the door in a Rastafarian greeting.

Sunshine nodded, looking regal with her black dreads tied high up in a scarf. We danced for hours enveloped by clouds of *ganga* smoke, and returned to the park late, sleeping on the grass in my favorite spot near a huge oak, with scarves and shawls wrapped around us.

At a drum circle happening in the park, I spied Star and Uncle John from behind. I studied the many embroidered patches on the back of his vest, then tapped Star's shoulder. She grinned merrily, saying, "Sister, oh my God, it is so great to see you again, beautiful! This is heaven here, right?"

We hugged a long time, then I pointed to Uncle John's patch of a man with his head between a woman's legs.

"I really love this patch," I said, laughing.

"I know! Isn't it awesome? It's what made me first fall in love with him!"

We laughed.

Sunshine left town saying she'd see me in Vermont, maybe.

"I really want you to camp with me at the National! And I want to hear your music, Sister. Come play your songs at Om Tea home."

"If I don't make it, I'll see you next time you're back in DC. I love you!"

"Me too, I love you!"

And she walked away to I-don't-know-where.

Late that night, a White House guard who was off duty, and drunk, assaulted us. We got the police and gave a report, and later detectives arrived.

"Please, get in," the lieutenant said to me, holding open the door of a black chauffeured car. In the back was a man in a suit with a clipboard and papers. He looked at me and gestured to the seat next to him.

"So, you were injured here tonight? Tell me what happened."

"We were sitting on the curb across the street from the guard house and entrance—"

"You mean right there?" He pointed to just outside the car window.

"Yes, right there, and a guard drove past yelling and cursing, and he threw a golf ball at us and it hit me and bruised me."

"Can you show me the bruise?" he asked

"Nope."

"It's okay," he said "we have witnesses, people saw it happen. Did you have any interaction with him before the incident?"

"No, I have no idea who he is."

"But you know a number of the officers here, right?"

"Um, yeah."

"But you don't think it's anyone you know?" "

"I don't think so, what's his first name?"

"Mike."

"No, I don't know him."

When the interview was over the man gave me his card. It said he was part of the Secret Service.

I hopped out of his car and walked over to a bunch of family waiting for me. Thomas, a lawyer, told me the man who threw the golf ball was part of the US Secret Service Uniformed Division.

"You might need to stay here in DC. We could sue them, we could have a serious lawsuit," he said.

"I don't know ... I gotta think about it."

I didn't want to let anyone down, but I couldn't stay. I missed the woods terribly when I was there, though DC is a verdant city with blossoms galore, and trees filled with bright green leaves. And there were so many people there that I loved!

One afternoon, Emmanuel showed up at the park. He'd led the prayers before dinner at Deb's while I was here demonstrating last winter, trying to stop the Persian Gulf War. I had not seen him since then.

"Emmanuel, I'm so happy to see you!" I said, "Have you seen Deb? I miss her so much!"

"Deb? No, no, I've been away."

"Away where?" I said.

"Oh, I was in Iraq, in the war."

"Oh my God ... wait, you were? And now you're back?"

"Yeah, I got blown up over there pretty bad."

But something was strange about him, different. His face had an animation I had never seen before; in the past he was always stoic and serious.

Next time I was at the Tree House, I asked about him. The activists there had started a safe house for people who need help after they return from Desert Storm.

"Oh yeah, you mean Simon, he's an outpatient from the DMH clinic, you know, the Department Of Mental Health. He's one of those people that Reagan put on the streets in the eighties. He goes on and off his medication, he's schizophrenic."

"So, he imagines he went to war?"

"Yeah, sometimes."

I was sitting on the steps of the Treasury Building with Sharon, where we'd taken to sleeping with a small group of family. The gigantic steps led to a marble platform flanked by columns holding the massive roof. It was an ideal spot for rainy nights.

"Hey family, we just flew in from Europe for the summer. We're headed to the National," a British man approached us. He was with a motley bunch, each carrying a backpack.

"Welcome home!" we said, getting up and hugging them.

I began talking to one boy with striking copper-colored hair and sparkly blue eyes.

"I'm Liam, he said.

"You're from Ireland?"

"Yes, from Galway, do you know it?"

"Not really ... some of my family is Irish, but they've been here forever, since before the Civil War."

He grinned and reached for my hand and we walked away holding hands, talking while I gave him a tour of Peace Park.

Liam was flirtatious, and adorable. I was hesitant; he had a puppy-love vibe. I'd been avoiding entanglements since Granola, afraid of more disasters.

But Liam was persistent, saying, "Come walk with me, beautiful girl," pulling me away to wander the city at night, exploring the shadows and ghostly monuments.

We landed at a quiet fountain near sleeping office buildings one night, and he sat down on the rim, pulling me onto his lap and wrapping his arms around my waist.

Then, he put his hands under my long skirts.

"Man, I love hippie girls without underwear," he said into my ear, pulling me closer, holding me tighter.

I now spent my nights with Liam, wrapped up together on the lawn near silent marble buildings, or along the hedges behind the park.

Days, I was working for friends who owned a T-shirt business. I created an inventory system for them, my specialty at my corporate job.

I also went to Greenpeace headquarters and asked if they could help me with the bleach situation at Rainbow. They offered me a desk with a computer and phone so I could do research.

I called author Debra Lynn Dadd, who wrote a book on the dangers of chemical cleaners and listed natural alternatives. I told her I was looking for proof that peroxide was an effective disinfectant. She told me that things like hydrogen peroxide, even though they might be effective, are not studied because they're not profit makers. Natural things tend to be cheap and common.

"Why do you keep ignoring me?" Liam asked.

"Listen, Brother, I'm really sorry. I'm just being an activist, and so many of my friends are here. I'm distracted."

"Yeah, but it's more than that," he said.

"Yeah, well, you are nineteen, and you are here for the summer; I just don't think we have a future."

"But you're only a few years older than me, how can that matter?"

"It just does, I don't know. Listen, I still want to hang out with you, just not every minute, that's all.

I woke up in my sleeping bag on the familiar marble terrace at the Treasury. There was a letter left on top of my bag. It was from Liam saying that I broke his heart and other things I don't remember. He left town before I even woke up.

I told Thomas I was sorry, but there was no way I could stay for the lawsuit. I felt bad, but also desperate to be back in the forest where the trees outnumbered the people, and the stars filled my vision as I went to sleep.

"Can we leave this town now?" I asked Sharon. "Star is gone, Sunshine is gone, and Liam hates me."

She laughed—she still laughed at my antics—but a more somber tone had taken over. I often yammered about my hopes, always plotting my next move towards saving the world. Sharon followed along, never speaking of how she felt or what she wanted herself.

To me she was inscrutable.

THIRTEEN

June & July 1991
Green Mountain National Forest
Vermont

Now I see the secret of the making of the best persons,
It is to grow in the open air and to eat and sleep with the earth.

Here a great personal deed has room ...
Here is the test of wisdom,
Wisdom is not finally tested in schools,
Wisdom cannot be pass'd from one having it to another not having it,
Wisdom is of the soul, is not susceptible of proof, is its own proof
...
Now I re-examine philosophies and religions,
They may prove well in lecture-rooms, yet not prove at all under the spacious clouds and along the landscape and flowing currents.

Here is realization,
Here is a man tallied—he realizes here what he has in him,
The past, the future, majesty, love—if they are vacant of you, you are vacant of them.
***

The Green Mountains of Vermont were sprawling, gently sloping hills of emerald. Tiny, picturesque towns dotted the landscape, and then gave way to endless forest. When we finally reached the parking lot deep in the woods, a skeleton crew of family camping in RVs greeted us.

"Welcome home, family! The main circle is gonna be almost two miles in, so we're working on getting more black tubing to pipe the water from the spring. We got West Coast family working on collecting donations. For now, you need to haul the water from down here to your camp," said one of the Brothers.

"We have a medicine kitchen and we like to set up near CALM. Are they here?" I asked.

"Yeah, a couple of them are here, TC has been setting up, and Water will be here any day. You're gonna need some help getting your stuff in, right?"

"That would be great, we can totally use some help."

He introduced me to Badger, a starry-eyed 15-year-old in a wide-brim hat who lived in a converted school bus with his family. "Badger here's got a wagon, he'll help you haul in your kitchen," he said.

CALM was located across from the main circle where nightly meals would be served. Afterwards, drums would play 'till morning. During the day council would meet there and discuss Rainbow issues by passing a feather; the speaker holding the feather had the floor until he passed it to another speaker, or rather *if* he passed it, as filibustering often turned the meeting into a trial.

When the speakers were through they took votes, votes that required full consensus to pass, which almost never happened.

A steep knoll with a wide, flat top sat directly over CALM—it was beyond perfect for us. After lugging everything we owned two miles, we built Om Tea Home.

A golden-haired girl named Gypsy I had not seen since West Virginia appeared. Now nine months pregnant, she glowed, her face freckled from sun.

"Oh my God, Gypsy! Look at you!" I said.

"Sister, I know. Can you believe it? I'd love to have him on July 4th, but I think he'll be here before that."

"That would be such a blessing," I said, July 4th being a holy day in Rainbow culture, "he'd be a sweet, sensitive Cancer. Still, Geminis are my favorite people, they're so much fun!"

"I'm gonna camp with you guys; Sharon's gonna take care of me, and TC is gonna deliver the baby just down the hill."

"At CALM?"

"Yes, well, they're setting up a teepee for me to give birth in."

After that, a gaggle of pregnant women moved in with us. It was sweet, and Sharon was amazing at caring for them. People with children usually camp together at Kid Camp, but it was located along the main circle and our place was quiet and a bit removed. Plus, CALM was right there.

"Sisters! I'm home!"

Fire-Catcher dropped his backpack on the ground early one morning. We hugged him tight, saying, "Welcome home, we love you!"

"Is Ocean here yet?"

"Nope, not yet," Sharon said.

"Six-up!" we heard someone call from the trail below—Rainbow code for cops; when rangers or State Police were in the forest, people ran ahead like squawking crows, warning us as they approached.

"How you doing today ma'am?" A polite state trooper said as he and a few other cops walked into our camp. "Mind if we look around?"

"Uh, okay, I guess," Sharon answered.

After a quick glance around, they were on their way, and the crier called out "six-up!" again while walking towards the next camp.

During setup, they allowed vehicles in on the main trail to bring in heavy supplies. A Brother I knew drove up alongside me in a pickup truck as I walked back to Om Tea Home.

"Hey beautiful Sister!"

"Hey Papa Dave!"

He stopped the truck. "Come're Sena," he said, waving me over.

I walked over to him, resting my hands on the door.

"Come have dinner with me," he said, a slow smile spreading across his face. "I just got in today, I was hoping to see you."

He pressed my hand, looking into my eyes.

"Okay," I said, pulling away. His unexpected attention made me nervous.

"Come on now, ride with me," he said, pushing the debris on the seat next to him to the floor.

Papa made me dinner in his RV. I never connected with him before, though I'd seen him at every Gathering. He was at least twenty years older than me plus a Rainbow High-Holy, so we hung out in different crowds.

"Where are you from?" I asked him, as he lit up a fat joint and passed it to me.

"Tennessee," he said. "I find you so interesting, you seem so much older than you are. What's your background?"

"I don't know, my father said I was born forty."

"Forty, aye?"

"Yeah, I was the only adult in the house, my mother was a helpless mess, my father, that's another story. Once, he was taken to the psych ward in a straitjacket while on a bad trip, and the doctor was Dr. Hendrix. He loves to tell that story."

"Really? Your father took LSD? So, he's a hippie?"

"Yeah, he is."

"And now you're an activist, he must love that. What about your mother?"

I sighed audibly; my shoulders slumped as I looked down at my hands.

"Never mind," he said, standing up. "Don't think about that now."

He stepped behind me and massaged my shoulders, squeezing them hard.

"Just let go," he said.

We talked for hours, until it was late.

"Thanks for inviting me over but I better go home. I gotta crash," I said.

"No, you should stay here with me," he said, flashing a mischievous grin.

"No, I really gotta go," I said.

"Well then, let me walk you home."

Papa continued to pursue me, and eventually I stayed the night with him. I didn't tell Sharon ... or anyone.

"You know the more time I spend with you, the more I admire you."

We were just waking up, still warm and naked under the covers.

"Aw, Papa Dave, that's such a sweet thing to say." I nuzzled my face into his bare chest, biting my lip. This is awesome, I thought, but how will it end?

"No, I really mean it, you're special, very spiritual, very caring ... just very special," he said, squeezing me tight.

"But ... is this, I mean, are we together now?"

"Sure we're together, you're here with me now, right?" He laughed.

Though more questions filled my mind, I didn't ask them.

Papa Dave moved into the Gathering, pitching a large tent. I stayed there a few nights, then one night I appeared as usual and he had someone in the tent with him.

How can this be happening to me again?! I thought, sitting on the pine needle floor outside his tent. The lantern light cast shadowy figures, and I could hear voices rising and falling.

Hot tears slipped down my cheeks as I walked home on the dark path. I slept under a blanket of stars, drinking them in as I fell asleep.

I stopped talking to Papa Dave after that, I was so hurt. I got that people had prior connections, or "Gathering lovers," but couldn't they just say so? Why did they make me find out the hard way?

"So, it didn't work out with Papa Dave?" Sharon asked one morning as we sipped hot tea together.

"What? How do you know about that?"

"A little bird told me."

"Really? Who?"

"TC."

"Fuck, so he knows too? These older Brothers are such gossips, they're like old ladies!"

"Is it a secret or what?" She shook her head and frowned.

"You know everybody here is so judgmental, and I can't seem to get away from losers. I don't want people to know how hard I slum! God help me!" I covered my face with my hands, and fresh tears wet them.

Gypsy had given me a beautiful sheer scarf of black and yellow that I wore wrapped around my head and tossed over my shoulder. At night, I wore a woolen shawl over that. Though it was summer and the days were balmy, the nights were chilly.

The Vaishnavas arrived, and I went to their camp evenings to cook with them, eat vegetarian Indian food, and chant Hare Krishna.

After I met them last summer in Ithaca, Sharon and I drove to Brooklyn to hang out in their temple. One of the requirements to stay with them is to chant for four hours a day, starting at 4 a.m. We did, it was super challenging, but it clears and quiets the mind so much it is miraculous.

We also cooked food while reciting special prayers, then brought the eatables to Tompkins Square Park and gave them out for free. *Prasada*, it's called, and eating it can bring enlightenment.

I started a speech fast, wearing the black scarf over my face, only exposing my eyes. It reminded me not to speak. I continued to go to evening chanting, but I chanted silently. I prayed the fast, or the chanting—or something—would fix my screwed-up head, and my heart, broken by life.

A man approached me, smiling brightly.

"Hello," he said, folding his hands together and bowing.

I smiled under my veil.

"You're from Iraq?" he said.

I shook my head no and wrote on my pad that I'm speech fasting, and from New York.

"Oh," he said, "I thought you were here on a peace mission from the Middle East. But you're Middle Eastern, right?

I shook my head no.

"Well, my Sister, you should go there. Or maybe you can create peace from this side?"

I shrugged. If he only knew how hard I had tried to do that.

"Okay, well, my Sister, blessed be!" he said, and he bowed again.

"Rainbow Bear! Rainbow Bear! I yelled, running over to jump into his arms. "I'm so happy you're here my favorite Brother!!"

"Oh, well, you know Rainbow Bear was coming, honey, I'd never miss my family reunion." He sat down on a thick log near the fire and pulled me onto his lap. "You know Rainbow Bear loves you honey, right?" He chuckled and his big belly shook.

He was staying at Welcome Camp near the beginning of the trail, while Om Tea Home was two miles in. Bear had trouble with his legs—it was hard for him to walk, so I hung out at his camp. We sat around joking and laughing and greeting the newcomers.

"The Kind Ovens have pizza," someone called out.

"Rainbow Bear, you want me to get you pizza?"

"Oh yes honey, Rainbow Bear would love that!"

I rushed off to get him some before it was gone. When I returned, he was grumbling. "I'll tell you Sena Bear, some of these people around here are gonna get a hurtin'!"

"Why Rainbow? What happened?"

"This guy was talking about things he wanted to do to you, sexual things."

"What!"

"Yeah, he was saying that you were sexy and a lot of other things and I growled at him like this: Grrrrr, don't you talk about Sena Bear like that!"

I handed him the pizza, "That's crazy," I said.

"It's disrespectful! You're a Bear! But you know, Rainbow Bear will always protect you, honey!"

Star and Uncle John arrived. She plopped her huge backpack on the ground and bounced over to me with arms outstretched.

"Sister, beautiful Sister, you will not believe what just happened. I was in the parking lot and this Brother said, 'Hey Sena!' He thought I was you! Then, when I was walking up Jojo said, 'Hey Star, you know that Sister who looks like you? She was down here the other day asking after you.' And I was like, 'Yes! I'm on my way to see her, I just got in.' So, Sister, I got all your cosmic messages!"

"That Sister who looks like you? Not *a* Sister that looks like you? Oh my God, that is such an honor!" I said, tugging the ends of her long black coils.

We laughed and hugged long, and shared tales of the past month.

"Love works, fear don't," Kendo said, wearing his ever-present black beret and goofy smile. He sat with Bear and me at breakfast one morning and we talked about *A Course in Miracles*, his personal bible. The main thesis is that fear is the opposite of love. I was fascinated, as I always am by religions.

"Love works, Kendo don't," Rainbow Bear joked after he left.

"Come on now, really, he doesn't work?"

"Nah, he's okay, it's just a joke. He's not a true Drain-bow."

Barter Lane was along the trail that led up to the main circle. Money was taboo at Gatherings except for the donations that went into the Magic Hat at dinner. Alongside the trail, people set out brightly colored cloths covered with handmade jewelry, beads, books, and crystals. Those were traded for candy, marijuana, rides, and other valuables.

One bright afternoon I meandered along the lane admiring beaded chokers. In the distance, I saw a group of people naked and sitting in a circle in a sunny meadow. I spotted a tow-headed mess of dreads and I knew it was Helena!

"Helena!" I called out and soon we were hugging and talking rapidly.

"Oh my God, Sena, I thought about you so much! How was Kentucky?"

"Oh, it was beyond gorgeous, but the Gathering was contaminated with the Klan."

"What? At Rainbow?"

"Yup, wait, are you from the South?

"I'm from Florida, Tampa."

"Oh, cool! I love Florida! It's because we were in a rural, moonshining area. Apparently, the Klan are moonshiners."

"I didn't even know there was moonshine, I thought alcohol was legal. Isn't it in the Amendments or something?"

"Girl, you sound just like me!"

We both laughed.

Helena never stopped smiling, and her smile was so infectious there was no way not to smile back. Whenever I talked with her, I grinned until my face hurt.

When I got back to camp, a sweet surprise awaited.

"Ocean, welcome home Brother!" I said, hugging him hard. "I missed you!"

He was sitting on a bench drinking tea with Sharon.

"Me too, I missed y'all, but listen, I'm not going to camp here. I'm going to the West Coast with family. I really want to get back to surfing. Where is Fire-Catcher?"

"He's here, he went to fetch water."

We sat in silence listening to the crackling of the fire and the din of revelers in the distance.

Ocean was so warm, and kind, and innocent. I'm glad he didn't get involved with me. I don't think he could've weathered it, and I was starting to think no one could. A deep sea of darkness surrounded me, always threatening to pull me in.

Gypsy went into labor the day before summer solstice. I sat on the ground with Cat outside the teepee while she was inside giving birth. It was a long time, hours, but eventually her screams of pain stopped and abrupt silence replaced them. It felt as if the world stopped for just a moment, and then there was a crying baby. An entirely new person was now inside that teepee! And she named him Forest Moon.

Cat and I wept and hugged each other tight. She pulled back and put her hand on her belly. "In a few months that's going to be friggin' me! God, Mama Sena, am I ever going to find River?"

"You will Cat, I know you will."

A few days later, a reporter showed up from *Time* magazine, wanting to take pictures of the baby.

"We don't allow cameras here," I said.

"Why is that?

"It was a rule when I got here. Some people say it's steals your soul, but I feel like cameras separate you from the experience."

"Yeah, but they let others share the experience with you." he said.

"That's true, I was traumatized by the pictures of the Vietnam War in *Time* magazine as a child. I still remember them clearly and they affect me, even now."

Sharon emerged from behind tarps and said that Gypsy did not want to be interviewed or photographed.

"Sorry," I said.

"I understand," he said, walking off and giving a small wave over his shoulder.

"Happy birthday, my soul Sister!"

Lemongrass came striding into my kitchen the morning of our mutual birthday. She had arrived a few days earlier, and we discovered we shared a birthday.

"Lovin' Oven's made me a cake, I want to share it with you," she said.

We sat down in the grass and ate the cake with our hands. It was a small cake, with rich chocolate frosting. The inside was still warm.

"Lemongrass, you're never in DC. Every time I'm there I never see you."

"I'm going back after this, I'll be there all through the fall Sena-love. Come visit me," she said, putting her long arms around my neck and pulling my forehead to hers, "I want to hang out with you!"

"Me too," I said.

After the cake, we laid back on the grass, looking at the sky. "When I was a kid I would do this for hours," I said. She reached over and held my hand in silence.

I came back to camp later, and in walked Zack.

"Daddy! Oh my God, I can't believe you're here!"

"I told you I was maybe gonna come last time you called. Happy birthday!"

He camped with us, and I told TC he was here. That night, TC, Water, and Papa Dave showed up at our fire.

"Everyone wants to meet Sena's father," TC said, and they hugged him. We all sat around the fire and talked.

"So Zack, do you ever get over to the original Woodstock site?" TC said.

"No, I tried to go to the original concert, but all the traffic was stopped on Route 17. There was no way there once it really got going. Did you go?"

"Yeah, I was there."

"No shit, TC, you were at Woodstock?" I said.

"Yeah, Sena Bear, I'm an old-time hippie."

"Well, I know you're old," I said, laughing.

"She always makes fun of my age," Zack said, "you should've seen the grief she gave me when I turned thirty."

"Zack, you should come over to Bethel and hang out with us. We meet there every year on the anniversary of Woodstock. Family over there wants to build a permanent memorial on the site."

"Really? I love that idea," he said.

"I'll write you directions before you leave, then you can meet us over there next month. The fifteenth. We'll be there before that though," TC said.

Papa Dave passed my father a joint and he took a deep inhale. "Sena talks a lot about you, she really loves you," Papa Dave said.

I didn't look at Papa.

"I know, she's always been my favorite; she's just like me."

"Except she doesn't like that old music from the '50s. I put on some Buddy Holly and she completely rejected it; she said, 'That's my father's music!'"

My father chuckled, "She grew up in the '70s, so she never learned to appreciate the good stuff."

"What! What about Zeppelin and the Allman Brothers?" I said.

"Those are her favorites," my father said. "I'm a Grateful Dead man myself. And Dylan; Dylan is a poet, a master, beyond human."

They chatted awhile about music.

I was stuck with Papa Dave. He was camped not far from us, and was always at CALM. He acted like we were still great friends, ignoring my icy demeanor.

Then, as he often did, my father turned to teasing me, " ... and she was always the biggest crybaby on earth," he made an ugly crying face to imitate me.

"Yeah, he's talking about when he brought me home Sundays to my abusive mother. I would cry for hours sitting in his van. I never wanted to go home."

That stopped the teasing; everyone fell into an awkward silence.

As I walked up the steep trail towards the Vaishnavas camp, a man stopped and turned to see me behind him.

"Oh, hey, Sister Sena!" Diego said, "So good to see you, come on with me, we've got a little DC enclave up past Gypsy Kitchen."

"Okay," I said, giving him a hug and following him. I was excited to see some of my friends.

We continued on together up the pocked trail.

"Man the clothes here really depress me, I don't know who told people the potato sack look is back? I don't know why people aren't wearing revealing clothes; I like sexy dresses, you know, that show the body off."

"We call it a prairie dress," I said, and of course, I was wearing one.

"Well, it's really unattractive."

Whatever, I thought, but I didn't say anything. I didn't like his vibe and I never had.

"Listen, I heard from some of my staff that you really helped them out and that you have some amazing office and business skills."

"Yeah, I do," I said. "Your staff ...?"

"Yeah, you didn't know I owned T-Magic?"

"Nope."

"You went to business school?"

"No, I was a business manager and I seem to have a knack; I am compulsively organized, great with numbers, and good on computers."

"Well, I own a few companies. I'd like to talk to you about maybe coming to work for me?"

"Oh, I don't know, I'm not intending to live in DC."

"Where're you gonna live?"

"No idea."

"What about New York, you're from New York, right?"

"Yup, but I haven't thought of going back there and working. Plus, I'm from the sticks."

"Yeah but I can set you up in New York City. Wouldn't you want to live there?"

"I never thought about it."

"Well, if you ever want to just get in touch with me."

Then he handed me a joint and told me to keep it for later.

Later, I ran into Sharon on the trail and she told me that Prairie was at our camp and looking for me. "She says she wants to sing Natalie Merchant with you," she said.

I followed her back home; I was long over whatever anger I might've had towards Prairie.

"My beautiful Sister," she said, and we hugged a long time.

"I really missed you at these past Gatherings," I said.

"Me too," she said, "I've been out west."

I didn't ask about Jai.

"I thought we could sing together ... 'Verdi Cries'?" she said.

"You might be the only person I know besides me who knows all of her lyrics. I'm such a fanatic. Sharon, tell her how many concerts I dragged you to."

"Oh, a few," she said, laughing while she stirred her ever-brewing caldron of tea.

We sat cross-legged on the ground, hand-in-hand, and sang that gorgeous song together a cappella.

Ben appeared in our kitchen one day.

"Oh, my Brother! I'm so happy to see you!" I hugged him tightly.

"When did they let you out?" Sharon asked.

"A few weeks back. I stopped in Virginia to see my mother."

"Was it really bad there, in jail, I mean?"

"It was like being indentured. All I did was roadwork. The guys there were okay but you know … they weren't family. There's nothing like being with family."

"True," I said. "I hope you can recover from all that now."

"Yeah, I will, and I sure won't set foot in Kentucky ever again!"

The Fourth of July came, and everyone gathered in the main circle at sunrise to maintain a silence that ended at noon with drumming and reverie. The silence was the time to meditate on and pray for world peace. Zack was there beside me when the silence was broken, and a sunbow was spotted emerging from the clouds, leading everyone to cheer.

"It makes me so happy you're here, and that you love nature so much," Zack said.

I inhaled deeply, "That smell of the forest; pine needles, damp leaves, and dirt, that's my favorite scent on earth. I want to wake up every day on the forest floor."

"You have no idea, Sena, no idea how good you have it, how lucky you are, how free you are … when I was your age, I couldn't do any of this."

"Because you had kids?"

"Yeah, because I had kids."

"I don't feel lucky at all, I just feel … lost … like … like I'm always looking for home."

He stayed silent. He had never offered me a home and he sure didn't have one to offer me now.

Sharon and I wondered about the money from the Magic Hat. It was used to buy supplies in town like coffee and sugar, a priority at Rainbow, while things like fruit, which we wanted for the pregnant Sisters, was not.

When we heard an announcement for a banking meeting at dinner we decided to attend, hoping we could get some provisions. The meeting was a small group of what we called High-Holies: older people who had been attending the Gatherings for decades. They seemed shocked that we showed up, and uncomfortable when we sat down with them.

We watched them give themselves large amounts of money to pay for things like gasoline, since they were considered essential crew, or they were bringing homeopathic medicine, or they were carrying the supplies for CALM. I frowned disapprovingly at Papa Dave. It's not that I thought they didn't deserve the money, maybe they did. It's that they did it in secret. Up until this moment, I thought all the money in the Magic Hat went towards food. I scowled, and picked at the grass under my crossed legs. I despise the culture of secrets!

Sharon spoke, "Listen, Water, everyone, I need fruit at my kitchen, melons, oranges, hydrating stuff with Vitamin C. I've got a few pregnant and nursing moms, as you know."

They quickly voted to approve her request and the next day a large box of fresh fruit was delivered to our camp.

Just a few days later, drama broke out.

"This is it, Sena, Sharon … I'm closing down your kitchen!"

"No, you're not, Water," I said.

"Yes, I am, and I told you if you keep promoting this anti-bleach movement this would happen. Other kitchens want to follow suit now, I can't have a public health outbreak."

"Well there's no way in hell I'm putting bleach in my rinse water and besides, this is a tea kitchen."

"It doesn't matter. People can get sick if they're putting their dishes in the same water."

"I'm getting TC, and whoever else I can. You can't make these decisions on your own, you need a council!"

I hurried down the hill, barefoot in a bright silk sari, blue and gold fabric flowing over my shoulder then falling on the ground behind me. Water ran after me.

"Sena, why are you doing this? You know better than this."

"Because I'm an environmentalist, Water, not a fucking armchair environmentalist and I thought you were too!"

"I am Sister, but I have to think about public health."

"Don't you think the people who pour sodium fluoride and other crap into the public water system say the same thing? There's not only one way to do things!"

"TC!" I called out. He was sitting in a camping chair alongside Papa Dave under the CALM tarp.

"What's up Sena?" Papa Dave said.

"Water is trying to shut my kitchen down, you guys have to help me. Are you environmentalists or not? We're bringing dozens—maybe hundreds—of gallons of bleach into this forest and it's not okay. I haven't bought that stuff in years and I won't use it in my kitchen. Plus, I boycott corporations that make toxic crap. I use white vinegar and hydrogen peroxide and you have to tell Water that's acceptable."

"No, it's not, Sena, I've been telling you for months, I've been warning you that I will shut you down," Water said, walking over to us inside of CALM.

"All right, everybody take a breath," Papa Dave said. "Sena, you go back up to your camp. Water and TC and me are going to have a talk."

"Yeah, I'm sure you are—fucking men! I'm so sick of this bullshit patriarchy, I didn't leave mainstream society to live under the rules of a bunch of fucking men!"

"You're cute when you're angry, Mama Sena," TC called after me as I walked out of CALM.

"Shut up, TC!"

I stormed back up the hill and told people in my kitchen what was happening. Sharon said, "TC will fix it, he's a peacemaker."

"What are we going to do in the meantime?"

"I'm serving tea," she said.

"This is going to blow over, Water's just mad because we went to the bank meeting," I said.

"Seems that way," she said.

Later Papa Dave came up to see me. "Listen, we're not going to shut down your kitchen but at least stop advertising you're not using bleach, alright?"

"So now it's censorship? First, it's unfair rules we're not allowed to protest, then it's old ways of doing things we're not allowed to improve, and now you want me to be silent. You guys are exactly like Babylon!"

"Look, I know you're mad at me for some reason but you don't have to be so angry."

"Right, for some reason, right, and now you're gonna tell me how to feel. You think we're here getting away from 'the man'? You *are* the man! This is bullshit and none of it is counterculture, it's right in line with all the things we stand against!"

"Okay Mama Sena, I can't talk to you anymore, you're impossible to deal with. I'm going to go talk to Sharon."

"Whatever, Papa, you do whatever you want."

One night as we sat near the fire a girl called out to us from the dark, "Sisters, Sisters, can you help me?"

Sharon and I jumped up and went over to her.

"I was raped," she said, "this guy, Jupiter, he raped me."

Sharon grabbed an army blanket and wrapped it around her shivering shoulders, then directed her to sit by the fire.

"What happened, Sister?" Sharon said, ladling hot tea into a cup then handing it to the shaking girl.

"I met this really sweet Brother, Jupiter. Well, I was hanging out with him and he offered to give me a massage, so I went to his tent with him. He seemed so nice. And then, he got really mean, he was so scary, and he hurt my arms, look and these bruises." She pushed up the sleeves of her dress showing us bluish marks on her arms, like fingerprints.

Her lip quivered as she spoke, and she took a sip of tea. "He forced me, I mean, he had sex with me when I kept saying no. I was crying, begging him to let me go. I couldn't get free."

The tea was valerian, a powerful herbal sedative that soon had the girl asleep in Sharon's bedroll.

We went down the hill to talk to the men at CALM. Sharon's face was full of fury, her eyes alight; it was rare to see her this angry.

We gave a brief description of Jupiter and asked them to put out the word to Shantisena to look for him. We wanted him captured and given to the police.

By the next morning, he had been found.

"Sharon, Sena, they got the guy, the rapist. They're having a council meeting over on the other side of the main circle," Little Hawk said, his hands on his knees while he caught his breath, "I ran all the way here, you gotta go now."

"Wait, they're having the council now? Why didn't anyone tell us?" I said.

"They didn't want you to know. That's why I came to tell you. I know you're taking care of the Sister and I don't think it's right, you should be there."

We were livid. We strode across the huge main field and found a small circle of people sitting in high grass off to the side.

About eight men were there including Water, Papa Dave, TC, and a guy from the peacekeeping force holding the perpetrator tightly by his upper arm. The boy sat cross-legged on the ground looking down at the grass, forlorn.

"We are going to be part of this meeting, we're up there picking up the pieces from his crime and we're not gonna let this happen to anyone else, this is bullshit! Why weren't we invited to this meeting, Water?" I said, busting into the circle with Sharon in tow.

"We're just trying to get this done peaceably."

"Well, there is no peace, he has to be turned over to the police, I will go with you."

"We're not turning him over the police, he is family," Papa Dave said.

"I don't give a fuck who he is," I said.

TC said, "Dammit, Sena, you know you're always up in arms and this is why we didn't tell you."

Sharon jumped in. "Well what about me? I'm telling you that we have a severely traumatized rape victim up at our camp and this guy will strike again. You don't have any way to protect people from him."

"Yes, well, Red Hawk here has a plan, he is going to tie himself to this Brother, tether himself to him. They will eat, sleep, and drink together." "How is that going to help him? He's sick, he needs help," I said.

"And you think he's going to get it in jail? Come on now, Sister," Papa Dave said.

"No, I know, I'm totally against the prison system, but we don't have any other system and I'm more against people getting victimized by known criminals."

"He's just a really messed up kid," Water said.

Sharon said, "Messed up? Messed up? You think that's what being messed up is? He's a rapist, and he hurt this girl."

"Yeah," I said, "and rape is an act of violence. You should know that Water, you're running a medical scene. He raped her and he will strike again and every girl here is a sitting duck if you let him stay."

The men overruled us, dismissing our fears, and Red Hawk left with the rapist, vowing to keep track of him. But within twenty-four hours, he had lost him in a sea of thousands and the rapist, Jupiter, was never found again. "Sharon, I don't know if I can be part of this community anymore. I am so traumatized by the rapist being let loose. I get that we don't want to turn people over to the cops, but I don't see any other choice we have, and so many of the people here act just like the authorities; everything they rebel against is who they are, I don't get it. So much power tripping, so much hypocrisy … I came here to get away from that shit."

"Let's decide later, after the New Mexico Gathering," she said, "I'm really upset too, so maybe it's not the time for us to make a decision. It is really discouraging how much patriarchy we're still living under. I still can't believe they tried to have that meeting without us, and then let a rapist go. Our concerns didn't even matter."

When we finally left Vermont, with Cat and Fire-Catcher in tow, we decided to go to the Blueberry Festival, a regional Gathering in North Carolina where wild blueberries were ripe for picking. We would be high in the Smoky Mountains at a relatively small Gathering where we could chill out, recover, eat blueberry pancakes, and think about the future.

FOURTEEN

**Late July 1991
Smoky Mountains
North Carolina**

Here is the efflux of the soul,
The efflux of the soul comes from within through embower'd gates, ever provoking questions,
These yearnings why are they? these thoughts in the darkness why are they?
Why are there men and women that while they are nigh me the sunlight expands my blood?
Why when they leave me do my pennants of joy sink flat and lank?

***

"I'm Sheriff Burton," a bearded young man in a uniform said, reaching his hand out towards me.

It was late afternoon and the magnificent Smoky Mountains surrounded us. We spent hours climbing hills at barely twenty miles per hour, the putt-putt of the Volkswagen straining as we went higher into the clouds. Now, in the parking area of the Blueberry Festival, we stood outside the van drinking in the eerie beauty of the fog-ringed peaks.

"Your friends over there said that you could help with all manner of issues. Is that there correct?" he said.

"Yes, that's right." I reached out to shake his hand and there was a feeling, a feeling that was not supposed to be there. He was a man wearing a badge.

We talked about parking and other logistics.

"Oh, so where can I find you? Where are you camping?"

"We decided we're going to camp here in the parking lot. It's small, there are no gatekeepers, so we're gonna do parking lot duty."

After dark, the sheriff returned in civilian clothes with two of his friends and some seriously nice bud. We all sat in the tiny living room of my camper van and talked.

"I didn't know sheriffs were allowed to smoke pot."

"Well, this one is allowed. Besides it's homegrown from the garden, no more harmful than the tomatoes I grow."

"I agree, but it's a lot stronger than tomatoes," I said.

"Yeah, I reckon it is," he said.

"I ran into the Ku Klux Klan," I told him, "and they gave me business cards, is that for real? Do you really have the Klan with hoods and stuff? I've never seen them up north. I don't really think they could survive where I'm from."

"Oh, we got 'em all right. There are not too many but they stick together. Why thar's some towns 'round here where they got a stronghold. I don't even go there. When the old sheriff hired me, he told me to never go messin' with 'em. They got a lot of hate in their hearts. You'd do best to avoid 'em."

He looked like us although his beard was neat and his long ponytail was clean and shiny. We talked until late into the night. His friends left us alone at one point, wandering down into the Gathering.

"So, you ever think of stayin' anyplace?" the sheriff asked me.

"You mean like here?"

"Well, yeah, you say you're a mountain girl, this here is the most beautiful mountains anywhere."

"It really is stunning here," I said. "I'm supposed to go to New Mexico next though, I was hoping to see the West."

His smile was warm, and when he left, he hugged me a long time. I sighed and rested there in his arms.

I went to sleep thinking forbidden fantasies, like being a sheriff's wife in the mountains of North Carolina.

But I was on a mission; I couldn't stop and take up a mundane existence. I needed to save the world, stop the wars, and end slavery.

And what about my past? No one was going to accept that or ever understand.

I had desire for love, even for a partner, but the fixation that absorbed me was finding some sort of spiritual balm that could offer relief from the vise-like grip of psychic pain that plagued me, and the grief that engulfed me, and absolution for my sins, and crimes, and mistakes, and everything I could never forgive myself for.

I questioned each day whether I could even make it through that very day. Sometimes it felt like I was clawing my way through, hour by hour. I thought of killing myself a myriad of ways. It was my golden parachute—if I could not find relief from the searing agony of consciousness, then I could release myself from the mortal coil.

But, if I could connect with God and if I could stay connected, I might have relief, mercy, forgiveness, even redemption. I prayed every day as I had my whole life, but what about every hour? Every minute?

Then I'd never be alone, no matter how many people left me.

FIFTEEN

August & September 1991
Jemez National Forest
New Mexico

Allons! to that which is endless as it was beginningless,
To undergo much, tramps of days, rests of nights,
To merge all in the travel they tend to, and the days and nights they tend to,
Again to merge them in the start of superior journeys,
To see nothing anywhere but what you may reach it and pass it,
To conceive no time, however distant, but what you may reach it and pass it

***

On the way to New Mexico, we visited Tennessee. In my dog-eared copy of the Rainbow address book, I found a couple in Nashville and called them from a phone booth telling them that we wanted to visit the city. They were friendly and welcoming and immediately invited us over for dinner.

As we sat in the living room of the sprawling Nashville home, I took a small magazine off the table and started to read.

The man seemed excited that I picked it up.

"Please take it," he said.

It was called *Daily Word*. I assumed it was a tract so I didn't think much of it. Later, I lay on my bed and slowly read. This was one of the most beautiful and visionary versions of Christianity I had ever seen.

In the morning, I asked him about it.

"Oh, that's our church they are the most loving church on earth. They are called Unity. I'll give you a book of theirs."

"I've never heard of it."

"They are mostly in the south, I think, they started in Missouri about a hundred years back."

The book was called *Meet it with Faith*, and it seemed to have a remedy for all the problems of life: turn to God.

We stayed a few days, spending evenings walking around Nashville listening to music. During the day, we helped with housework and hid from the blistering heat.

Then we were off, headed west towards New Mexico. We decided to stop in Oklahoma and call a man we met at the National who called himself Oklahoma. He was a gentle-natured schoolteacher. When we called, he seemed shocked.

"I told you I was going to call," I said.

"I know," he said, "but people always say things. I'm so excited you guys are here! Meet me at McDonald's and you can follow me home."

I stood outside McDonald's with a huge glass jar that I used to make alfalfa sprouts in my van. I turned on the spigot and begin filling the jar with water to rinse the sprouts.

Oklahoma pulled up and got out of his car, hugging us, then he eyed the jar filled with greenery.

"Are you guys gardening in your van?"

"Kind of," I said, pouring the water back out on the ground.

"Well, come on, let's go to my house, you can garden there!"

We followed him home and stayed the better part of a week. He offered us money to do work at his house and we cleaned, did landscaping, mowed, and every night I made a beautiful dinner for all of us.

Then it was time to leave, and we drove off early one day, landing in Santa Fe around dusk. We planned to hang out there a day or two then head to the Gathering. We hit the health-food store and immediately ran into family.

"Sisters, where are you staying?" they asked.

"We don't know yet," I said.

"Everyone is camping down at the railroad tracks, just a few blocks south of here."

We went to the tracks and sure enough, there was a rag-tag bunch of family in town for the Gathering. We parked and walked past an RV.

"Sharon! Mama Sena!" a girl called out.

We turned and saw Helena. I ran over and hugged her.

"Who are you with? I'm so happy you're here!"

"I'm here with Jay and Grace," she said.

"We are camping in our van here a few days till we go to camp. Come find me there!"

Cat went to sleep early, and soon Sharon and Fire-Catcher followed.

The train yard was abandoned and ghostly, old railcars sat silent around us. I walked over to the tracks. It was dark, but a group of people sat upon the long-abandoned rails. I sat with them, and we talked about the upcoming Gathering. Then, Helena appeared.

"What's going on with you, Sena? I really want to travel with you."

"Yes! You should, I would love that. We totally have room for you."

"Let's see what happens at the Gathering. I was going to go to California after this to meet up with a boy. What about you, what's after here?"

"I don't know, I've got so many things to tell you. My father was at the National, for one."

"Really? I wish I got to meet him."

"It's just I've been trying to get space from him, you know, it's so hard. I feel lost when I don't talk to him. It's weird. But also, he's crazy. Like seriously, he's bipolar, un-medicated, and he pulls me down."

Just then, a man came over and sat down across from us on the tracks.

"How you doing, Sisters?" he said.

He had flowing wavy brown hair and a super-handsome face. His broad grin was mischievous, like a Cheshire cat's.

"I'm Zack."

"Really? That's my father's name!" I said, flashing a huge smile.

"Sena! Oh my god, I don't believe you!" Helena said, chuckling.

In no time I was leaving the tracks with Zack to get high. High, that is, on sleep deprivation.

"It's this whole new thing I've discovered," he said, "it's better than any drug. And it's natural, it's all about brain chemistry."

I was intrigued but way more interested in being with him than I was in getting high. He was philosophical, and brainy. Plus, he was crazy and that was my exact type, apparently.

I walked around art-filled Santa Fe with him until dawn, looking at pottery through store windows. We sat on a bench and watched the sunrise. Soon it was daytime, and the hustle-bustle of the city began. The park was full of people walking dogs, jogging, or cutting through on their way to work.

I was exhausted. "Let's lay down there, under that tree."

"Okay," he said, "I give in to sleep. I'm beat."

We lay down on the bare grass. The blades were cool and dewy. I could see people's feet as they walked by. Soon, I was in a deep sleep.

"Sena? Sis, hey wake up!" It was Grace and Helena. "Sharon's been looking for you ... she was worried."

"Oh, okay, shit, it's evening now, right? I better go back with you then."

I roused Zack and brought him back to the tracks with me. Sharon shook her head and laughed at me.

"So, he's our new passenger?"

"Yes," I said, with a foolish smile.

"Alright, but hey, Sister, please leave me a message when you go off, you know I worry."

I agreed but I was irritated. I once liked her protectiveness but lately I felt smothered. I felt she judged my endless love seeking, or maybe that was just my self-judgment?

Most likely, we both judged me.

Up in the remote Jemez Mountains, we were a world away from the city. As soon as we got there, Zack went elsewhere to camp. Nothing ever happened with us; I soon realized he was way too crazy, even for me.

Besides, I was avoiding Gathering entanglements since Papa Dave burned me a few months back. It still smarted.

I continued to wear shawls and clothes that covered my head and sometimes part of my face. I really wanted to focus on praying. I really wanted to focus on God.

The Gathering was small but I was so excited Helena was there. I told her everything that was going on with me, and it helped to be able to tell someone without feeling judged.

I met a guy named Sam, who had long blond dreadlocks and lived in a house off the grid in Albuquerque. We talked many hours about spirituality, the environment, and reggae. We were both huge reggae fanatics.

"Where are you going after this? He asked.

"I don't know, we haven't really planned our next move."

"You should come and stay with me in Albuquerque, I've got some great roommates ... you'd really like them. I live with three women!"

I wrote his address in the notebook I always kept with me.

"I just might come by," I said.

Tripper was at the Gathering and I hadn't seen him in months, since Kentucky. He had turned me on to speech fasting there, and one night we kissed while exchanging handwritten notes. I sat down next to him at a campfire and when I gave him a hug and tried to catch up with him, he interrupted me.

"You know, you really hurt me."

"Oh my God, I did?"

"Yeah, I thought we had something special and you just ditched me."

"No I didn't. Tripper just listen—"

"No, I don't want to listen. You need to listen, you can't just go around being a heartbreaker."

"What are you even talking about?"

"I'm talking about all the men that you've rejected." He stood up. "I'm going to start a support group for men that were dissed by Sena."

"Come on, stop, Tripper, it's not funny."

"It's not meant to be funny."

"Look, Tripper, I'm really sorry."

He walked away and soon he was walking around camp trying to collect people who felt rejected by me.

Helena came and found me.

"There's a guy going around looking for people who got their heart broken by you?" She was laughing.

"I know, it's absurd, I don't know what to do. Tripper's just mad at me I guess …"

"What happened with you and him?"

"Nothing! That's the thing, sometimes I'm interested in somebody, then I spend a little time with them, maybe I kiss them or cuddle with them, and then sometimes I figure out they're not right for me. But when I try to stop it, it turns into a disaster. Dating here is a fucking nightmare! Imagine if all the guys you rejected you saw at breakfast the next day?"

"Oh shit, yeah, that sucks, what are you gonna do?"

"I don't know, I still love them, I still want to be friends with them, but it's like they want to get married after one day. Unless someone else comes along, then they ditch me anyway."

"Wait, what are you saying now?"

"Nothing, Helena I am just so fucking burnt out."

She put her arms around me.

"I'm so sorry my beautiful Sister, I love you."

"I love you too."

I sighed deeply, letting her cuddles comfort me.

Cat came running into camp one day, pulling a handsome, freckled guy by the arm. "Family! Hey family, look at who's here: this is River!"

"Oh my God, I'm so happy you guys found each other!" I went and hugged him.

"Looks like I'm going to Montana to have this baby!"

"Montana?"

"Yes, that's where River lives and he's taking me home!"

"I'm so happy for you, but I'm going to miss you so much."

"Well, I'm going to go back to Santa Fe for a little while before we leave. He's got a job to finish up and then I'm going north."

The Gathering was uneventful and soon it was winding down. Fire-Catcher decided to go to California with some people and maybe catch up with Ocean.

Sharon heard about a Rainbow house in Santa Fe. "Maybe we can go stay there for a little, while we decide what we want to do next?" she said.

"Okay," I said. "Let's take Cat with us until River comes to get her."

Helena and I hugged a long time.

"I wish I wasn't going to California, I would just come with you," she said.

"Don't go, just blow him off."

"Well, I can't, he's going to teach me guitar and that's my dream—to be a musician. I'll find you, don't worry. Where are you going?"

"I'm going to stay at a house in Santa Fe and I might be able to get you a phone number. Actually, Grace knows about it so let's see if she has the number."

She did, and Helena wrote the phone number on a scrap of paper and shoved it in her rucksack.

"Oh, you know what, I think I'm going to Albuquerque. Sam says I can come and stay at his house. But I don't have the number there. Just call the house in Santa Fe if you need to find me."

"So you're not gonna stay with Sharon and do the kitchen anymore?"

"I don't know, right now I really don't want to. I'm so down on Rainbow right now, and, well, you know ..."

There was a cool scene at the Rainbow house in Santa Fe. Grace was there, newly broken up with her boyfriend. She and Sharon seemed inseparable and I was glad. I had never seen Sharon connect with anyone in the years that I knew her.

We tried to talk about what we were going to do next but we couldn't really come up with any plans.

"I'm thinking about going to Albuquerque for a little while and staying with Sam, just maybe hanging out for a bit. Maybe we could have a little time apart ... you could take the van."

She was sitting behind the steering wheel and I was in the passenger seat of our van. She turned the key off, and the hum of the Pancake engine turned to silence.

"Why do we need time apart?" she said.

"Because I always feel like you're mad at me, I always feel like I'm in trouble, and we don't really talk anymore. I don't know what you want or what you feel, ever."

"Well, I'm not like you, I don't just wear my heart on my sleeve and say everything I think."

"But I want to know what you think, you have a brilliant mind. I just want to talk about why you're angry with me and what your issues are with me."

"I don't have any issues with you Sena, I don't know what you're talking about."

We ended in a kind of cool stalemate. We agreed that she would stay in Santa Fe, and I would go to Albuquerque with the van for a week or two.

"Surprise my Brother, I'm here!"

I showed up at Sam's door one morning.

"Hello, oh my dear Sister, I am so happy you're here. Come have some breakfast with us, meet my roommates."

He flipped his long locks back and pulled me close, hugging me tightly. I barely cleared his waist, wrapping my arms around his lanky frame.

"I was hoping I could stay a week or two, check out Albuquerque."

"Definitely! I have a cabin in the backyard and you could stay there with me. It's all off the grid."

"That sounds so cool!"

Sam was at work most days so I had a lot of time alone, more than I'd had in years. The days were long and hot. There was a giant cottonwood tree with a swing and I spent hours lounging there, writing poems in my notebook.

I made a Gambian groundnut stew my former boyfriend Sa'eed had taught me how to make, and it was a hit. I was so happy to use a real kitchen. I love cooking for people, and playing in the kitchen.

I was in the driveway late one morning cleaning out my van, trying to figure out what I would take if I gave Sharon the van and I was on foot with only a backpack.

One of the roommates, a girl named Sandy, pulled in next to me.

"Hey, whatcha doin'?" she said.

"Trying to decide what to do with my life, so, nothing much."

She laughed. "Why don't you come inside and have some lunch with me?"

We made grilled cheese with tomato on sourdough bread and then sat at the table together. No one else was home.

"So, you're with Sam?" she asked.

"No, no," I said, "I mean, I liked him at first but then he told me he's totally hung up on his ex. Of course, that probably made me like him more because I love unavailable people."

"Oh no, really? Well, me too."

"Yeah, it sucks, right? My mother left when I was fifteen but really, she left before that. When I was thirteen my mother suddenly considered me an adult, she tried to fix me up with men and let me stay out all night and drink. I feel like she broke something inside my head that makes me only want people that are unavailable, or nuts, or just plain fucked up," I said.

"I can relate to a crazy mother. My mother made me wear gloves to school as punishment and one time she made me wear a heavy overcoat in May when it was hot. I was adopted, but I don't know why she adopted me, it felt like she never wanted kids. She beat us, and made us kids stand for hours as punishment."

"Oh my God, that's horrible! I'm so sorry, my girl."

"Yeah, well, she totally disowned me since I'm a dyke. She's a Christian fundamentalist, so, you know, I'm gonna burn in hell."

We moved to the living room, where heavy drapes were drawn against the blazing desert sun. We put on a k.d. lang album and sat in the dark listening to her croon sad songs over moody strings.

"I'm always looking for a boyfriend, always looking for love, but lately all I think about is this girl, Helena. She's not like anyone I've ever met. She ... she makes me feel alive. Like, excited to be alive and most days I don't even want to be here. It's like I'm trapped on earth, trying to make the best of my supernatural prison."

She reached over and took my hand. Her face was girlish, and I realized she was much younger than the other roommates.

"I've tried to kill myself twice and I've ended up in the psych ward, so I hear your pain, Sister. I'm always looking for love too. Tell me more about Helena. Where is she?"

"She's in California with some guy, I don't know."

"Have you ever had a girlfriend before? Have you ever been in love with a woman?"

"I don't know, sometimes I think so. A few years ago I had this best friend, this girl, Jenn, and we used to drink together, it was before I quit drinking. But even when we were sober, she was always flirting with me. She wanted to dress me up in her lingerie. She was married but her husband was away, he worked overseas."

"So did you wear the lingerie?"

"I did and nothing happened but one night when we were both drinking, she hit on me and we fooled around the whole night. I really wasn't that drunk because I remember all of it."

"So what happened after that?"

"Okay, so when we woke up in the morning she was freaking out, 'I'm not gay, I'm definitely not gay," she said. "Well, I am,' I said, 'I'm at least half gay!' I was pretty happy but she was having all kinds of remorse."

"I think you should definitely find Helena, you should see what's there."

"Do you have a girlfriend?"

"Oh yeah, I'm with a woman who doesn't believe in monogamy, she's much older, and she breaks my heart every day."

"Wow, I thought only men did that."

"Nope." Fresh tears rolled down her cheeks. I put my arms around her and she cried while I held her. It seemed so wrong to me that someone who went through that much pain as a kid then grows up and suffers more. Is there no mercy in life?

The days went by slowly and I spent a lot of time with Sandy. She was raw and hurting, and every chance I got I tried to be there for her.

Then, it was time for me to leave and face my own life.

"I better head back up to Santa Fe and deal with Sharon and our kitchen," I told Sam one afternoon.

"I get it, you should definitely go, but you know, I think the world of you, Mama Sena, you're a saint, you're the best person I've ever met."

"No, no, I'm not, believe me."

"I don't believe you."

"Well, I'm just a messed up person who prays a lot."

"No, you help everyone around you. My roommates benefited so much from you being here and so did I. All that amazing food you made, and you cleaned my house, you're better than you know."

"Yeah, I'll tell that to people who hate me."

"Nobody hates you!"

"You'd be surprised."

I drove the hour back to Santa Fe and showed up at the Rainbow house where Sharon was staying. She and Grace gave me a cold welcome and I knew I'd probably made it worse by leaving.

"Grace and I want to take the van and go up to Taos for a little while."

I was in the laundry room tossing my clothes in the washer. Leaf bits and burs floated on top of the water and I scooped them out with my hand.

"Look, Sharon, you can have the van. I can't go back to Rainbow and I'm not gonna take the van from you. Just take it."

"But what are you gonna do?"

Her hands were on her hips, her face reddened.

I turned back to the washer. "I don't know. Maybe go to DC, to the Tree House?"

Her voice rose. "You do whatever you want Sena, you always do!"

"But what does that mean?"

"Nothing."

"Do you want to talk about our issues so we can fix them?"

"I don't have any issues, you're the one who has issues."

"Okay, so what does that mean?"

"It doesn't mean anything. I don't want to talk anymore." She left the room in a huff and I followed her into the kitchen where she was filling a glass of water. The people there scattered.

"Look, I'm sorry Sharon, I'm so sorry. I can't say it enough, but I don't know how to fix things."

I took things out of the van the next day, whatever I thought I could carry; a bunch of clothes, five books, and a plastic case filled with my beading supplies.

I cried the whole time. I was losing my dream of family and community, and it was back to the harsh world.

The last few years I knew what I was doing next and where I was going. Now, I felt completely lost, adrift in the world, alone.

SIXTEEN

October 1991
Santa Fe
New Mexico

Listen! I will be honest with you,
I do not offer the old smooth prizes, but offer rough new prizes,
These are the days that must happen to you:
You shall not heap up what is call'd riches,
You shall scatter with lavish hand all that you earn or achieve,
You but arrive at the city to which you were destin'd, you hardly settle yourself to satisfaction before you are call'd by an irresistible call to depart,
You shall be treated to the ironical smiles and mockings of those who remain behind you,
What beckonings of love you receive you shall only answer with passionate kisses of parting,
You shall not allow the hold of those who spread their reach'd hands toward you.

***

I hugged Cat goodbye, petting her silky blond hair for the last time. My eyes filled with tears.

"My dearest Sister, I will miss you so much!"

"Me too, so fucking much, but I'm really, really happy! I'm going to go chill out in a house, I'm going to be with River, and we're going to raise this baby."

She was large at this point, nearly seven months pregnant. River picked up her bag and carried it out to the car. I walked out with them, waving while they backed out of the driveway.

Something I really hated about Rainbow was the countless goodbyes.

I went back inside the sprawling ranch house. Unfurnished, it had plenty of floor space for family crashing in their sleeping bags, though just a handful of people were here now.

I lay on top of my sleeping bag listening to Burning Spear with a portable tape player.

"I can't believe you listen to this shit," a Brother name Marc said.

"Shit? Are you crazy! This is some of the most spiritual music on earth, and it is pure political genius."

"I think the lyrics are full of hate."

"What are you talking about?"

"Total destruction is the only solution? That's not loving," he said.

He sat down on his bag nearby, scowling.

"Even what you are listening to right now, 'Raid them Jah, someone's got to pay?' That's hate speech."

"You are taking it out of context, this is a brilliant album about the suffering Africans went through being kidnapped and enslaved. In the beginning of the song he talks about his entire family being slaughtered, his sister being raped—"

"I know, I know the history, but singing lyrics hating on everyone now, saying someone's got to pay, that's just evil."

"If you heard the whole song you'd understand it better. He's coming from a place of personal devastation," I said.

He was so agitated I didn't argue anymore with him. I'm always uncomfortable with lyrics that call for the harm of people, but that's just a small part and it comes out of anger and hurt, and the Old Testament, which is something Rastafarians prize.

Marc reminded me of myself; sermonizing, and filled with unmovable opinions.

I started to socialize a lot with the guy who owned the house, Red Wolf. He was warm, and quiet, and he listened to a lot of female folk music. I'd never met a guy into that music.

He saw me reading the *Daily Word*.

"Do you like Unity Church?

"I love their writings. A Brother in Nashville turned me onto them."

"But have you ever been to the church?"

"No, I never have."

"Do you want to go? There's one here in Santa Fe."

"Oh my God, I totally want to go!"

"Well, let's go on Sunday then."

We went to the most positive uplifting service I have ever seen, not that I had seen many church services. We met people there; a couple invited us over for lunch. Everyone was friendly and welcoming.

Soon after that, I began sleeping in Red Wolf's bed.

Red Wolf and I had outrageous chemistry. I had more in common with him than anyone I had ever met. The spiritual thing was particularly unique but he didn't ask me to stay in Santa Fe and our romance remained undefined, which for me was unusual. I started thinking of going to DC. I could go to the Tree House and find Lemongrass and maybe Sunshine.

One night Red Wolf and I went on an ice cream run and brought an assortment of Ben & Jerry's back for everyone.

"Kick down, kind Sister," a Brother named Jester held a bowl out while I dished out the ice cream.

"For sure, Brother, we got this for everyone," I said, filling his dish with Chunky Monkey.

A group of us sat around the table, eating. The phone rang and I jumped up and answered it, as I often did.

"Hello?"

"Hi, um, this is Helena, I am trying to find a Sister named Sena and —"

"What! Oh my God Helena, it's me!"

"Oh wow, Sena, I can't believe it's you! I'm in Albuquerque because that's where you said you were going but I realized I didn't know where you were in Albuquerque."

"I was at this Brother's house but now I'm staying here."

"How far is it to Santa Fe?"

"An hour."

Then she was talking to someone in the background.

"Mama Sena? This man just offered to give me a ride, I will be there in an hour!"

"Holy shit, I'm so excited! I'm gonna save you some ice cream."

Soon she stood in the kitchen with us, smiling, telling us animated stories of her travels in her honeyed voice.

"It didn't work out with Mike and I decided to come try to find my girl!"

She put her arms around me.

"How did you get here?" I asked.

"I hitchhiked. I bought a guitar in California and I hitched all the way here with it and this guy who gave me a ride put it in the back of his pickup truck and it fell out and smashed on the road."

"What, that's crazy!"

"I know! I'm gonna have to buy another one because I'm in the middle of learning to play."

Later when we all went to crash Red Wolf asked me, "Do you want Helena to sleep with us?"

"Yeah, that would be so great."

The three of us got in his bed with me in the middle. I slept in the dress I was wearing, a floral light-blue gown with a crocheted neckline and sleeves, only taking off the striped pajama bottoms I had on underneath.

Soon Helena was sleeping and just as I was dozing off Wolf's hand was on my shoulder, then he kissed me and soon, we were making love in the darkened room. I prayed we didn't wake Helena.

Red Wolf left for work while I was still asleep and when I awoke Helena was sleeping with her head resting on my shoulder. She looked like a cherub with her rosy cheeks and golden hair.

Helena and I took to walking around Santa Fe hand-in-hand, often singing. I taught her all the Public Enemy songs that I treasured, and some LL Cool J for fun. She taught me Gershwin, and the Dead.

When I was with her the world seemed to melt away, as if we were the only people on earth. I had never felt anything like it.

One afternoon a man in a business suit approached me on the street. "Oh, wow, your hair is so beautiful. Can I touch it?"

"No," I said, jumping back as he reached his hand towards my curls.

"Oh my God, girlfriend, I've never seen that happen to anyone."

"It happens to me a lot."

"Are you serious?"

I shook my head.

"I bet it wouldn't happen if you had dreadlocks."

"I've been thinking about it seriously the past month and I'm definitely gonna do it."

"It's just knots, all you have to do is stop combing it."

"I only comb it in the shower, with tons of conditioner," I said, "so all I have to do is stop?"

"Yup, that's all!"

Helena had a fascination with me that was unlike anything I had ever experienced. She wanted to know my thoughts on everything. We were both loquacious. We would talk so much my jaw would hurt but I couldn't stop talking with her.

"You know I came here to travel with you?" she said.

"Yeah, I do. I was planning to go to DC and I thought you could come with me."

"What's in DC?"

"Just some really cool family but my big dream is to go to West Africa."

"Seriously, Africa?"

"Yeah, totally, it's the Motherland, the source of all humanity. I think the Garden of Eden is there, if it's real."

"Do you think it's real?"

"I don't know. It's a myth that says there was once a perfect time and I want to think there was, and that we can get back to that, you know, back to the garden ... like in the song 'Woodstock.'"

"Oh my God, Joni Mitchell is such a genius!"

"I know, I worship her!"

I stopped combing my hair and in days, I had discernible dreadlocks. I put painted ceramic beads on some of them, and I made a beaded sheath in the colors red, gold, and green; the colors of the Ethiopian flag. I slipped it over one of the long locks.

Sam called to see if I was still in town.

"Did you hear Israel Vibration is playing in Albuquerque?" he asked.

"What! No, I didn't, I so wanna go!"

"I know you love them, that's why I called. I can come get you, you can stay here for the night."

"Oh, my sweet Brother, thank you so much. I have a Sister here I'm going to bring with me."

"That sounds cool," he said.

The evening of the show we got a ride to Albuquerque early and hung out with the guys setting up the theater. Sam was gonna meet us later, after work.

"Do you think I could meet the band?" I asked one of the guys as he bent over a heavy speaker while rolling it past me.

He stopped and took a break, hands resting on his hips.

"Yes, Sistren, wi si yuh inna there an wi try fi get yuh backstage."

"Oh my God, thank you so much, I'm so excited!"

The show started hours late. People joked that the band was on Jamaican time. Then, they took the stage and mesmerized the room with soulful wailing about peace, justice, and God. Helena and I danced for hours in our flowing dresses and sandals.

The guy from set up came over to us during intermission.

Yuh cya guh back there now just guh dung dat hall," he said, pointing to the right of the stage. "Guh inna di doa pan di lef."

I made a prayer sign with my hands, "Thank you Brother, thank you so much!"

"One love, y'all now, okay?"

"Girlfriend, what did he say?" Helena asked.

"He's speaking Patois, he said we can go back there, down the hall by the stage, and something about the left … "

Helena and I crept down the hall afraid we would be caught and tossed out of the show. Sam had refused to come with us. We saw a door on the left and walked through and there sat Skelly, one of the three members of the band.

"Hi Skelly!" I said.

"Waa gwaan my Sistren?" he said.

"I'm such a huge fan of your music!"

We sat and talked with him, while staff came in and out.

"Where are you going after this?" I asked.

"Oh, we gwaan through sum more towns den up to DC."

"Oh my God, really? I'm going to DC too, I'll come see you guys there."

"Mi wi be a guh home afta dat."

"Where do you live?"

"Mi live inna Brooklyn."

"Brooklyn! But I thought you like to be always in nature …" I started reciting lyrics from one of his songs.

"Well yuh kno all di lyrics gyal!"

"Yes, I love lyrics, it's poetry."

"Surely it is di words of Jah flowing through mi."

"Jah live," I said.

"Uhman yuh kno Jah too?" he smiled and continued, "Yeah yuh get 'dem locks."

Then intermission was over and we said goodbye.

"Yea cum an si wi inna DC," he said.

Helena and I were back in Santa Fe, spending the days talking, singing, and laughing. We built our own language largely comprised of private jokes and song lyrics. She showered me daily with compliments and kindhearted observations; I had never known anyone as affectionate as her.

"Girlfriend, what got you so interested in Africa?"

We were lying in the grass at the park watching the clouds drift past.

"I went to tons of reggae shows in New York City at a club called Sounds of Brazil. They also had Afro Cuban music. I saw Senegalese music and I fell in love with Baaba Maal. Then, I met people from West and East Africa and they are amazing ... warm, friendly, and kind of innocent. Most were college students here going to school.

I dated this guy for a bit, Sa'eed, he was from Gambia, a tiny country next to Senegal. It's was once part of Senegal, but the British took it back from the French ..."

Helena rolled her eyes.

"I know. Anyway, he told me lots of stories about West Africa. The clothes are so incredibly colorful and the music is so rich. The culture is so different than here, and it's ancient, not new like American culture."

"I'm surprised you don't want to go to Jamaica or even India."

"Reggae is my favorite, that's true. India has my spiritual roots but I'm afraid to go there because my health really sucks. Like, I'll probably end up sick."

"Oh my girl!"

"I know, but I feel so incredibly connected to India I don't even know if I have to go. I know that sounds weird but you know people think I'm Indian, too."

"I could see that."

"I guess that won't happen in Senegal!"
We laughed.

I went to see Nelson Mandela just after he was freed and it was extraordinary. I never thought he would be released. Winnie Nelson was there with him. Lots of people were wearing T-shirts that said: 'It's a black thing, you wouldn't understand.' Sa'eed asked me what it meant.

"Well, it means that their experience ever since they got to this country is completely different than ours, meaning Europeans."

"But I always wanna understand, Seen, why are they so angry?"

"Because of hundreds of years of slavery, and the oppression they live under every single day."

"Here in America?" he said, and he looked genuinely surprised.

"Yeah, here in America it's really bad, there's complete racial inequity, it's institutionalized. A lot people here are really racist, and super ignorant."

He looked perplexed. Later, the anthem for the United Kingdom played and he and his friend stood while Sharon and I remained seated.

"Come on, Sena, stand up with me," Sa'eed said.

"Never, and I don't know why you're standing! Why are you standing for the anthem of the oppressor? England colonized your country ... enslaved your ancestors ... stole your countries wealth!"

He ignored me. He wasn't political.

"Bastards! I can't believe the way they're treating this woman!"

I was listening to the Anita Hill hearings on the radio. I still followed the news when I could by listening to the local NPR station.

"She's a friggin' professor, she's got everything to lose and they talk like she's lying for no reason! Are people ever going to believe women?"

"God, the way they're grilling her is so disturbing!" Helena said.

"I've got to stop listening, I can't take it!" I said. Then I kept listening anyway, day after day.

"What do you think about leaving soon?" Helena asked me.

"I definitely think we should leave. If I don't leave soon I'm gonna end up a housewife in Santa Fe."

"Really girlfriend?"

"I don't know, this guy is just so perfect, but I don't even know how he feels. And I really, really want to go to Africa!"

I told Red Wolf we were leaving.

"Let me give you a present," he said, and he handed me a book called *The Way Out*. He opened the cover and wrote his parents name and address there.

"You can always find me through them if I'm not here," he said.

"You're from West Virginia? I love it there!"

"Me too," he said.

Then, it was time to leave. We had sixty-nine dollar 'Go anywhere' Greyhound bus tickets. Red Wolf drove us to the station.

I hugged and kissed him goodbye and held him tight, tears filling my eyes.

"I will miss you," I said.

"Me too," he said, and he carried my bag over and handed it to the bus driver, who stored it in the belly of the bus.

I got on the bus and waved to Red Wolf out the window one last time. He smiled his usual impish grin, his blonde hair falling over his eyes in the bright sunshine, and he waved back, slowly.

And that was it. That was the last good man I would ever be with.

SEVENTEEN

November 1991
Tree House
Washington DC

Allons! we must not stop here,
However sweet these laid-up stores, however convenient this dwelling we cannot remain here,
However shelter'd this port and however calm these waters we must not anchor here,
However welcome the hospitality that surrounds us we are permitted to receive it but a little while.

***

"Sena Bear!" Lemongrass saw me across the room, "What are you doing in DC? I'm so, so happy you are here!"

"We just got here a few days ago, I'm on my way to New York, then to West Africa. Do you know Helena? We're traveling together."

"No, hey Sister," she said, leaning over and embracing Helena.

"What are you two doing in Africa?"

"We want to learn about culture, live really simple, see a different life, away from Babylon, where all our roots are. I just want to live someplace peaceful and mellow, where there is not all this hate and fighting."

"Oh my Sena, I love you so much!"

Then, she got down on the floor and started kissing my feet!

"No, no, stop, Lemongrass, get up!"

I held onto her arm, pulling her up toward me. She stood up and draped both arms around my neck. She was tall and willowy. I gazed up at her face and got lost in her sky-blue eyes. She was so sincere, so kind; she always made me feel so loved.

Then, people were around us, talking and passing joints.

"It's 4/20," Lemongrass said.

"What's that?"

"It's the criminal code for smoking marijuana in Cali."

"Really? I said, taking the joint passed to me.

Later Helena said, "You and Lemongrass looked so beautiful together, like Anais Nin and June Miller!"

She was referring to a movie that was both of our favorites called *Henry and June*.

"Yeah? Sometimes I think I'm so in love with her, I don't know what to do."

"Maybe just tell her," Helena said.

I smiled and lay down next to her in the dark, the streetlight shining through the window like a poor man's moon.

My dear friend Peter had given us the key to his room since he was leaving town for work, so we scored a private bedroom with a full-size bed.

"How does anyone sleep in cities?" I asked, with a deep sigh.

A horn blew in the distance to illustrate my point.

"Oh, girlfriend, I love cities, look at all the beautiful people we see every day!"

"It's true, it's just that I miss the woods so much. I guess I need to focus on the living forest of people."

We spent the days cleaning, doing laundry for some of the roommates, and walking around DC hand-in-hand talking about our plans to travel. Most evenings we cooked food for anyone who wanted.

We went to a music store, and Helena bought a new guitar. She practiced daily, sometimes for hours. I often read my new poems to her and one day she said, "I gotta make this poem into a song, it's amazing, girlfriend you could write songs!"

She set it to music, and sung it over and over for weeks.

Your eyes meet mine
Why does my heart ache so?
Pulling me into a lake of emotion
laughing, laughing while I'm drowning

We took the bus one day into an African neighborhood to get shea butter and coconut oil. I had been using coconut oil for years as a moisturizer, now I slathered it on my dreads. We wandered down the street looking for the African Trade Shop and two men approached us.

"Hello Sisters, who are you?"

"Who are we?" Helena asked.

"Yes, you seem completely different from anyone we have seen here."

"Yes, this is true," agreed the other man.

Their English was formal like British English, but the words were rounded with a soft accent.

"Where are you guys from?" I asked.

"We're from the Cameroon."

They shook hands with us.

These men were handsome, with almond shaped eyes and high cheekbones. Their cheeks had small lines traveling across them in a pattern.

We talked with them for a few minutes and they directed us to the store.

"Oh my God, girlfriend! Those were the most beautiful men I've ever seen!"

"Maybe we should visit the Cameroon?" I said.

"They were so sweet, and so friendly," she continued, "we should definitely try to meet more people like that. They seemed genuinely curious."

"I know! It's a completely different vibe from here in the West."

"What were those lines on their faces?"

"Oh yeah, that's scarification. They cut them with a blade when they are babies, then rub an irritant into the wound to make scars. It identifies the tribe they're part of."

"Holy shit!"

"I know, it's so hardcore."

A few days later, we were walking to the grocery store and I saw posters for Burning Spear and Israel Vibration in concert.

"This is what Skelly told us about, but I can't believe we're gonna see Burning Spear too! I've never seen him; he's one of my all-time favorites."

"I know! I know!" she said laughing, as if she didn't listen to me playing my cassette of *Hail H.I.M.* a few times a day.

On the day of the concert, we went to the venue in the afternoon seeking the local promoters. There was a group of young guys moving in equipment. They stamped our hands for later and we had to be careful all day not to wash the ink off that would get us into the club later that night.

I wore my new favorite dress, one that Helena had given me. It was a gorgeous moss green, with light brown splashes of color. It skimmed the tops of my feet, covering the Job's tears necklace I kept wrapped around my ankle like a bracelet.

When we arrived, the guys we met earlier invited us backstage. We were sitting with Israel Vibration and in walked Burning Spear.

"Your music means everything to me," I said, "I must've listened to *Marcus Garvey* a thousand times!"

"Tank yuh mi Sista," he said, "one love, yah." He gave me a quick hug and was off.

I stood there star-struck and before I recovered, in walked Sunshine.

"Holy shit, my Sister! I'm so happy to see you!" I said. "Look, I still have the necklace you gave me." I showed her my ankle, decorated with the white beads.

"Yeah, that's cool Sena," she said, but she didn't really smile.

She stood with a Sister with long dreadlocks and light-brown skin. She smiled shyly at us.

"This is Roots," she said, and then I introduced them to Helena.

"So what are you guys doing?" Sunshine said.

"We're on our way to West Africa, we're staying over at the Tree House right now."

"Oh, yeah, Africa, aye?"

The people around us started to hustle about.

"Sistas di show starting now," one of the entourage said, "gwaan out there!"

We all rushed out of the dressing rooms to see the show.

"We'll come and see you at the Tree House!" Sunshine called to me, as we dissolved into the huge crowd.

"Who was that?" Helena asked.

"A girl I crushed on for a long time ... but it wasn't good."

"Why, what happened?"

"I don't know, it's hard to explain."

A couple of days later the doorbell rang. I looked through the narrow glass framing the door. Sunshine and Roots stood together on the porch of the old mansion. I opened the heavy door and ushered them in the living room where Helena and I were busy folding laundry.

I cleared a spot on a small loveseat. "Here, Sisters, sit here."

Helena and I sat across from them on wooden folding chairs.

"Do you guys want some water?" Helena asked.

They shook their heads and Helena brought them glasses of water.

"Sisters, tell me about your plan to go to Africa," Sunshine said.

"We want to start in West Africa," I said. "I want to see Senegal and Gambia. Then hopefully Sierra Leone and Ivory Coast, along the shores. I do want to see Ethiopia, of course, then maybe Zimbabwe ..."

"Sisters, that sounds amazing! I love the South; I want to go back there again soon."

"You've been to Africa? Helena asked.

"Yes," Sunshine said, "I'm surprised Sena didn't tell you. My mother lives in Zimbabwe."

"Wow, that's so cool! My mother and I lived in Central America when I was little, and I got to see the culture and speak Spanish," Helena said.

"Really? What did your mother do there?" Roots asked.

"She was a dancer, she was in a dance troupe."

"That's awesome, do you still speak Spanish?"

"*Un poquito*," she said, pinching he fingers together to mean "small."

"So what were you guys doing backstage?" Sunshine asked.

"Sena's an Israel Vibration groupie," Helena said, laughing.

"Oh yeah? Roots is good friends with Wiss."

"Really? We're on our way to New York now so I hope to see them again before we leave."

"Yeah, you should go check him, he lives in Brooklyn, they all do. I can write him a note, maybe you guys can bring it to him?"

"Yeah, we would love to!" I said.

She pulled a notebook out of her bag, wrote for a moment then scribbled the address of an apartment in Brooklyn and handed it to me with a folded letter.

"He lives with family, I think cousins, but Apple lives in the same building downstairs."

"Give thanks to the most high! I can't believe I have the home address of Israel Vibration in my hand!"

"Oh Mama Sena!" Sunshine said, laughing at me. "You're such a sap."

"She's very sentimental," said Helena, "it's one of my favorite things about her."

"I just like cheesy stuff, really, I can't help it," I said.

"Yes, you're a cheese ball," Helena said.

Soon, Roots and Sunshine said they had to go. We all stood up together.

Sunshine turned to me. "Sister, I love your dress, it is so beautiful, it looks like a moss forest. Trade dresses with me."

She dropped her bag, removed her shawl, and started to lift up her long dress.

I looked down at my dress. It was the gorgeous green and fawn one Helena had given me, and it was now my favorite dress. I wore it constantly; even taking it off and washing it so I could put it back on.

At this point, I wore it every day.

"No, I'm sorry, I don't want to trade this."

"Sister, don't be selfish, give me the dress!"

"No, Sunshine. I'm keeping this dress."

She dropped the fabric of her dress and it fell down over her long underskirt.

Silence embraced us all a time, and then Sunshine spoke.

"You've really changed, Sena."

"Well, I hope I see you again, I love you," I said, and I hugged her. She was mad, but in that moment, I felt how I had become completely free from her grasp.

"So … that's what happened," I said to Helena after they left, and she took my hand and squeezed it.

The only thing I cared about now was Helena. She was the sun in my sky. I woke up to her voice like music and I went to sleep talking to her until we conked out, exhausted. Her faith in me, her adoration for me, was the strongest elixir I had ever encountered.

I was reading a book by Paul Bragg called *The Miracle of Fasting*.

"This could be the answer to all my problems," I told Helena, "I'm going on a fast for health."

"Oh that sounds great girlfriend, I could never do it though, I love food too much."

"I fuckin' love food too but it often makes me sick. It's like my stomach hates me."

The next day I started my fast and by the day after I was seriously hungry. Helena went to the post office without me; I stayed behind to clean the kitchen.

Some of the roommates came in with a tray of brownies and quarts of ice cream. I broke down and took a bowl of ice cream and a brownie. We all sat on the kitchen floor in a circle eating.

Helena walked in, her cheeks rosy from the cold.

"Oh my God, girlfriend! Are you eating brownies? And ice cream!"

"Yeah," I said, and she cracked up.

Taking a bowl and scooping ice cream into it, she sat down next to me. She put her arm around me and pulled me close, kissing my cheek repeatedly.

"You crazy girl!" she said, "breaking a fast on brownies and ice cream!"

Diego spent a lot of time talking to us, asking us about our plans, and smoking us out, though Helena really didn't smoke pot.

"I'm trying to get her to come work for me," he said to Helena, "but she doesn't want to live in a city."

"Oh I know, she's not a city girl, but we're still traveling, we want to go to West Africa."

"Yes, I heard that," he said, "just call me when you get back."

"I don't know if we're coming back," I said.

"Really?"

"Yeah, I want to live in West Africa, maybe, I mean it's so fucked up here. Every five minutes we're at war. Then, when the soldiers come back, they're homeless on the street! No American should be homeless and especially not war veterans. It just infuriates me."

"It's not going to be better in Africa … there's plenty of war there."

"That's true," I said, "but we're going to go check it out. Each country is different. I want to live someplace chill and peaceful, without slavery, or racism. Somewhere people matter more than money."

"Yeah, okay," he said, scoffing at my plan, "call me when you find that!"

That night I told Helena, "There are some crazy countries in Africa. My old boyfriend is Ethiopian and you can't believe what he went through."

"What happened to him?"

"So, the king was deposed and the military took over and they came and took his father away and shot him because he published a democratic newspaper. My boyfriend, Negus, and his siblings had to be smuggled out of Ethiopia into Holland for safety. He speaks, like, seven languages."

"Really, girlfriend! That is unbelievable. Is he a Rastafarian?"

"No, no, he despises Haile Selassie. Even though he has dreadlocks and everyone gives him 'the greeting' he does not say anything, he simply nods, but then later, under his breath, he says, 'fuck that bastard.' It's a trip. He says Selassie purposefully starved people by refusing to take aid during the famine and that's part of why he was taken down. He thinks it's a joke that Jamaicans think he's the second coming of Jesus."

"Wait, girlfriend, they think he's the second coming of Jesus? Serious?"

"Yeah, that's what Rastafarianism is. Selassie made this amazing speech to the UN and the whole speech was turned into a song by Bob Marley and it was pretty profound, lemme play it for you on the stereo."

We went down the back stairs leading to the kitchen, then through the swinging door into the dining room where there was a hi-fi, and we listened to the song "War" from *Rastaman Vibration*.

"Wow, that really is a profound speech," Helena said.

"I know, it's easy to see why people would look to him as a savior. Plus, Ethiopia is the only country in Africa that was not colonized by Europeans, so there's a mythical quality to that place."

I called my old friend, a dear man from the Dominican Republic who took over my apartment when I left and told me I could always visit.

"Yo, yo, Louis, can I come visit with my friend, maybe stay for a couple weeks or a month?"

"Absolutely," he said, "mi casa es tu casa!"

We jumped back on the Greyhound and headed to upstate New York, where Louis's living room had two sofas we took as our beds. I was back in the town where my family had lived for generations, in the dilapidated apartment complex on an old dairy farm where I spent the first nine years of my life.

Where my sister's grave was.

It felt a bit like home.

EIGHTEEN

December 1991
Suburbs
New York

Allons! the road is before us!
It is safe—I have tried it—my own feet have tried it well—be not detain'd!
Let the paper remain on the desk unwritten, and the book on the shelf unopen'd!
Let the tools remain in the workshop! let the money remain unearn'd!
Let the school stand! mind not the cry of the teacher!
Let the preacher preach in his pulpit! let the lawyer plead in the court, and the judge expound the law.

***

I scoured the *Village Voice* classified ads for low-cost airline tickets and found a company called Air Hitch offering one hundred dollar tickets.

"Yeah," the agent said, "you pick a city, and give me a range of dates you can leave, then I get you on unsold seats ... it's like you're hitchhiking on an airplane. I give you twenty-four hours notice."

We sat across from him in his tiny cramped office, his desk covered in paperwork. He leaned back in his chair and smoothed his unruly locks. His office smelled of stale coffee and cigarettes.

"But can we fly to West Africa? To Gambia or Senegal?"

"No," he said, "I can only get you on direct flights. Why not go to Europe and travel by land?"

"Can we let you know in a few hours?" I asked.

"Of course," he said.

Helena and I walked outside to talk it over.

"Let's go to a bookstore. I want to look for a guidebook, and then we can look at some maps." I said.

We walked hand-in-hand though the narrow streets of the Village until we came to the Strand Bookstore. We studied a map of the world, and I bought a thick book called *Africa on a Shoestring*.

We began walking back towards the travel agency.

"*Muñeca*, why don't we go to Spain, then we'll be close?" Helena said.

"Girlfriend, I forget you speak Spanish!"

"No, I don't, I don't speak Spanish, I just know a little, *un poco*."

"Well, you better brush up if we're going to Spain," I said, smiling. "Let's look in my guidebook and see what it says ... okay ... so, there's a whole section about Spanish North Africa. No, wait, okay ... it says we can take a ferry from Spain across the Mediterranean to Spanish North Africa, and cross into Morocco."

"North? But we want to go to the West."

"Yeah but we could go to Morocco and then travel by land."

"Oh shit, are we going to go to Muslim countries?"

"Yeah, I think so, the whole north is Muslim."

"Are we going to have to cover our faces?"

"I don't know, I don't think so, I mean, it's not Saudi Arabia ... we'll just do whatever they're doing then we'll figure out how to get down to West Africa. We are only going to be passing through."

We walked back to the Air Hitch office and each bought a one-way ticket to Madrid, Spain.

"*Muñeca*, I'm so crazy excited! We should celebrate!" she said, kissing my hand while clasped in hers.

"You're the sweetest person I've ever met!" I said, while she smiled her infectious grin, her eyes flashing. "And, yes, totally, let's celebrate! Have you ever had Ethiopian food?"

"No, I never have."

"Oh my God, it's the most amazing food! I'm going to bring you to the restaurant that Negus always took me to."

We walked for hours until we reached the nineties. Insulated in our private world, we did not care how much or how far we walked—it went by in an instant while we were absorbed in endless chatter.

"Girlfriend, I really hate your parents!"

"I know, they're fucking assholes." I said.

I was telling her about how I lost my home and all the horrifying shit that went on in the years leading up to it.

"I can't even imagine," she said, "my mother was so protective, so loving, always there taking care of me until she died, but it's like you never had anyone, yet somehow, you're Mama Sena."

After an hour or so of walking through Manhattan, we arrived at the restaurant. I pulled open the thick glass door and the warm aroma of cinnamon and cumin wafted over us. We stepped down into the dining room and there sat Negus! The backpack he always carried was next to him sitting on a chair, and books were spread out on the table before him.

We walked over to him; he looked so happy to see me.

"Hey, girl, where have you been? Your phone is disconnected!"

"Well, you shouldn't have disappeared without giving me a number. I live on the road now."

"What!" he said.

"Yes, this is my best friend Helena. We are going to West Africa together."

"You must both sit with me and tell me what's been going on."

We ate *injera* (flatbread) with *shiro* (lentils), and *atakilt wat* (cabbage and carrots) with our hands, as was the tradition. The bread is a large thin crepe, you tear off a piece then use it to scoop up the food. The delicately seasoned dishes were served on silver plates that crowded the table. We talked for hours about the African continent, reggae music, our travels, and politics.

When we left, I gave Negus the number for Louis's house.

"You can find me here," I said.

I brought Helena to my father's house to meet my grandmother and my half-siblings. I gave one of my young sisters my beading kit, as I was not planning to take it to Africa.

"My mom says you're a dirty hippie and I'm not allowed to take anything from you," she said.

Helena and I laughed but the underlying dynamics broke my heart. My stepmother had long worked to destroy my relationship with her children, calling me names was just the tip of the iceberg.

I once thought that she worked to oust me because I was not her biological child, but it was now clear to me she treated her own children even worse. The cruelty and chaos that ruled my father's house sickened and disturbed me.

Tragically, no one had learned from the past (which I believe always looms as prelude). I had long talks with my father after my sister was killed, and he swore he was going to do everything different with the children he had now. His words were empty, though, and I watched the tragedy unfold while powerless. I protested, lectured, and begged him to keep his promise. His response was hostility. He took no input from anyone, not even me.

We went to my grandmother's small rooms in the front of the house.

"I am so happy to see you!" She hugged me and took my hand, her hands slightly shaking. "I'm so glad you're back home. Are you staying here?"

"No," I said, "this is my friend Helena, we're going to go to Spain and West Africa together."

"Oh no, am I going to worry about you forever? I've been waiting for you to come back, I've been hoping to dance at your wedding," she said with a sigh.

I am as far away from marriage as I am from the moon, I thought, but I didn't reply.

"Oh no, no, do you hear that?" she cried.

Through the wall, you could hear my stepmother yelling at my 11-year-old brother.

"Every day she screams at my boy... my poor boy ... she tells him horrible things, she says he'll never amount to anything. He's just a little boy."

Tears ran down her face. "Why does she do that?"

"Gram, she's very sick, she's mentally ill."

"But the things she says to him, and she screams and screams, I just can't stand it."

I started to cry too.

"*Muñeca*, I'm so sorry about what went on at your family's, you poor girl!" Helena said that night when we were back at Lou's.

"Yeah, well, welcome to my nightmare. I don't know what to do, girlfriend. I called Child Protective Services on her and they told me to call back when she got arrested for DWI with a child in the car. They don't really care about emotional abuse. I'm really scared for my brother, I mean, she's destroying his self-esteem and my father, he has no self-esteem. I'm always scared of how it's all going to turn out. My sister didn't even make it out of this family alive."

Louis drove us to the bus stop that went to Port Authority. It was only a couple of miles from his house. We were going to go tool around New York City and then visit Brooklyn.

After a long day walking around Manhattan, we took a subway to Brooklyn and after stopping a few people and asking directions we finally found the apartment where Wiss lived.

He stood in front of the open door of his apartment on the third floor. We had pressed the buzzer saying we were here with a letter from Roots. He let us in and we raced up the stairs, giddy.

"Hello Wiss," I said, "I love your music so much!"

"*Welcome mi Sistren, come inna di yaad.*"

"*Yes I*," I said in Rasta slang, and we walked in to find him surrounded by his wife and children.

"We brought you a letter from our friend Roots in DC," I said, and handed him the letter. He tucked it away in his pocket.

"I'm Sena and this is Helena."

"We love your music, Sena plays it all the time," Helena said.

"*Tank yuh, please sidung an ave sum tea.*"

We sat down to drink tea with his wife. She was welcoming and kind.

"Where are you from?" I asked her. Her accent was very different from her husband's.

"I am from Bermuda," she said.

"Wow, what is it like growing up in Bermuda?" Helena said.

"Well, it's very boring," she laughed, "I would ride my bike everywhere. It is not very big at all. I love being in New York."

"Really?" I said, "You don't miss the beach? Or the slow pace of life?"

"No, no I don't," she smiled. "I love it there, it is so beautiful, but I'm happy to be here. There is much more to do here."

We talked a bit about our travels and our plan to go to West Africa.

"*Yeah? yuh adventuras!*" Wiss said.

"We are," I said. "We met Skelly in Albuquerque. Is he nearby?"

"*Nah him lives far but yuh wa fi cum an si Apple?*"

"Sure," I said, and we said our goodbyes to his family and followed him down the stairs to the first floor.

"Him lives inna here," Wiss said, tapping on the door.

Then, Apple was standing before us with a large grin.

Later, we walked through the darkened streets of Brooklyn to the subway station.

"I still can't believe we went to their house! I wish we could've seen Skelly too, God, I hope I wasn't an obnoxious fan. I'm just so in love with their music ... it's that old roots style."

"No, no you weren't at all girlfriend."

We got on the train and made our way back to Manhattan where we jumped on a bus.

Negus called and said he wanted to visit. He also asked Helena and I to come down and see some reggae with him and we did.

Louis lent us his car so we drove Negus back uptown on our way north to the George Washington Bridge.

"What's your plan from here?" he said.

"We're going to go to DC for New Year's and then Florida to visit Helena's father. Then we fly in February from JFK to Spain."

"Oh no, no, you should stay here with me."

"Yeah, I've heard that one before."

"No seriously, I really, really want to spend time with you," he said, "especially if you might not come back from Africa. Then I'll never see you again."

I asked Helena that night, "Would you mind if I blew off Florida and stayed here with Negus?"

"No, not at all, girlfriend."

We had not made a plan for travel yet, so Helena decided she was going to hitchhike and skip New Year's Eve in DC.

"I don't really like you hitchhiking, I was in jail with a girl who murdered a woman who picked her up hitchhiking. Then, there was Angela, my classmate ... there are serial killers out there."

"Yeah, but we can do it in a safe way. We can go to a truckstop and I can get a ride from there and you'll know who I went with."

"Well, I guess, I'll pray and God will send us an angel. Call on Kali if you need help, call on God. I always do and it works. It's probably why I'm still here."

Louis and I drove her to a truckstop and sure enough, she got a ride to Florida from a trucker. We wrote down his plate number and name and we hugged goodbye.

"Girlfriend," I said, "I don't know if I'm doing the right thing, staying here and letting you hitch ..."

"Don't worry," she said, "it's fine, we'll be going overseas in a couple of months and we'll be together all the time."

"But I'm going to miss you so much!"

"Me too, girlfriend, but I'll see you so soon."

When Helena got to Florida, she called me from her father's house.

"Sena, that guy tried to rape me!" she said, "He was such an asshole!"

"What the fuck! I'm gonna call the cops," I said. "No, I'm just gonna kill him!" I said, and I let out a groan and sat down of the floor of the kitchen. "I knew you shouldn't hitchhike, I knew it!"

"No, no, I got away and in the end nothing happened."

"Well what the fuck did happen?"

"I don't know, we were talking and I was expressing my opinions probably a little too freely, and all of a sudden he freaked out and pulled over and said he was going to rape me! He was so angry his face was beet red, and I thought of you and I just started praying for God to help me; praying, praying so hard and saying 'Please God, please Goddess, help me!' And then he stopped and he said, 'That will teach you a lesson.' He drove me to a bus station and bought me a ticket to Tampa and told me, 'Here, don't ever hitchhike again!'"

"I'm so sorry, I'm so sorry my girl! I can't believe I let you go alone."

"You didn't know!"

"Yes, I did, fuck, why did I ignore my gut?"

"*Muñeca*, it is not your fault. I love you and I'll see you soon. And listen, I don't think I've heard you say "fuck" this much, ever!"

"I'm from New York, it's mandatory."

She laughed but I was still doubled over in pain. How could I have thought it was okay to let her go like that? What if she had been raped, or killed, how would I live with myself?

I only saw Negus once, and I never heard from him again. I really had no way to reach him. I finally called the Ethiopian restaurant and asked for his cousin who I knew worked there.

"Ahmed," I said, "this is Sena and I was with Negus, I mean, I was his girlfriend, a while back."

"Yes, yes, I remember you," he said, "it's been some time."

"Yeah, well, I've been away, and now I'm back and I was supposed to see Negus but I can't find him."

"Oh, I think he has returned to Boston."

"Boston?"

"Yes, he has relatives there."

"Is there any way I can reach him there?"

"I'll try to reach him for you, I'm not sure where he is staying."

I got off the phone angry and confused. Why would Negus convince me to stay here if he were leaving town? And why would he then leave and not tell me? The obvious answer: it is what he does and this wasn't the first time.

There is a saying that goes: most men lead lives of quiet desperation. But I lead a life of quiet self-destruction. It's an urge within that drives me towards people that are bad for me, and even towards people who are just simply bad.

I called the Tree House to talk to my friend Jessie, telling her what happened with Helena and Negus.

"Girlfriend, that's so fucked up!" she said, "Why don't you just come here now, before New Year's Eve? You can stay in my room."

"Okay," I said, and I made a plan to head back to DC, this time alone.

NINETEEN

January 1992
Washington DC
Tampa & Key West, Florida

Jessie and I spent the day cleaning the kitchen, rearranging furniture, and working with other roommates to set up different areas, such as the basement, which became a stage for the bands playing that night at the New Year's bash.

A house meeting was planned for five o'clock and Diego asked me to attend.

"We're going to need volunteers for the door. I've got a sheet of paper to sign up; it's a one-hour shift. I'm gonna take eight to nine. Who wants to go after me?"

"I'll take nine," I said.

"Awesome, so the way you work the door is you try to assess if they're family, activists or what? Just be careful of who you let in but don't worry. Ask them who they know that lives here. Don't be afraid to turn people away."

After the meeting, Jessie and I went to chill out and get dressed. We wandered into the bedroom next door, which was shared by a lesbian couple.

"You guys want to smoke a bong with us?" Jessie asked them.

"Sure," Kathy said, and we sat on the bed with them.

"Sister, did Diego talk to you about coming to work for him? I'm the one who told him how amazing you are and all the stuff you helped me do in the office," Kathy said.

"He did but I'm going with Helena to Europe and Africa."

"Is she … is she your girlfriend yet?" she smiled mischievously.

"She's my best friend, I don't know what else. Speaking of that, I need to call her, can I use your phone?"

"Absolutely," Alice handed me a black handset.

"You know you kinda look like Alice in Wonderland?"

"Everyone says that; it's the long blond hair."

"And the headband!"

I knew Helena's father's number by heart.

"Girlfriend, I miss you so much!! How am I gonna do New Year's Eve without you? I'm sitting here with Kathy and Alice and Jessie and everyone says hello!"

"Tell them I said hi! I'm gonna go to a party with some of my old friends. Why don't you come to Tampa? Come hang out with me here, it's beautiful."

"I'll look for a cheap plane ticket … I'll let you know in a few days."

"That'll be great! It's like six weeks till we fly so we might as well hang out where it's warm."

Someone set a giant pot of brewing mushroom tea on the stove. The grand Washington mansion was lit with strands of white Christmas lights, and the tables were covered with veggie snacks. We set cones of burning incense throughout the house, and the air filled with sweet-smelling smoke. We turned the outside lights on and a trickle of partygoers began to arrive.

Diego came over to me, "Do you want to try some mushroom tea?"

"Well, I don't know, I mean, I don't take drugs."

"They're natural, we harvested them outside in the south where they grow. It's not like peyote, that makes you puke, it's much more mild."

"I'll try a little," I said, and I took a cup and lightly sipped. I went easy but I still felt the effects. Despite years of abusing them, I have always been a lightweight with substances.

"Help yourself, it's here for the taking. I gotta run and get on the door, I'll see you there."

I walked slowly through the large parlor. The air was now thick with marijuana smoke and the room loud with people talking. The tea made me smile and laugh about nothing. Soon, I made my way to the grand hall where Diego was letting people in the door. It was my turn to do the door.

I sat on the intricately carved staircase, sipping my tea. Diego reappeared with a burning joint and handed it to me.

"We always take care of the door person," he said.

When my hour was over Jessie came to take over and I told her I'd cover her shift.

"Really? Really Sena, you want to do that?"

"Yeah, I kinda like the spot."

"All right, I'm gonna bring you whatever you want: cake, cookies, how about some hash?"

"Yeah, that all sounds good. Just make sure I don't pass out while I'm supposed to be answering the door."

When eleven o'clock came I took over that shift too. I spent the entire evening sitting on the fancy staircase, opening the door and welcoming people, and accepting gifts and visits and appreciation from all the housemates.

A few days later, I grabbed a local paper and looked in the classifieds and there was a ticket to Tampa. Actually, there was more than one! These were the days when people could easily resell a plane ticket; no identification was required when flying.

I called one of the numbers and spoke to a man who told me it was his wife's ticket and I could simply travel as her.

"She bought a round-trip because it was cheaper but she doesn't need the return. I'm at the Pentagon, you can come pick it up here."

Later that day, I walked through those hallowed halls in knit Peruvian mukluks, and a military man handed his wife's plane ticket to me: dreadlocks, nose ring, flowing Indian dress, all. I had recited a Yogananda prayer in my head during the long walk there, as I often did, that said in part ' ... I have no enemies, I am a friend to all.' The man was warm and friendly and he reminded me that prayer *always* works.

"Oh my God girlfriend! I missed you so much!" I said to Helena as she rushed over and gave me a huge hug and kiss. The air was warm and I started to peel off my layers, stuffing them into my backpack.

"You have to meet my friend Aria from high school, she's awesome, she drove me here."

"Thank you so much!" I said, hugging her also.

Soon we arrived at a neat ranch house in a quiet suburban neighborhood.

"Dad, I'm here with Sena. She's going to be staying. remember?"

"Oh yes, come in," he said.

Her father sat perched on a stool in front of a large canvas covered with tiny faces. He squinted through his glasses, detailing the expressions on each face with a tiny paintbrush. We walked through the house towards Helena's bedroom. She had sliding doors that went outside to an in-ground pool.

"I can't get over this place! It's so beautiful and your father, wow, he's really talented."

"He was a lot older than my mother when they got married."

I sat on her bed, which was on the floor surrounded by books and crafts. I pulled a book off of the shelf: *I Was An Autodidact*. I flipped through the pages and read the jacket.

"Oh my God, I'm an autodidact! I didn't know there was a word for it."

"You must be, you're one of the smartest people I've ever known and you didn't even finish high school."

"It's because of books. I can't stop reading, it's a compulsion. Once, I was at a garage while my father was working on a car, there was nothing to read except matchbook covers so I read every cover in a box full."

"That's funny! Me too, I love books so much ... so listen, Aria and I talked about going to Key West. What do you think?"

"I think it sounds amazing!"

"Okay, then I'll tell her we're going, but let's chill out here for a few, alright? My father wants to take us out to dinner."

"That sounds great," I said, picking up a small box with jewelry making supplies. "Do you mind if I make a pair of earrings?"

"No, girlfriend, use anything you want in there."

I fashioned a pair of wire earrings from I Ching coins and tiger-eye stones. I put them on and wore them for the next year straight.

The drive to the Keys is spectacular. My favorite part is the seven-mile bridge. It's low and it stretches out across the ocean, as if you were driving on top of the water. Eventually, you cannot see land in any direction and there you are, out on the ocean in a car.

Later that night, we three sat on the stoop of a house playing music. We met the homeowner in town, and he told us he has rooms for rent and invited us to stay with him. We ended up sleeping for free on the small porch.

Throngs of people continually passed, and sometimes stopped to talk with us. Two guys stopped one evening, a black guy and a white guy, both with dreadlocks.

"So where are you guys from?" I asked them.

"Oh, we're from a teeny tiny town in New York that you've never heard of."

"Try me," I said.

Then, they said the name of the tiny town I started out in!

"Holy shit! I'm from there too," I said, "from Field Road."

"What?" The black kid said, "*I'm* from Field Road!"

His name was Darius, and it turned out we went to elementary school together. I don't remember him, I was a year older so he was not in my grade but his cousin Lynelle used to come over to play before we moved away when I was nine.

They joined us on the porch and we played music for hours.

"Can me and Darius crash out here with you guys?" Cody asked.

"I think so, we just have to ask the guy who owns the house."

We asked him and he said if we could all fit it was okay. We spread our bedrolls on the floor, plus there were some old couches, and the five of us slept outside with soft sea breezes blowing over us, and the methodical sound of crashing waves in the background.

We hung out with them for a couple of days and then Cody said that they were headed back to Miami where they lived.

Darius turned to me, "I really want to hang out with you, but I need to go back. Can you come up to Miami?"

"I don't know, I'm not the driver, maybe," I said, and he gave me his number.

About a week later, the three of us drove out of the Keys on our way back to Tampa.

"Would you mind if we took a detour to Miami?" Aria said, "I wanna visit someone."

"Hey, I wanna visit someone too."

"You mean Darius?" Helena said.

They left me at Darius's house with agreement that they would come back to pick me up in a couple of days. He lived with his parents, a sweet elderly couple who'd retired to Florida.

We went up the stairs to the top floor that he occupied and holed up there watching *The Emerald Forest*, a movie about native Amazonians I was obsessed with, smoking pot, and philosophizing. He was on his way to Jamaica next, so we talked a lot about Rastafarianism, which he had a keen interest in.

When Aria and Helena picked me up they had a guy in tow. He was with Helena and I immediately disliked him. He was a super flaky kid she knew from Dead tour. Back in Tampa Helena started ditching me to be with him and I could not complain. It seems that is what we did to each other and if anyone had set the tone, it was me.

I spent my time reading books, and cooking. I hung out with Helena's father, and he told me wonderful stories. He was a fascinating man who had done many things; designed handbags, composed music, danced professionally, and dabbled in acting.

"I once met Marilyn Monroe, and I didn't even know it was her. We were in the same acting class in New York City, and a group of us went out to lunch. I remember she had this very distinctive bulbous nose ... she was very plain, not glamorous at all. Later, my friend told me who she was and I was so surprised!"

Helena finally ditched the boy and we resumed our nightly marathon discussions on almost every subject on earth. We talked about past boyfriends one night lying on her bed with the glass doors open. A warmish breeze came in.

"Let's go for a walk outside," I said, and we left the house in the dark of night and walked the blocks of her neighborhood, talking.

Besides our voices, our footsteps on the pavement were the only sounds. The streetlights shined a dull beam of light downwards on the blacktop, leading the way.

"My first boyfriend got a woman pregnant, she was in her thirties, and the next boyfriend date raped me. We were drunk. I was fifteen, and we were kissing and all of a sudden, he had this look of rage. It was so weird, at the same time he was trying to get me to fool around with him. I kept saying no. I fought him, but I was too drunk.

"I still clearly remember the look on his face and how I didn't want to because he looked so scary. It was so not sexual ... it was like he hated me all of a sudden." This was the first time I had ever talked about it outside of therapy to anyone. I didn't like to even think about it.

"Oh my God girlfriend! I'm so sorry... that happened to me, too. This boy named Matt, he was a football player, I was at a party drinking. It was bad ... "

"I am so sorry for you! It makes me want to kill him. Fucking alcohol, and, you know, dozens of women have told me about their rapes, it's a fucking epidemic! What the hell?"

I took her hand and squeezed it. "I'll protect you," I said, and she smiled.

We went out a few times to see a local reggae band. One night me, Helena, and Aria were waiting on line and Helena gasped, "That's him, that's Matt, shit, what am I gonna do?"

"I'm gonna go confront him! Fuck this, my friend Loretta did it for me," I said, starting to walk towards the guy she pointed out.

"No, Sena, no," she said, grabbing my arm and crouching down on the ground. "Come down here, stay here, don't, don't."

"Why not? He should be exposed as the lowlife he is!"

"He should, I just I don't want him to see me, I don't want to confront him, please."

"Okay, it's okay, I understand, I'm so sorry sweetie. Let's leave."

We left the line and went back to the car. There was no way we could be in that club with him there.

"We need to think about getting back to New York for our trip in February," I said, "and let's not separate anymore, let's make sure we stay together."

"We will *Muñeca*! You know, I always wanted to have a friend like you, like, you know, an older tough girl who can protect me."

"I can totally protect you," I said, "but I can't believe you think of me as tough. I'm not tough."

"Oh my God girl, you are so tough!"

In the end we took the Greyhound, which we affectionately called "the hell hound," back to New York state.

I studied the guidebook intensely. I could now look at the African continent and identify every country. I also learned that our passports were invalid in both Syria and Libya, and that we may not be able to get into Morocco or other Arab countries if we had an Israeli stamp on our passports.

"Oh shit, wait, why can't we go to those two countries?" Helena said.

"They both have harsh dictators. We bombed Libya a few years ago and killed Gaddafi's daughter. Al-Assad is a major human rights violator, they have fake elections in Syria where there's only one candidate, but you have to vote by law!"

"That's insane! How do you know all this shit, is it in the guidebook?"

"No, it's from years of activism … probably from listening to WBAI. I followed the Iran-Contra debacle on there for years."

"Well, I lived in a kibbutz as an exchange student so I *do* have an Israeli stamp."

"Shit! And what does this even mean? Should I not tell people I'm part Jewish?"

"I don't know, but I'm gonna get rid of my passport so we don't have to find out."

Helena tossed her passport away and applied for an emergency replacement. We raced to Manhattan and spent most of the day on a lazy line. She showed her ticket to Spain to stand in. By that day's end she held a brand-new passport in her hand, the golden eagle on the cover shining like newly polished brass.

PART THREE

TO AFRICA

TWENTY

February 1992
Madrid, Valencia, Roquetas de Mar
Spain

To take to your use out of the compact cities as you pass through,
To carry buildings and streets with you afterward wherever you go,
To gather the minds of men out of their brains as you encounter them, to gather the love out of their hearts,
To take your lovers on the road with you, for all that you leave them behind you,
To know the universe itself as a road, as many roads, as roads for traveling souls.

***

We are the only Americans on the flight, and only ones who speak English. Our Air Hitch is on a Spanish airline that mainly ferries tourists between Madrid and New York City.

The plane was full of rowdy drunken Spaniards returning home from vacation. They sang songs and we smiled and clapped along with the rest of the people on the plane. We had never seen a plane like this, with its party atmosphere and freewheeling attendants.

Helena smiled her beautiful sunny smile.

"Girlfriend, do you think you can remember the Spanish you used to know?"

"Not really, I mean, I understand more than I can speak except for curses, and they're not gonna help us get on a train," I said.

We both laughed.

We got off the plane at night in Madrid. People on the plane welcomed us to Spain as we disembarked. We approached the line at Customs and a sign directed us to hold our passports in our hands. When the woman behind the glass asked for them, she quickly identified the navy blue cover and pushed them back toward us without stamping them.

"*Americanas*," she said to the guards, and they waved us forward into Spain.

"Damn, I wanted a stamp from Spain," I said, "and I can't believe we can just stay here indefinitely, that's crazy."

"Man, being American is so VIP," Helena said, and that turned out to be more true than we imagined.

Madrid was chilly, and the darkened streets near the airport were silent with hulking industrial buildings. We hailed a cab and asked the driver to take us to the youth hostel, where we found cold sparse dorm rooms and rented two beds for the night for a few dollars. There was no heat or hot water.

We sat on a bench in the interior courtyard so Helena could bum a smoke. A jovial African man handed her his bag of tobacco and invited us to the community room party, where a gaggle of young travelers hung around a tinny radio blaring American pop. We met a man from Ghana name Kwame and we told him how we were going to go south to Almeria to take the ferry to North Africa.

"You should visit Roquetas de Mar, that's where I stay. It's right on the beach and it is near to Almeria."

"That sounds good," I said.

"I have a nice room with two beds in an apartment there. You can go and stay in my room, tell them I sent you. I will be traveling for some more months."

"Oh my God, that's so generous, Kwame!" Helena said.

"Oh," he said, "I am very happy to help and I hope you visit my country. Do you have a pad and pen?"

I wrote down his address in Roquetas de Mar.

The next day we were in the train station, and I was nearly in tears trying to read the train schedule.

"What are we going to do, how are we going to figure this out?" I dropped my backpack onto the floor of the station and sat on top of it trying to calm down. Announcements for trains blared in rapid Spanish over the intercom system.

Part of the problem was the schedule was in military time, and, of course, in Spanish. Helena and I took turns trying to read the table and somehow figured out which train went to Valencia. We quickly bought tickets and then settled into the worn leather seats.

The Spanish countryside was picturesque, evolving from tiny towns to boundless orange orchards. Once in Valencia, we bought a shopping bag full of oranges for a dollar and later ate them in our five-dollar hotel room.

The building we stayed in was ancient, the tiny room stuffed with antiques. I sat on the windowsill, taking in the view from our third-floor window. The houses were crowded together in a sea of tile roofs punctuated by tall steeples topped with crosses. I had never seen buildings this old before, and I have long been fascinated with the past.

"Let's go sit outside and play music," Helena said, unzipping the soft backpack that held her guitar. She grabbed the strap and tossed it over her shoulder.

We walked until we spotted a small park, the *Plaça de la Reina*, and we stood along the sidewalk, playing music in the warm afternoon sun.

We noticed a McDonald's directly across the street.

"I can't believe there's a McDonald's here," I said, "I wonder who eats there?"

As evening fell, we knew the answer. Spaniards in chic dresses, pressed suits, and fancy shoes walked past us, trailing a cloud of cologne, heels clicking the sidewalks. Through glass walls we watched them order at the counter then carry their plastic trays to the dining room. We crossed the street and peered through the door to read the menu. It was so expensive!

"Do you think they think that's how we eat in America? No one can make that at home!" Helena said.

"Yeah that's true, you have to cut down a rainforest to raise cattle, for starters," I said.

"What? That's horrifying! But it does seem like people are super interested in anything American."

"I know! I had no idea before traveling."

The next morning, Helena coaxed me to eat breakfast.

"I never eat breakfast, my stomach doesn't like it."

"I know, but if you eat a healthy breakfast … it's just oranges! My mom would never let me skip breakfast, she thought kids should eat really healthy and she stuffed me with fruit and vegetables."

"My mother was a teenager who didn't like fruits and vegetables and I stuffed myself with Entenmann's chocolate donuts until I was sick. We didn't have any food rules; we could eat when and what we wanted."

She handed me a peeled orange and I ate it.

"This is possibly the best orange I've ever had in my life," I said. She handed me another and I decided from then on to only eat fruit for breakfast.

We went to an outdoor market to look for groceries. We bought a large bottle of chamomile liquid soap, and at another stall we bought luscious red tomatoes and ripe avocados. Helena asked a woman at the counter for *pan integral* (whole wheat bread). She handed us a long loaf and my new favorite sandwich was born: Avocado and tomato on whole wheat, yum!

We returned to our room to make our lunch on a small wooden table.

"I'm so glad you brought this knife," Helena said, cutting open the avocado with the hunting knife my father gave me as a kid.

We went back to the park in the afternoon. A woman stopped and gave us a donation; we had put out a small coffee can we found.

"Are you Americans?" she asked and we smiled and said yes.

"How long have you been in Spain?"

"Just a few days," Helena said.

"Oh my and you're working already!"

She walked on and we marveled at the fact that she considered busking work.

A young couple approached us and told us they wanted to sell their art on the sidewalk and would we mind if they stood with us.

"No, we would love it!" we said.

They laid down a few blankets, then placed a collection of sketches on top turning our part of the sidewalk into a small art gallery.

They were from Holland and travelers also. We talked with them for hours and they asked us if we wanted to come with them to a fundraiser dinner at the squats to raise money for political prisoners.

"Definitely," we said.

"I can't believe there are squats in Spain," I said.

"They probably have them in every city," Helena said.

Diederik and Evi came to our hotel in the evening, walking up the tiny narrow staircase to our room. It was more of a boarding house than a hotel, really. They had a kind of punk look; he was tall, with long brown hair, she was petite with short blond hair and a nose ring. They both wore American jeans and black tops.

We walked through the city with them, sharing tales of our travels. Helena and Evi laughed and talked side by side, Diederik and I lagged behind.

"We have a bit of a problem," Diederik told me, dragging his fingers nervously through his hair. "We are here trying to quit heroin."

"Heroin?" I said, "Really? Jeez, I'm so sorry to hear that."

"Yeah, it's really bad," he said.

"I can't imagine," I said.

Given that Helena and I relentlessly read ingredients and refused to buy anything with hydrogenated oil or high fructose corn syrup, I could not fathom taking a street drug. Unlike in my reckless youth, I now worried about what I ingested. I was afraid of dough conditioners!

We turned onto a narrow, quiet street and walked in the center of the road, flanked by unlit abandoned buildings. We went through the door of one and the inside was packed with people. The room was dimly lit with candles and oil lamps, and there were dozens of long tables to sit at and eat. For a two-dollar donation, you get a bowl of hearty vegetable soup. I handed the server eight *pesetas* and soon she returned with four bowls of hot soup.

Helena was playing Gershwin in the late morning sun, and Evi sat near her, smiling. Diederik was sitting on the sidewalk near large charcoal drawings he laid out on a blanket to sell. A British couple stopped and sang along to "Summertime," delighted with the live performance.

An African man approached us and said, "Hello young ladies, what brings you to Spain?"

"We are on our way to Africa!"

"Oh, yes?" he said, then he greeted Diederik and Evi.

"I am Adedayo, I come from Nigeria. I have bought some of their art, it is very nice, very nice. You should come to my house, come and visit," he said.

"We will," I said, and he offered to come back and fetch us later.

It was evening when Adedayo came to meet us. Diederik had carefully rolled up his drawings, and he and Evi had left to return to the squat where they were living.

"That's an American restaurant, yes?" he said, pointing to McDonald's. "That is the food you eat in America, yes?"

"No no, that's fast food, it's the cheapest food in America. It's bad for you. We don't eat it."

"Really now, really? I cannot believe this. I have went there and I thought it was very good."

We laughed. "Yeah, it tastes good, that's the problem."

We walked through Valencia with him to his apartment. Once there he offered us food.

"We are vegetarian, I said.

"Oh, okay, what does that mean?" he asked.

"We don't eat meat."

"You don't eat meat? It is like that in America?"

"No, not really."

"I don't understand."

"Well there are all different diets there and some people don't eat meat, most Americans do."

He still seemed perplexed, but I was learning that the concept of individualism is unique to America.

"Okay," he said "maybe I can give you some fruit? And some cheese and crackers?"

We shook our heads yes and noshed with him.

"I have extra rooms here, you should come and stay here," he said, "I have a couple that stays in one of my rooms."

"We're only gonna be here a few more days, we're getting ready to travel to Almeria."

"Yes, well, come and stay here until then. I would be honored to have American visitors."

We decided to stay with Adedayo. Helena was trying to raise the money for bus tickets so we did not have to break into our savings (which I was wearing in a hidden money belt under my dress). We brought our bags over the next day and that night, we watched Spanish news with Adedayo.

"I'm going to sleep everyone," Helena said, shortly after the young German couple who stayed here also went into their room. I was sitting on a chair adjacent the sofa where Adedayo sat. He took his remote control and changed the television to porn, like, 1970s American porn.

"You want to watch this together?" he asked.

"No, I said, "I'm going to bed."

I went into the room where Helena was sleeping on a full-size bed. I got in next to her.

"Is everything alright, girlfriend?" Helena asked in a sleepy voice from under the covers.

"Yeah, fine, I mean, we have to leave here tomorrow."

"Did something happen?"

I told her and then said, "There doesn't seem to be a lock on this door and now I'm nervous that he's going to come in here."

"No, I don't think he will, and we'll be gone tomorrow."

The next morning I asked Adedayo if he could tell us where the bus station is.

"Of course! I will take you there," he said, and he walked us there. In fluent Spanish he asked for bus tickets to Almeria.

"Do they have one to Roquetas de Mar?" I asked.

He spoke to the clerk and then said, "You have to get on a different bus once in Almeria."

We got on the bus and sat near the back. Almost immediately, a man started harassing Helena. I could not sit next to her because there weren't two open seats together, so I was across the aisle. He was in the seat next to her.

"Stop!" she said, "No," while pushing him away.

"Let me switch places with you," I said to Helena and we swapped. I narrowed my eyes and stared at him coldly until he looked away then snuggled his head down into his ratty coat.

We got off the bus early afternoon. There was not a bus to Roquetas de Mar until later that night so we sat on a bench with our bags, unsure about our next move.

In moments, an African man in a shiny black Mercedes pulled up and asked if we needed a ride. We told him we were going to Roquetas de Mar. He spoke little English but he smiled and nodded for us to get in the car.

"I have my knife," I said, "and there are two of us."

In hindsight, I realize that is crazy logic. Still, we hopped in the backseat and he drove along the highway hugging the coast of the Mediterranean. The ride was made even more spectacular by the ethereal music the man was playing. The car was filled with music I'd never heard the likes of before. It was Enya, and it was the perfect soundtrack to the breathtaking views.

We got out of his car in a charming town with whitewashed buildings and tiny cobblestone streets. We were instantly lost.

We found a little park and sat down and soon a man approached us. He said he was from Morocco and we told him we were on our way there.

"Oh," he said, "you must come to dinner with me at my home. I will make you authentic Moroccan food."

Helena looked at me questioningly and I pulled her aside.

"I don't like this guy," I said to Helena.

"No, girlfriend, he seems really nice."

"I don't think so. He seems creepy to me."

"Well, I don't think so and we need someplace to hang out and he can tell us about Morocco and then we can figure out how the hell we're going to find this address. Maybe he can help with that?"

"Okay," I said, "but it's against my better judgment."

I always second-guessed myself, worried that my past had made me untrusting. In reality, it has made me *too* trusting, but I didn't know that then.

Muhammad had a roommate in his twenties named Mustafa. Muhammad made us a Moroccan dinner of couscous and salad with bright cherry tomatoes—minus the lamb.

Mustafa made goo-goo eyes at me over dinner. Helena and I were learning if we spoke rapid English to each other, no one could understand us.

"We can't stay here," I said.

"Well it's getting night so let's stay here. Muhammad said he'll help us get there tomorrow."

"Alright," I said, not feeling comfortable but not knowing how to make another move.

They lived in a small one-story house with two bedrooms, a living room, and kitchen. Muhammad made up beds for us on the couches. He was polite and unassuming but I still did not trust him.

Helena and I lay in our beds talking as we did each night.

"Mustafa seems into you," she said.

"Yeah, I'm just not interested."

"How come? He's gorgeous."

"I don't know him and I can't converse with him because he really doesn't know English ... I get attracted to people's minds, you know."

Soon I drifted off to sleep and I woke up to someone touching my face. It was Mustafa leaning over me and kissing me.

"Stop! No! Stop it!" I yelled.

I burst into tears he mumbled an apology and quickly left the room.

"Girlfriend, girlfriend, oh my God are you okay?"

"Yeah I'm fine," I said, choking on my sobs.

"Why are you so upset?"

"I don't know but I don't like people kissing me while I'm asleep."

"No, I understand, that's so fucked up. Do you wanna talk about it?"

"No, he just scared me that's all."

The next morning Muhammad tried looking at some maps of Roquetas de Mar but he didn't really understand the address the way it was written. Neither did we. After a time he said he was going to work and he would see us at lunch.

"A friend of mine is coming for lunch so we can ask him," he said.

While we sat around the table at lunch, Mustafa complained to Muhammad that I rejected him. It was in Arabic but I heard my name.

"Wait, what is he saying?" I said to Muhammad.

"He's saying he was upset because he thought you liked him but it turned out you didn't like him." Before I could respond he said, "I told him you have… the… hmmm, how do you say *alhayd* in English? I told him, 'Sena does not feel well.' Like, here see the mark on Muammar's pants? He kills the sheep, um, he killed sheep today … and there is *dam,* you know, dam?"

Helena looked at me with concern.

"Wait, what is he saying *muñeca*? You are bleeding … oh shit."

"Just say nothing." I said to her in my rapid American English.

Muhammad continued, "I told him you don't like to be kissed now because you have a … alhayd … "

I continued to feign not understanding what he was saying and the conversation died out. Soon siesta was over and the men left to go back to work.

"Girlfriend we got to get out of here, I don't want to ever sit around the table with three men discussing my period in Arabic as long as I live!"

We both laughed but it smarted.

"How did he know?" she said.

"I don't even wanna think about how he knows, I have no friggin' idea!"

We took our time since we had the house to ourselves for a few hours. We took showers, collected our clothes, and repacked our bags. We studied the map again, thinking if we got to town, maybe someone could direct us from there. We started out, walking along a sidewalk that ran alongside the beach.

"Oh my God we are strolling along the Mediterranean! And the air here is both sweet and salty!"

"We have to swim in it girlfriend!" Helena said.

"It's pretty cold but yeah, we have to before we leave here. Did you swim there while in Israel?"

"I did, and the Dead Sea too. I was all so gorgeous."

We listened to the waves breaking as we walked along the outskirts of town. We walked slowly, lugging heavy backpacks, bedrolls, and a guitar.

Night descended and we continued climbing a seemingly endless steep hill. We came along a stretch of road where the surface of the sea shimmered with refracted light from the town ahead. "I think we are close now," I said to Helena.

It was dark. A carload of young men drove by and catcalled us. We ignored them until they made a U-turn and headed back towards us. They pulled the car off to the beach side of the road and we watched them begin to get out. We started walking as fast as we could.

"Holy shit, what are we gonna to do?" I said, my voice now shaking from fear.

"Girlfriend, you gotta pray! You always pray for everything and it always works."

"Yeah, you're right!"

I stopped and grabbed her hands, pressing them together and folding mine over them.

"Heavenly God, please, send us an angel right now! We need your help; we need your protection! Help us now, God!"

The men across the street—there were four or five of them—began crossing the street to our side and just then a man came up behind us out of the darkness and said, "Hello my sisters."

We raced towards him, grabbing onto his arms and peppering him with questions, "Where did you come from? Thank God! You're our angel! How come you know English?"

He chuckled and said, "I am from Gambia, I live right here, in this house."

As we talked with him, the men retreated, crossing back over the highway and getting back into their car.

"What made you come outside just now?" I asked him.

"Well, let's see ... I was sitting in my house and I thought I should go outside and smoke a cigarette and when I came outside, I saw two sisters and I couldn't believe it. You are here from Germany ... or England?"

"No, we're American."

"Really? Really, now? I have never met Americans before. What are you doing out here alone walking at night carrying all this stuff?"

"We're lost," we said.

"Oh, well, I am a cab driver, this is my car right here," he said, touching the trunk of a dusty brown Mercedes. "Tell me the address you are trying to find."

I showed it to him.

"Yes, I know where that is ... oh, my name is Ali, I will be happy to drive you there".

"Oh bless you! You don't know how much you're helping us. I believe that God moved you to come outside just when we needed you," I said.

"Of course he did."

We tossed the heavy bags in Ali's trunk and hopped in the backseat, breathing huge sighs of relief, and soon we were at the door of the apartment with Ali. He really was our guardian angel.

"Kwame sent us. He said we could use his room?" I said to the boys who answered the door.

"Oh yes, he wrote to us about you. Welcome, welcome," said two boys from Ghana.

"This is our friend Ali," I said.

They led us to the end of a long hall, pointing out the last room on the left. Inside was a neat, good-sized room with two twin beds.

"Here, you can lock the door when you're inside," one boy said, showing us the lock. "And here is the bathroom but there is only cold water."

We told Ali we were fine and we were going to stay. We were so glad to put our stuff down and have a room!

"I will come and visit you again, alright?"

"Yes, yes, please do that and thank you, thank you so much!"

Roquetas de Mar was cold and it was the off-season so it was a ghost town, mainly occupied by migrant farm workers from West Africa. We went into a tiny grocery store and Helena asked directions to the nearest beach in halting Spanish. The woman shook her head and answered briskly.

"Uh oh," Helena said, "I don't think I can understand Spanish even if I can speak a little."

"Oh, I understood, she said to go down to the second street and go left."

"How do you understand Spanish so well?"

"I can't really speak it but I listened to it being spoken around me for years. You know, when I was a teenage gangster."

This was now how we got by; she could speak a little and I could understand a little.

The beaches were fairly deserted but the Mediterranean still looked inviting. We spent a day on the beach and swam; though it was chilly, I just had to dip in the mythical Mediterranean.

We met men, almost constantly. It would've been hard not to since the town was mainly men, and we were young, friendly, and American, though I cannot say for sure who had more fascination with who. As we walked back from the beach, a few men approached us, asking us where we were from. One man pulled Helena aside and said, "I like your friend very much, she is very *gordo*!"

"Oh my God, I can't believe this!" Helena said when we were back in our room. "This is blowing my mind! I want to arrange tours for people to come here from America. Like if you live in America you think the only thing that's attractive is Christie Brinkley! These guys are all asking me about you!"

"You know you kinda look like Christie Brinkley a little."

"Yeah, I'm boring vanilla blond!"

"No, you're tall and skinny, you could totally be a model!"

"Models are boring. I want to be dark and exotic and curvy like you!"

"You're crazy!"

Kwasi was the older of the two boys in the room across the hall from us. They were around twenty and both had come to Spain for work, crossing the border illegally and spending time in jail. Now they both worked six days a week on a commercial farm.

"The work is very hard," said Kwasi.

"We have to send money home to our families," Kofi said.

Kwasi seemed to do most of the cooking. He showed me how he made fufu from boiling white flour into a stretchy mass.

"You are supposed to make this with cassava," he said in broken English, "but they do not have them here." He also boiled whole potatoes and split them in half in order to dip them in stew.

"Kofi, how come your English is better than Kwame's but you're both from an English-speaking country?"

"We don't speak English at home. We speak Ashanti, our tribal language. Very few go to school, they must pay a lot of money. Those people speak English. My brother's friend, he went to school, and then he taught us at home."

It turns out very few countries have public school systems like we do in the United States.

Helena and I hung out with them a bunch, often eating our evening meals together. There were other roommates in the house too, some men from Nigeria we also befriended, but it seemed like they didn't socialize with the Ghanaian boys.

One night at dinner Kofi announced that he and Kwasi had given Helena and I Ashanti names.

"You, we are calling Asantewaa," he said to me, "and you," he turned towards Helena, "you we name Agyeman."

"This is so cool," I said, "what do the names mean?"

"Let's see, Agyeman, Agyeman travels around, all around, doing magic. He is a great magician."

We immediately started laughing.

"Asantewaa, she was a great Ashanti queen … when the British came she got on her horse … and she fought like a man!"

"Oh my God, girlfriend! How do they know? How do they know!" Helena said, floored.

"I have no idea!" I said.

We went out one afternoon to get groceries and change money at the bank. "This is so weird," I said, "the bank is closed? Is it a holiday?"

"I haven't heard anything," Helena said. "Let's go over and check the grocery store." But it too was locked and closed.

We went back to the apartment and talked to a Nigerian man who lived there named Oladeji.

"Oh, sisters, it is siesta, everything closes for a couple of hours."

"Oh, that makes sense. We don't have that in America. People would literally riot."

"Really?" he said.

"Oh, yes, our stores are open 24 hours a day."

"Now that cannot be."

"Yes it really is."

"Listen ladies, why don't you come with me to my friend's house for dinner? I'm going by there soon."

"We don't want to be any trouble," we said.

"No, no, no trouble, you are welcome."

"But we're vegetarian," I said.

"That is no problem, you will talk to Bisi, she will have things for you."

We sat in the kitchen with Bisi, in her second-floor sprawling apartment. The smell of spices wafted in the air, and the walls were decorated with carved masks, beaded animals, and colorful prints. The men congregated in the living room.

"I'm so happy to meet you," she said, "I never met Americans before. Where in America are you from?"

"I am from New York and Helena is from Florida."

"I have a lot of family in New York City!"

"Yes, there are many African people there. I have friends from Senegal and Gambia. What tribe are you from, are you Yoruba?"

"Oh, I am Yoruba! You know Yoruba? My husband too, he is, and Oladeji. Gowon, he is Hausa but everyone gets along."

Helena asked her what she was making.

"Oh, see, I am making a goat stew."

"I'm so sorry but we are vegetarian," I said.

"Oh yes, I know, I am going to make something special for you!" she said, throwing handfuls of eggs into boiling water. Do you like eggs?"

"Eggs are fine," we said.

"Why don't you go talk to the men for a little while? They want to hear from you."

We went into the living room and started to talk to Bisi's husband.

"I am looking for a second wife," he said, "are either of you interested?" All the men laughed.

"Does Bisi know about this?" I said.

"Of course! Everybody does it in Nigeria!"

He was loud, gesturing with his hands. His English was impeccably British.

"Why do you have the hair like this?" Gowon asked. "Don't you want to put cream in it? I like the hair with the cream in it. I like it smooth."

Helena rolled her eyes, looking at me. She didn't say anything because we weren't sure we could speak American English covertly in this crowd.

"We're going to go back to the kitchen," I said, taking her hand and leading her back down the hall.

We walked in as Bisi was peeling the hard-boiled eggs. She leaned over the simmering pot and tossed the peeled eggs into the goat stew before we could stop her.

I looked at Helena with horror. She looked helpless. We were desperately trying not to be rude or to make people fuss over us but I knew for sure I could not eat that food.

"Bisi," Helena said, "your husband was telling us he is looking for a second wife ... "

"What!" she said, "he is just joking with you. If he tries to get another wife do you know what I will do? I will put this pepper in her eye!" she said, grabbing a vial of ground hot pepper. "That's what I will do! I will put this in her eyes and his too!" she said loudly.

Then she laughed and we laughed with her.

"But they do have it in some places?"

"Oh yes, they do, in the country, in the north, but we're from Lagos. We do not do that."

She scooped the eggs back out of the stew and put them into two bowls, which she then carried past us. "Come now," she said and led us down the hall to a small room. At this point, I was praying for help. She set the bowls down on a small dining table and told us to enjoy, then she closed the door and left.

"Give thanks," I said, "she's leaving us alone to eat."

"Oh my God, what are we gonna do, girlfriend?" Helena asked, looking around the room. She walked over to the window then grabbed her dish, trying to push the food out the window, but narrow iron bars blocked her access. She began to take tiny pieces and push them through the bars.

The door opened and we froze, but it was Gowon.

"What are you doing?" he said.

"Please, can you eat this food for us?" Helena said.

"You do not like it?"

"No, we can't eat it. Don't tell Bisi!"

"Alright," he said and he ate the food.

"We can't eat it, it's against our religion because there's goat in it, but we don't want her to know. Don't say anything, please," I said.

"No, no, I will not," he said, looking at us strangely.

Later we were back in the living room with the group. Bisi said, "We want to dress you in African clothes, my clothes, we want to dress you African and take some pictures, okay?"

"Okay," we said, following her into her bedroom. We put on African dresses. They were made of long wide fabric, sewn together under the arm then straight down the sides. The cutout neckline was scalloped and embroidered. The one I wore was silky bright purple with large white polka dots.

We went back to the living room and took a series of pictures. Later Oladeji gave us copies and those turned out to be the only pictures we had from the trip.

Ali came to visit us one evening at the apartment, and when he left Helena said, "He likes you."

"He does not."

"Yeah, he does girl, he's gorgeous."

"Yeah, he is really handsome."

"Are you interested?"

"No," I said. "You can have him."

She cracked up. "This is how it is here … I have to take your rejects!"

Mustafa and Muhammad came to the door one night looking for us. Mustafa wore a black leather jacket and both of them smelled strongly of cologne.

"We were worried … you disappeared!" Muhammad said.

"Well, we needed to find this place. How did you find us?"

"Some people in town told us you were here."

We invited them inside but they stayed in the doorway.

"We wanted to make sure you were alright. Would you like to come out with us for a little while?"

"No thank you," we said, "you're welcome to have a cup of tea with us."

The Ghanaian boys sat behind us, speaking in hushed Ashanti at the table.

The Moroccans glanced over and said, "No, thank you. We will be going."

When they left Kofi asked, "Who are those men? Are you mad at them?"

"No, not really, we just didn't want to go out."

"They are from the north?"

"Yes, they are Moroccan."

"Yes, well, we don't like people from there so much."

"But they're from Africa!"

"We do not even get along with the Nigerians that live here. We stay separate."

"But Nigeria's only like two countries over from you!"

Back in our room Helena and I got into an hours-long discussion about racism, nationalism, and tribalism. We were shocked to find out that people from different countries in West Africa would dislike each other.

"Ever since humanity began this is how it's been, tribalism or nationalism dividing people. They were like, 'you stand on the east side of the creek and we stand on the west side so we're going to kill you!' Krisnamurti says nationalism is the scourge of the earth and it caused two world wars."

"But Sena why? Why are they like that?"

"It's that evil nature in humans. It's like we have the ability to be gods on earth or demons on earth. I think when people are unhappy inside, they look for people to hate and they look for ways to group others together."

"This is so crazy! Do you think they don't like Ali because he's from Gambia?"

"Probably."

The next day Kofi and Kwasi questioned us.

"You girls stay up late into the night talking, so much talking!"

We started laughing.

"We do not understand ... what do you talk about?"

"We're trying to solve the problems of the world," I said, but they still looked at us quizzically.

Ali came over again and offered to take us to a party.

"Sounds great," we said, and we told the boys we'd be back late. They gave us a key to the front door and asked us to put it under their door when we came back in. They would need it in the morning.

Ali drove us in his cab.

"Who's going to be there?" I said.

"Oh, I don't know, a lot of people, some good friends. Maybe some beer."

Soon we found ourselves in a spacious apartment with a large group of maybe fifteen men. We were the only women.

"Ali," I said, "we're the only women here!"

"I know. Our women don't come with us, they stay home, in Africa."

Everyone wanted to talk to us and we ended up sitting on a love seat together answering questions about America for hours. The most popular question was: Do you know what I have to do to get a visa?

We spoke rapidly to each other as usual so no one could understand us.

"Do you think we're safe here?" I said to Helena.

"These guys seem pretty tame."

"Yeah, but the ratio is kind of disturbing. Do you think they want to be with us so that they can get to America?"

"I don't know but I can't get over how much everyone wants to go to the US! Everyone we meet asks about going to America."

"I know, I feel like we're celebrities here just because we're American."

The party was uneventful. There was no alcohol because many of the Africans there were Muslim, mostly people just rolled tobacco and smoked.

Helena developed a romance with Kofi. She started spending time across the hall evenings, while I sat and drank tea with Kwasi, or even better, lay on my bed in our room reading books.

One night I fell asleep while she had still not returned to our room. I was awoken late at night by Kwasi coming into the room.

"Agyeman will stay with Kofi. I'm going to sleep in her bed."

"Okay," I said, drifting off again.

Then, I awoke again and he was in my bed trying to convince me to sleep with him.

"No!" I said, "Go back to your bed!"

"But I have loved you all this time, you know that I love you!"

"Well, I don't love you and you need to leave!"

He grabbed my wrists and rolled on top of me, pinning me to the bed.

This happened before when I was a teen and drunk. I swore I would fight to the death if I were ever in the situation again. Now, I was totally sober and I thought strong enough to fight, but I wasn't. This was a migrant farm worker, he did physical labor all day. He was shockingly strong.

I kept fighting anyhow, and in minutes he was back in the other twin bed.

"I'm sorry," he said.

I didn't respond.

"Listen, Sena, I'm really sorry."

"Go fuck yourself you evil bastard. Go back to your room."

He slunk out of the room, and I kept one eye open the rest of the night.

I felt like I had lost a fight and gotten beaten up, bad.

The next day when I awoke Helena was back in her bed and the boys were long gone to their field work. I said I was sick but really, I was injured.

I went to take an icy shower, and inspect the damage. My arms and legs were dotted with bruises, and I had tiny cuts, like paper cuts, that stung with every move.

I spent the day in bed reading my books and writing poetry. I was not crying or talking about anything that happened. I was stoic.

The boys came home and went into their room across the hall. Next, they came to see what we were doing; Helena told them I was sick. They left but after some time they returned to our room together. Kofi was sitting on Helena's bed next to Kwasi, who started telling him something in Ashanti. Kofi was often the translator, as his English was far superior to Kwasi's. Then Kofi said something to Helena in a hushed voice.

"What! Oh my God, Sena! He says he forced you to have sex and that's why you're sick! Is that true?"

"No," I said.

"Girlfriend are you sure? Are you sure? What happened?"

Kwasi hung his head, resting it in his hands, looking at the floor. Kofi looked troubled.

"I don't know ... nothing. I just don't feel well. I'll be okay."

We never spoke about it again. There was no way I could tell her, I didn't even tell myself. I banished it completely from my thoughts. How could I protect her if I could not even protect myself?

Over the next few days there was tension between the Ghanaian boys and the Nigerians. It had something to do with us but we never got the full story. What did happen is a knife fight broke out in the living room, and we retreated to our room, locking our door.

"We gotta leave here," I told Helena, "we just need to go."

"Yeah, okay muñeca, let's go."

She told Kofi we were leaving. He started arguing with her and then with me that we would be sold into white slavery.

"You cannot go, it is not safe, you just cannot go! I would say the same to my sisters," he said.

The next day as we packed to leave, he lured us in his room to look at maps with him, then promptly left the room and locked us in from the outside, telling us through the door, "You cannot go! It is not safe."

I started pacing the room. "I really don't like being locked in, this is bullshit!"

Finally, hours later, he let us out. We agreed that we would stay awhile longer but the next morning when he left for work, we left.

We hauled all our bags to the bus station and got on a bus to Almeria. While we were packing Oladeji came by and I told him that we were leaving. I said goodbye to him, or tried to, but he insisted on coming with us to see us off. He rode on the bus with us and sat at a café while we drank tea and spoke rapid English so he couldn't understand us.

"What should I do with him girlfriend?" I said.

"I don't know, he's gotta go back home."

"I know, there's a bus back in the evening. Is he just being chivalrous or is he pursuing me?"

"Are you kidding girlfriend, he's totally into you!"

"Fucking fuck fuck!"

We decided to get a hotel room for the night so we could take the ferry in the morning to Spanish North Africa. We stopped at a bank and I made a note of the exchange rate for when we got to Morocco.

Using the guidebook, we found an inexpensive room in a frigid stone house filled with ancient fixtures. Oladeji insisted that he was going to stay overnight and see us off to the boat. So, we got a room, and he got his own room. Only when we all settled in, he was there, gently tapping at the door.

"What's up Oladeji?"

"I came to see you," he said, sitting down on one of the smushy twin beds. I sat next to him and Helena lay down on the other bed, next to the wall.

He started to roll tobacco and offered Helena a cigarette.

"No thanks," she said, "I'm exhausted. I want to go to sleep."

"Yeah me too," I said.

"It's okay," he said, "you can turn the light off."

I did and laid back on the bed, then he started to rub my legs through my long dress. "Stop," I said.

He paused, but a moment later he was doing it again.

"Stop, come on cut it out!" I said.

He sighed deeply then tried a third time. "No!" I kicked at him. "Why don't you go in your own room?"

"Girlfriend," Helena's soft voice came out of the dark, "why don't you sleep with me?"

I instantly sprang onto her bed and she put her arms around me, pulling me close. I snuggled up against her.

He sat in silence, smoking. With each drag, the cherry of his cigarette flashed in the darkness. Then, he left the room. When he closed the door, I jumped up and locked it behind him.

TWENTY-ONE

March 1992
Melilla
Spanish North Africa

We sat on the top deck of the boat where the water stretched out on all sides, surrounding us in bright blue from sea to sky. We reclined in the sun and soon we were gleefully watching dolphins jumping and playing in the surf.

We were crossing the Mediterranean Sea on a commuter ferry that took passengers from Almeria to a tiny stone fort city on the edge of North Africa called Melilla, the only part of Europe located on the African continent. While there, we will still be in Spain.

A group of scruffy young people soon joined us, three men and a woman from West Germany. They had bought a car in Germany, a Mercedes, and were driving it to West Africa to sell. Mercedes are the most commonly seen car here, though they were often beaten and dusty with age and use. Their plan was to drive the car east to Algeria, then go south to Niger, and then to Nigeria where they would sell the car for a profit and it would pay for their entire trip.

"Don't you have to drive through the Sahara?" I asked them.

"Yes, that's right. We really want to see the desert!"

"My guidebook says it's super dangerous, you gotta be careful."

"Oh we will, we have it all planned out."

"People constantly think we are German," Helena told them.

"We never see Americans like you in Germany, it's mostly military people. Then there's what we see on TV."

"It is so much more diverse than the homogenized version you see out of Hollywood," I said.

Soon the boys were rolling up tobacco and hashish an offering it to us to smoke. I took some though Helena refused. I took a ceremonious hit and immediately coughed, unable to tolerate inhaling the tobacco. Although I smoked occasionally as a teenager, I had stopped years before. Next, they offered us heroin, which I didn't even know you could smoke. We passed on that.

Hours later we disembarked and they went towards a different part of the boat where the cars were kept. In minutes one of the men came back and said, "Listen, hey, we just heard the president of Algeria was assassinated … they say the border is closed. We are not sure how we are going to go now, but you won't be able to cut through there to go to West Africa." Then he said goodbye and wished us luck.

Helena turned towards me with a furrow in her brow.

"Oh shit, are we going to be trapped here?"

"No, I read that we could take a boat if we go over towards the Atlantic, we can try that. There are other borders here too … Mauritania to the west … maybe we can go that way?"

Helena and I sat on a low wall facing the dock with our bags and guitar and I pulled out my guidebook. After a few minutes of reading I said, "So, yeah, there's a war in the Western Sahara in Mauritania so we cannot leave here by land. Nor can those Germans, now that Algeria is closed."

"Oh shit, what are we gonna do?" Helena asked.

"It says here that we can actually hitch a ride on a boat that's going to West Africa."

"Really?"

"Yup. I think we should try. We have to go to a port city though; we should go to Casablanca, I think. For now, let's figure out where we're going tonight."

We picked up our stuff, walking past the moored ferryboat towards the main drag and an affable, well-spoken man approached us.

"Mademoiselles, allow me to welcome you to the most beautiful city in the world, la!"

We smiled and told him we were Americans.

"Ah, ah, Americans! Wonderful, wonderful, my name is Muhammad and the police know me; you can see this policeman over there, he knows me," he said, waving to a policeman who tapped the brim of his hat. "I can be your guide, I can help you get through Customs to Morocco, and if you need a hotel I even have a room to rent you in my house. My wife is there, it is very safe. There is a key, your own key I will give you."

"How much?" I asked. "Just five American dollars," he replied.

We followed him home down narrow stone streets lined with attached houses until we reached the doorway of his house, behind a small gate.

The house was olden and dark with a narrow staircase and miniscule rooms. Giving us a skeleton key, he showed us how to lock the door on our room from inside. Later, there was a soft knock and a silent woman offered us bread and sweet mint tea. Through the wall, we could hear the muffled chatter of he and two women talking.

In the morning, Muhammad offered to take us to the border and help us get a taxi into Morocco. Then he offered to exchange our dollars for dirhams.

"The bank is closed, it is a Sunday. I can help you out. No charge."

"Great, I checked the exchange rate on the bank on Friday before we left. Can you change one hundred dollars?"

"Yes, no problem."

Then he told me the exchange rate and I debated him, but he insisted I was wrong so I figured I must be and allowed him to change the money for me.

The next day while at the bank in Morocco, I found out I was right about the rate, and he had stolen twenty dollars from us.

"Why didn't he just say he needed to make a fee? Why did he have to steal from us? I would have gladly given him twenty for taking us through Customs and getting us a taxi to Fez."

Helena shrugged. "Maybe he was ashamed, or maybe he thought we are rich since we're American."

After Muhammad gave us the dirhams, he walked us to a taxi stand and negotiated a ride for us to the Moroccan city of Fez. We paid the driver to reserve our place in the car then followed Muhammed to the Customs inspector.

He turned towards me, "This," he said, pointing to the area my scoop neck left exposed, "this you must cover. You cannot show this skin in *Maroc*, it is Ramadan."

"Ramadan?"

"Yes, our holy month."

I dropped my backpack on the ground, unzipped it and grabbed a woven indigo sweater, pulling it over my head on top of the dress.

"Is this good?" I said.

He looked down at my suitcase and pulled out a multicolored shawl, wrapping it around my neck and shoulders. "This is good now," he said.

He chatted with the Customs inspector in Arabic, promised us an easy entry into Morocco, and then departed saying, "Enjoy your visit to *Maroc*! *Allah yusallmak!*"

I placed my backpack on the table as instructed by the inspector, unzipped it and removed my books. I carried a number of them with me, and it made my pack ridiculously heavy. But I couldn't live without them.

"So, you are Christian?" The inspector asked, slowly looking over each book. "This is a book for Christians, yes?"

He held the Aquarian Gospel of Jesus the Christ in hand.

"It's an alternative form of Christianity, it's actually a channeled book about Jesus," Helena said. I interrupted her. "Yes, we are Christians," I said, meeting the man's stern eyes with mine. He stared hard at me with a serious face. I was intimidated, but probably not as much as I should have been. I thought I understood things about the culture but truly, I knew almost nothing. The inspector put the book down and picked up the *Koran*, then my book on Reggae, Alice Miller's *For Your Own Good*, and Walt Whitman's *Leaves of Grass*. He frowned but said nothing, placing each one of them back on the pile. Then he picked up the *Bhagavad Gita*, a book of Hindu Scriptures. "How many of these do you have? You have only one?"

"I have only one," I said. "You will not leave this here, in Maroc, you will keep this, correct?"

"Yes, I will."

"You cannot leave this here."

"I won't." I smiled nervously.

Later, when I decided to leave it in Casablanca, I searched it for markings that it belonged to me. I was afraid it would be traced back to me.

"Don't worry," my friend said, "the Hindus smuggle those in often. Me, I go to jail if I have it, you, you don't have to worry."

"Jail?"

"Yes, Hindu religious books are illegal here. Only Islam, Christianity, and the Jewish religion are recognized here."

"Oh, right, they all worship the same God ... that Middle Eastern Jehovah God."

"Yes, they're called the Abrahamic religions, and they're the only ones Islam considers legitimate."

We repacked our bags and hauled them to the waiting taxi we had engaged. Only now, there were two men waiting by the car. The driver pointed for us both to go into the front seat of the ancient Mercedes. We did, and then the two men got into the back seat. Then, two more men!

Helena and I looked at each other as the car drove away. We wore frozen grins as we contemplated our situation.

"I guess this is how taxis work here," Helena said.

"Yes, hopefully we will see Fez soon."

"Do you think we're really going to Fez?" she said, "I hope this isn't the thing everyone warned us about ... "

"The white slavery thing?"

"Yeah, I mean it can't be real, right? Whoever even heard of that?"
"I never did. I don't think it's real," I said, smiling to hide my fear.

TWENTY-TWO

March 1992
Fez, Morocco
North Africa

Helena and I talked animatedly to each other in the front seat. We both had a stiff smile that we would talk through so that we did not alert the men in the car to our absolute panic.

The driver was singing along with mimicry to The Police blaring on the radio and he smiled at us.

The car crawled along roads pocked and pitted with holes, then sailed along nonexistent roads; brownish desert flatland where there was no road, and yet the driver went doggedly on seeming to know the way.

Hours went by as we drove through tiny villages where children were riding donkeys, herding goats, or carrying parcels wrapped in burlap.

Suddenly the driver veered off the road towards a sprawling single-story house made of mud brick. He pulled up near the door and a cloud of red dust kicked up.

Helena and I looked at each other with our big fake smiles.

"Shit, girlfriend, what the hell, why are we here?"

"I don't know," I said through my teeth.

The driver disappeared into the door of the house while we held our breath. Moments later he emerged with a woman carrying a large sack. She got in the backseat and we set off again.

She greeted us warmly in Arabic. Helena had been practicing French and I had been trying to learn some basic Arabic so we were able to say *bonjour*, and

as-salāmu ʿalaykum to the smiling young woman who instantly alleviated our fears by joining the car.

Men in full military gear stopped our car about an hour later. I had seen the red Moroccan flag with its single green star waving over the building they were near, and there seemed to be more of a road as we got closer to Fez. The driver stopped and rolled down the windows and an officer came around to our side of the car.

"*Passeports*," the man commanded. He was tall with a neat black moustache and a serious face. We smiled and handed him our passports. He opened them and smiled saying, "Ah, *Américaines*, huh? *Très bon, très bon. Bienvenue au Maroc!*"

I looked at Helena. "He's welcoming us, right?"

She shook her head yes.

"*Shukran*," I responded, (thank you in Arabic) and he chuckled then waved his hand telling the driver to go on.

When we got to Fez we walked around trying to find the *auberge* (youth hostel) that was listed in our guidebook.

"We are never going to find this place," I said. "Maybe we should take a taxi, it can't cost much?"

We approached a taxi driver leaning against his car smoking a cigarette while talking to a man on the sidewalk who had a blanket laid out where he sold a few different items, including single cigarettes. We showed the taxi driver the address and he shook his head yes.

The language barrier was much greater than I had anticipated and most of the people did not speak French but rather Arabic. Not that we spoke French either, but the English speakers we found all around us in Spain were not here.

When we went to pay the cab Helena and I had our first ever argument. It was about the exchange rate and what the cab was charging. I don't remember the details, but when we got out of the cab I sat down on the steps of the stone building that housed the youth hostel. Helena walked away and went around the block. I prayed she would not be abducted.

She returned shortly and sat down next to me.

"I'm sorry muñeca," she said, "I always had issues with my father with money and you know … I'm sorry."

"No, I'm really sorry girlfriend, I don't mean to treat you like you're stupid or you don't understand money. It's probably my control issues."

"No, you're always taking care of me and everything and I know how much you care."

We walked into the hostel. The man running it was named Faisal.

"Welcome to Fez," he said in pretty good English.

"Wow, how did you learn English?" I asked him.

"Oh, I know so many languages. People come here from so many countries. What will you be doing in Fez? Are you interested in buying a rug?"

"A rug? No, we are going to go to Casablanca by train. We are hoping to get a boat from there to West Africa, to Gambia."

"Oh, yes, I see, let me show you to your room. There's really no one here this time of year especially with the holidays on. There's no alcohol for sale during the whole forty days of Ramadan," he said.

"We don't drink," I said.

"Okay, good," he said, "also, it might be good for you to wear a scarf over your hair and if you can get them you should wear *djellabas*. That's the customary clothing for Ramadan. It is a very holy time of year."

We went into our small room. The walls themselves were stone.

"This building has to be a thousand years old," I said.

"It's so amazing," Helena said.

We decided to lie down for a while and take a nap. The trip here took much longer than we had expected.

Later that evening Faisal came to our door and asked us if we would like to go have tea with him at a friend of his who lived just across the street. We said yes and put scarves over our hair, made sure our skin was well covered, then walked across the street to meet with his friend Muhammad.

Muhammad was a handsome young man with an innocent looking smile. We sat down with him at his table and had tea. He spoke some English and we soon got into a conversation about law and order.

"I think America is too harsh," I said, "the prison sentences can be insane especially for drug offenders. People can get fifty-year sentences!"

"Oh yes, that's not good," he said, "they should just kill them."

"Wait, what?"

"Well, I don't think they do it right here, they should, you know, cut the hand … cut the hand off." He was making a gesture with his hand like a slice across the wrist.

I was horrified and speechless. I turned to Helena on my left and said, "I'm so hungry, maybe we should go eat?"

"Will you excuse us? We've been traveling all day and we need to get some food," Helena said.

"Oh, yes, of course, of course," Faisal said, "let me tell you where to go."

He took us to the front door and pointed out the directions. Helena put her arm through mine and we walked towards the restaurant, unsure how we were going to order although I had asked Muhammad how to order vegetarian food and he told me how to say "without meat" in Arabic.

We sat down in the crowded restaurant and pointed to salad that we could see in the open kitchen area, and French fries. Our waiter was patient and helpful. We sat there holding both hands across the small table.

"Can you believe it? Can you believe we are in Fez? This is spectacular!" I said, "This is an ancient city."

"Yes, it's unreal, I am so excited that we're here and that we are going to see West Africa soon!"

"Me too!" I said and as we ate our salad of dark green leaves and bright red tomatoes, I looked around the room and noticed we were the only women in the restaurant.

"Oh my God, girlfriend, this place is one hundred percent men! What the hell does that mean?"

"I don't know, maybe women can't come to restaurants?"

"We're gonna have to ask Faisal when we go back, I don't think he would've sent us here if it wasn't okay."

We walked home along the cobblestone streets in the fading light.

"How come all the men here look like friars or monks?"

"I don't know," Helena said, "but they do!"

They wore long woolen cloaks of dark brown, zippered up front with a pointy sort of hood.

"How was your food?" Faisal asked when we came through the door.

"It was really good," I said, "but we have a question. We were the only women at the restaurant? Why is that?"

"Oh, yes, women don't generally go out in the evening, it's only men. Though in some of the cities late at night you will see families come out—just during Ramadan."

"They come out late at night?"

"Yes, they come out and eat a meal before the sun rises."

"We were wondering about the clothes the men are wearing," Helena said, "We've only seen people in religious orders dressed like that."

"Ah, yes, that is the djellaba I spoke of, you wear it over your clothes. Would you like to buy one? Women wear them always, men generally only wear them during Ramadan."

"Maybe," we said, and we bid him good night.

After we got into bed we talked, as usual.

"I do love the spiritual vibe and all," I said, "minus the hand chopping!"

"Yes, it is very different, it feels really ancient, but it's so weird to see everyone on the street wearing the same thing though!"

"Yeah, you're right, I think they only have one religion here too."

"I don't know, probably. That's so crazy compared to the US with, like, hundreds of religions!" she said.

The next day Faisal took us to purchase the djellabas but they were very expensive and not at all in our budget. He tried to also show us rugs and we laughed. "Do you think we can carry rugs with our backpacks?" we said.

"No," he said, "but you can ship it back home."

"Oh, we're not living anywhere right now."

"What about your families?" he asked.

"Oh, no, no thank you," I said.

We decided to take a train to Casablanca the next day. We took a walk around the city to try to see it a little more before we left. We were only passing through but it was hard to keep moving when there were so many things to see!

An adorable couple sat across from us on the train and struck up a conversation with us by drawing pictures. They were Czechoslovakian, they worked for the railroad, and they were touring Europe and Africa with rail passes. They spoke Czech, Russian, some German, and no English, but somehow we agreed that we would venture together to the hostel in Casablanca.

TWENTY-THREE

March 1992
Casablanca, Morocco
North Africa

All parts away for the progress of souls,
All religion, all solid things, arts, governments—all that was or is apparent upon this globe or any globe, falls into niches and corners before the procession of souls along the grand roads of the universe.

Of the progress of the souls of men and women along the grand roads of the universe, all other progress is the needed emblem and sustenance.

****

"Listen, Fatima, I will give you two camels for the white woman," a man said to me, smiling, as he passed us on the street.

Helena and I burst into laughter.

Helena said, "Wait, girlfriend, is this what people worried about? Was he serious?"

"No!" I said, "or he wouldn't have said it in English!"

The two of us walked side-by-side though the busy city while the Czech couple followed close behind. We were all hungry after the hours-long train ride so we looked for a restaurant.

I spotted one, but it was closed. Then we looked for another and it was closed too.

'Why are the restaurants closed in the middle of the day?' I wondered aloud.

We came to a huge outdoor food market were people were making fresh bread on top of a grill. We four bought some and ate it as we walked through the market.

"Why are people staring at us? Do you think because we are foreigners?"

"Maybe," Helena said, "or maybe we're not supposed to eat outside?"

"Oh, yeah," I said.

The Czech boy smiled and shook his head yes, but I am quite sure he did not understand us.

We made our way through the city to the youth hostel, occasionally asking people to direct us, which turned into a hilarious ordeal involving the couple speaking Czech, us speaking English, and the people helping us speaking Arabic!

Somehow, we made it to the hostel. Again, the man at the counter spoke perfect English and we instantly plied him with questions.

"Is it a bad thing to eat outside when you are walking around?"

"Oh, it is illegal to eat during Ramadan, you have to fast from six until six, sunup to sundown. No food, smoking, or water is allowed. But for foreigners it is okay, but you," he gestured towards me, "you look like a little Fatima. Some people might have been confused because you're not wearing a djellaba, and then eating."

"Fatima? What does that mean?"

"It is the name of the prophet Muhammad's daughter. Here it means, um, you look like a girl from the north ... from the mountains."

I smiled. "So the restaurants are closed for Ramadan?"

"Yes, they will open at 6 p.m."

"How long does Ramadan last?" Helena asked.

"Ah, almost four more weeks. It has just begun."

We checked into the hostel and planned to visit the shipping port the next day.

In the morning, we walked across town to the shipyard and weren't able to find out much, but we took a sheet with a schedule of the ships coming and going and figured we would ask for help reading it at the hostel.

Back in the center of town we visited the bazaar again and bought oranges, then sat on large stone stairs in front of a closed bank. Helena played guitar and sang a new song she'd been writing.

"Hallo, willkommen in Marokko!"

A few young men approached us.

"Oh, we're American," I said.

"Really? I haven't met any Americans," the man said, now in perfect English.

"How do you speak English so well?" I asked.

"I have my master's in English."

"Really?"

"Yes. My name is Aamir and this is Driss and Muhammad. We are about to go on top of that building and smoke cigarettes and eat bread, do you want to come?"

We had met a crew of rebels.

"Yes we'd love to!" we said.

These boys looked different than the Moroccans we saw on the street. They were not wearing djellabas, for one. Aamir especially looked unique, he wore a black leather jacket over a black turtleneck and crisp blue jeans. Long black curls spilled down over his collar.

We sat on top of the building in the cold afternoon sun where we could see much of the city.

"You can play now?" Driss said.

"Sure," Helena said, grabbing her guitar case.

Aamir said, "You best not, we don't want to get caught."

"Why, what happens?" I asked.

"Six months in jail for us."

"What the hell! What about us?"

"Foreigners are allowed to eat during Ramadan, we are not."

"That's so weird that the religion is the law."

"Oh yeah, I'm not even allowed to have my hair long like this," he said. "If the police knew I was Moroccan, they would take me and cut my hair, but they think I am a foreigner. Maybe they think I'm Italian? I don't know."

"Where are you staying?" Muhammad asked.

"We're staying at the youth hostel and we're trying to get a boat to West Africa. Maybe you could help us with the ship schedule?"

"Let me see it," Aamir said, and I handed him the timetable

"We want to go to Gambia or Ghana."

"Yes there is one ship that is going to Guinea, would that work?"

"Yes that would totally work! We're going to try to hitch a ride."

"It looks like it goes in about ten days."

"Ten days?"

"Yes. It is called the *Pagaso*."

Later that day, Aamir and Muhammad walked us back to the hostel. It was facing a type of square where there was a park on one side. Some kids were playing there and they ran over to us, holding their hands out and saying, "*Raja, raja.*"

"What are they saying?"

"They are saying please, they are begging."

"We don't really have any money but I did bring toys. Is it okay if I give them some toys?"

"Yes, I think so."

I unzipped the side compartment of my backpack, which was filled with little dinosaurs and animal figurines. I gave one to each of the three kids. They yelled, "*Shukraan!*" and then ran off. We crossed the street and stood outside the door of the hostel and out of the side street a giant group of children emerged and ran towards us, screaming. They surrounded us, holding out their hands saying "*Damiya! Damiya!*"

"They are asking for more toys," Aamir said over the shouts of the children.

"What should I do?"

"Here," he said and he pulled forward the little boy who I gave a toy to earlier. He spoke to him in Arabic and told him that he would be in charge of the toys. I opened the compartment and gave the kids every toy I had inside.

"Will that work? Will he share them?"

"I don't know," he said, "but you would never be able to carry enough toys for all of them."

"Do they have toys at home?" Helena asked.

"No," he said. Then he and Muhammad bid us goodnight.

"I will come get you in the morning, I can be your guide," Aamir said.

"That would be so great!" we said.

The next morning Aamir and Muhammad came to the hostel and the worker came and got us. "There's some men here to see you," he said, sort of disapprovingly.

Helena grabbed her guitar and we were on our way.

"What would you like to do today?" Aamir said.

"We'd like to shop for some dresses."

"Dresses? Oh yes, yes, I will take you to where they sell them."

We walked through Morocco taking in the sites. This part of the city was very old, some of the buildings looked medieval. Everything was made of stone: the streets, the houses, even the benches. He took us to a stall that had piles of folded cotton dresses with beautiful embroidery and short sleeves. They were very long with a small slit on both sides so you could walk.

"Can we wear these on the street? I mean, with pants and long sleeves under them, of course." I said.

"Oh yes, people will love that."

Next, he took us to the market and we pointed to the man ladling batter onto a hot griddle where it became bread.

"What is that called?" we asked.

"*Msemen,*" he said.

"We think it's the best bread in the world! We are addicted it!"

"Yes, yes, it's very good, it's a Moroccan specialty."

We spent more time at the bazaar, now that we had a translator with us. There were baskets filled with fresh vegetables, many we had never seen, and a stall where they sold dried beans that had been pre-soaked in large white buckets.

"I wish we could get some of these and we could cook," I said.

"You could cook at my apartment," Aamir said.

"Really?"

"Yes, I will have to sneak you in but I know how to do that."

"Wait, why do we have to sneak?"

"Because it's illegal."

We bought chickpeas, the woman scooped them out of the water with a large strainer and put them in a bag, weighing them on a hanging scale. We also bought greens and carrots.

"I could make a dish out of this, if we could get some spices."

He took us to another stall where large, endless jars of spices lined the shelves.

"Which ones do you want?"

"Curry."

"Curry?"

"Or, you know, like ... red pepper... or chilies? And we need cumin."

"Yes."

He ordered in Arabic and the man took down the jar and scooped the ground spices into a plastic baggie. Aamir told us the price in dirhams.

"You have to be careful, they always charge tourists more," he said.

"Well, we come from the west so I'm sure it seems like we have so much more and I guess we do."

"No, no, you don't need to pay those prices," he said. "let the wealthy tourists do that."

Later, we sat on a bench in a small square playing music. Just across from us was a walled-in part of the city, you could only glimpse the city inside through a doorway carved into the sandy-colored stone.

"What is that?"

"Oh, that is the *Medina*. I will walk you in there someday, you can get lost very easily, the streets are confusing on purpose."

"On purpose?"

"Because of invaders; only people who live there can navigate the streets."

A large crowd formed and continued to swell. After each song Helena played, the entire crowd clapped and begged for more.

"Is this really happening?" I said.

"Oh people here love music, and they love to hear different languages. They don't hear anyone singing in English except on the radio."

Aamir brought us to his apartment building and told us we had to be careful not to run into anyone on the stairs. He was on the third floor.

"I will go first," he said, "and I will open my door and go inside and when you come upstairs, I will open the door and you must come inside quickly."

We did as he said, walking up beefy concrete steps in the dark hallway. There was no lighting at all, but each floor had a tiny window that supplied some light. When we reached the third floor, we slipped inside Aamir's apartment.

"Welcome, welcome," he said, inviting us into a dark and sparsely furnished one-bedroom apartment.

We sat down on a low colorful futon-like couch.

"Do you mind if I roll a cigarette?" Helena asked.

"No, please help yourself," he said, pushing a bag of tobacco towards her.

"Do you want to see my banned book collection?" Aamir asked.

"Banned books?"

"Yes," he said, leading me to his bedroom where a small bookshelf sat in the corner. He had books by Alice Miller, Sylvia Plath, and Erica Jong! I pulled one off the shelf.

"I love Erica Jong," he said.

"She's my writing idol! I can't believe you read these!"

"Her poetry is fabulous," he said, pulling a small book off the shelf called *Loveroot*. "I like American writers and I love poetry also."

"Me too! 'Loveroot' is a word in a Walt Whitman poem. You should see the books I have with me!" I said, walking back to the other room to my backpack and unzipping it. "I'm a fanatic too."

"Oh, my, look at all these books!" he said.

"Yeah, I was afraid I wasn't going to get them through Customs."

Muhammad said he had to go home, but other friends of Aamir's dropped by including Driss and a man name Ahmed. I had made food in the dark kitchen. At one point Aamir brought me a candle.

"I'm sorry," he said, "the electricity got turned off, but I do have gas for the stove."

"It's alright, I used to cook over a campfire. This is a little bit easier... maybe ... I mean there is a sink ... " I said, and he laughed.

We took bowls of food and passed them out in the living room. The men sat on the floor.

"This is very good, is this American food?"

"No, it's not. We don't really eat American food, we're vegetarian so we eat a lot of Indian food."

"Oh God, Sena cooks the hottest food, I had to beg her to let up on the hot pepper, I couldn't even eat it!" Helena said.

"It's true! I like food that burns my mouth," I said.

We asked him for a glass of water and he looked at us strangely. "Just water? Not tea?"

"No," we said, "just water."

I took out a bottle of grapefruit seed extract and squeezed a few drops into the glass before drinking it to purify the water. It did not cover the odor, which to me seemed metallic, but everything here smelled different than back home; the cooking smoke wafting through the air in alleyways, the streets after it rained, even the air itself was distinctly different, in a way hard to pinpoint but I can clearly recall in sense memory.

Later that night Aamir walked us home. "I will come again tomorrow. You should wear your new dresses," he said.

"Yes, we will."

The next day we walked around the city with Aamir showing us various buildings and sites. I noticed people pointing at us and laughing.

"Why are they laughing at us?" I said. "What's going on?"

"It's nothing, it is because you are foreigners in Moroccan dress, they like it, that's all."

"But why are they laughing?"

"It's just an unusual sight," he said.

We passed a bank. "Oh, we should go change money," I said.

We went into the bank and he spoke to the teller for us. I took out money to change and the bank teller's face lit up. He looked at the bills with wonder, then he called out to the other tellers and they came over and crowded around the man to look at the American money in his hand.

Aamir said, "They rarely see American money here."

"Really?"

"Yes, Americans usually go to the Citibank."

"There's a Citibank here?"

"Yes," he said, as I collected the dirhams off the counter.

When we returned to the hostel that night, Faisal looked up at us then rushed out from behind the counter. "No, no," he said, "ladies you cannot wear this outside."

"What do you mean?" I said.

"These are ... these are ... oh what do you call them in English ... nightgowns?"

"Oh my God, so this is why everyone was laughing at us!" Helena said, laughing.

"Yeah, Aamir played a joke on us," I said, "a pretty good one too!"

We decided to get a hotel room, since we were going to have to stay and wait for the boat. Using my guidebook, and Aamir, we rented a room inside the Medina. It was near the door, so we memorized the way in and out, and did not venture further alone. The streets were narrow, and broke off into forks and uneven crossroads, like a maze.

Our room had a window overlooking a well; a square stone basin with numerous spigots. We watched women fill buckets with Tide and water then wash the clothes by hand while stooped over. After, they emptied the buckets in the street, refilling them to rinse the clothes. Soapsuds splashed out leaving snowy-white foam on the cobblestones. Lines for drying were strung from house to house, some higher than our second floor window. Damp sheets, skirts, and jeans flapped in the breezes daily.

"You know, I don't think they have Laundromats here, I have not seen one," I said to Helena.

"Girlfriend, that's got to be crazy hard, washing sheets by hand!"

"Yup, I think we're going to be washing everything by hand while we're here."

The room was tiny, the plaster walls were a light gray marred by chips, dents, and even holes. We had two beds, and a small bowl and pitcher. The bathroom was down the hall--it was a hole in the floor framed by a porcelain basin. There was a faucet at squatting level, and a plastic pitcher to fill with water then splash over your bum. That was it, that was the bathroom. There was no toilet paper, there was no shower.

"How do we take a shower?" we asked Aamir.

"At the *hamam*, the public bath. There is one for women," he said.

We learned Arabic greetings from Aamir, and now we amused everyone we met by saying: *Assalamu Alaikum,* a typical hello, *Shukran,* meaning thank you, and *Inshallah,* meaning if God wills it; we learned to say this word often and after any statement about the future, as Moroccans did.

One day while Aamir was busy, Helena and I left our tiny room in order to drink green tea at a nearby café. We found that hashish was passed freely about and we were happy to smoke some.

The men crumbled hashish over tobacco, then rolled it into a cigarette. I was unable to smoke tobacco without immediately coughing, though I tried.

I had an idea. I pulled an apple out of my bag and using my hunting knife, I carved it into a pipe. I put a hole on one side, tunneled through the middle and made a hole on the top connected to the tunnel. Men crowded around me, handing me hashish just to see me smoke it in the apple. Everyone laughed and clapped.

"We gotta come here every day," I said.

"Yeah, maybe, but did you notice it was nothing but men here?" Helena said.

"There's nothing but men everywhere here! I don't know what it means."

"It means the women aren't fucking allowed out!"

I convinced her to go there with me anyway the next day and I brought my apple. There was a repeat of the scene from yesterday with no one drinking tea except us, and me smoking hash through an apple. Smoking cigarettes was forbidden during Ramadan fasting, as was drinking anything, including tea or water, so I have no idea how these men were allowed to smoke.

While we were sitting at one of the wooden tables, I saw Aamir and Muhammad walk by, headed to our hotel.

We ran outside to catch up with them and a man accosted us, hollering in Arabic. He was scruffy and unkempt, and I thought maybe he was drunk. Aamir and Muhammad came and started arguing with the man. Finally, they ushered us away while the man continued to yell at us.

"What is he yelling about?" I asked Aamir

"Nothing, it's nothing, he's just drunk."

"Yeah, but what is he saying?"

"Nothing, he is just saying you are western whores."

Though we wore long dresses that covered every inch of flesh and scarves that covered our hair, we were out in public, alone, and unescorted. We played music in the public square, and we lived in a hotel where men came to call for us and worst of all: we came from the sin-filled west.

"I know I'm not your type," Helena said, "I'm bland, boring, like Christie Brinkley. You like curvy women who look like you. Dark-haired, exotic women."

I sat in stony silence.

Then she said, "Well, I like that type of woman too … "

I looked at her softly but I didn't reply. I wanted to, but my throat was closed. I was unable to speak and I was so sorry. I knew what it was to fish for affection. I knew what it felt like to ache for a response. What I didn't know was why I was mute.

I thought she was the most beautiful person I'd ever seen. She glowed. There was light around her, like a halo, and she shimmered, like all those rippling lake surfaces I so adored.

She was so luminous everything around her looked dim, even in memory.

She was warm, steady, loving, thoughtful, and incredibly kind, everything I wanted to be. She was full of life and excited about each day and she made me feel that way too. I forgot about my obsession with dying, and I felt like I could live forever.

Later that night we lay in our twin beds in the darkness.

"Helena, I'm terrified for us to have a relationship because everyone I've ever been with is out of my life. My life would be over if I lost you, like, I will die without you, and if we don't get involved then we could stay together forever as best friends!"

"I understand girlfriend," she said flatly.

"I just can't lose you," I said, "I can't."

We spent many evenings having dinner with Aamir and sometimes his friends and then later sneaking into his apartment to all hang out together. A man named Reza was the clown of the group. He would put a kerchief on his head and start saying to Aamir, 'He's my wife! He's my wife!' Everyone laughed a lot but for us it was a little bit confusing.

"Aamir what is he saying?"

"He's trying to say that he is my wife, not that I am his wife."

Later when he walked us home, I asked him if Reza was gay. "Yes," he said, "but this is very illegal so do not talk about it."

Helena and I sometimes sat in the square across from the Medina and played music. Crowds would always form around us. She would play and sing and sometimes I would sing along.

On one chilly evening just as the sun began to fade, Helena and I sat on a bench with Aamir while she played songs. A young woman stood a few feet away smiling shyly. She wore djallaba and headscarf, as did most people here. Only a handful of women covered their faces.

Helena stopped playing and turned her guitar on its back, resting it on her thighs then flashing a wide sunshiny smile at the woman who was not much older than us. She leaned over her guitar and tried to talk to the woman.

A man in a dark brown djallaba came up and grabbed the woman by the arm. He pulled her across the street to another sidewalk where he argued with her loudly.

You could hear her voice softly protest and then he was hitting her. She was crying and then crouching down on the ground.

Passersby ignored the scene.

I turned to Aamir and plead with him, "We need to do something, we need to help her, how do we call the police!"

"No, we need to leave now."

"But she's being beaten up!"

"No, that's her brother. He's allowed to beat her."

"But why? Why is he hitting her? Why is he so mad?" Helena asked.

"Because she was talking to you. We need to leave here, now."

Helena shot me a look of horror, and we left with Aamir walking back to the auberge in silence.

We went to the shipyard to find out about the Pagaso, but it had not arrived as far as we could tell. We saw some European backpackers getting on a boat and we talked to them but the ship couldn't take any more people.

I learned Arabic for the shipyard, Aamir taught me how to ask them when the Pagaso was expected. I practiced for days, writing it out phonetically in my notebook. Finally, Helena and I approached the soldiers standing near the entrance to the shipyard and I repeated my question in Arabic to them. They leaned forward, listening keenly. One man shook his head and then began answering me in rapid-fire Arabic. Of course, I didn't understand a word and I turned to Helena, "What the hell was I thinking! That they were going to answer in English?"

She laughed and offered to try to speak French but that didn't work either.

"We're going to have to get Aamir to come here with us or we're never gonna get out of here on a ship," I said.

We were invited to dinner at the home of a prominent lawyer. Being American here was like being a celebrity.

"They are excited to meet Americans," Aamir said.

"We are far from typical Americans," I said.

"No one here knows what a typical American is."

We took the long journey across the city. We talked about the people we were visiting as we walked; Aamir told us about the latest case the lawyer was representing.

"It's a famous case," he said, "a man, a writer, he is Moroccan. While visiting Spain he did an interview. He said the Moroccan government are all crooks. They arrested him when he got off the plane."

We arrived at a lovely, sprawling apartment with the smell of lemon and cumin in the air. We waited for 6 p.m. when the fast is broken and breakfast would be served.

We sat on the floor around a large round table. A young maid placed covered dishes and clay pots on the table. The television was switched on and the king of Morocco came on and led the evening prayer and the breaking of the fast. After, we ate fruit, couscous, homemade yogurt, and bread.

"What will happen to the man who criticized the Moroccan government?" I asked the lawyer.

"I will defend him. If he loses, he will get five years."

"Five years!"

"Yes," he said, "we are working hard to change these laws, it is not like where you are from."

"That is very true," I said.

"By the by, has anyone told you that you look just like a little Fatima?"

As we got ready to leave some of the women asked us to wait and they came back with gorgeous djellabas. They insisted we take them and it turned out they had given us the very clothes off of their backs!

I put mine on, it was a beautiful fabric of crushed velvet in pale gray with long sleeves and a hood. Detailed embroidery concealed a zipper that ran up the front. To put it on, you stepped into it and then zipped it up all the way to the neck. It was worn over your clothes.

"Do you wear these in the summer?" I asked.

"Yes, we do, and it is very hot. We try to stay home as much as possible in the summer."

We walked home in silence. Aamir walked ahead, leading us back to our hotel room in the Medina.

"We're pretty shocked," I said to Amir. "we just didn't know it was this bad. We are very spoiled living in America, you can say anything you want ... even hateful stuff."

"I know," he said, "I would love to live there."

Back in our room, Helena and I were uneasy. I picked up the spillage from her side of the room, tossing clothes and papers onto her bed. Our room was near identical to my childhood bedroom; my side was military neat, my sister's side looked like a small bomb went off. An invisible line divided the room.

"I've read about things like this, like in Saudi Arabia," I said, carrying a bowl of water from down the hall so I could wash my face.

"Should I get you a bowl?" I asked when leaving the room to empty the water.

"Yes," she said, "I gotta take a bath."

"I don't know how you do that, it is freezing in here!" I said, as she stripped naked and used a washcloth and icy water to bathe.

"Muñeca, how many weeks has it been?"

"I know, I know, I would kill for a shower!"

"This is such a frightening place," Helena said, "five years in jail for a simple remark?"

She put her long dress back on and then went down the hall to dump the water.

A pall hung over us as we climbed into our beds.

"I can't imagine being afraid to criticize my government," Helena said.

"I'd be doing life!" I said.

Later, we heard a commotion outside and we got up to look out the window. It was past midnight and the streets were suddenly full of women, children, and men. Everything was lit up and open and people were going out to restaurants.

"Oh my God, girlfriend, these people are not fasting from food, they're fasting from sleep!" Helena said, laughing.

The wife of the lawyer, Meryem, was a kind and generous lady. She invited us on a trip to Marrakesh so one night, after breakfast, me, Helena, Muhammad, and Aamir got into her sedan. (Muhammad was her brother). Her three-year-old daughter sat in back with us in her car seat, she spoke to us in French for most of the trip. She kept warning us: "*Le chocolat a des insectes*!" A phrase her parents had told her to keep her from eating candy.

We saw a lightning storm; jagged forks of white sprung from above and touched the desert horizon. It was a spectacular sight. We passed a waving Moroccan flag near an outpost.

"Aamir, I meant to ask you, why is there a pentacle on the flag?"

"It is the symbol Solomon used to seal the ark of the covenant."

"I can't believe you know that! No one in America knows that, but how do you know, have you read the Bible?"

"No, the Koran has the Old and New Testament in it. It's the same stories."

"Yeah, but it is very different, though I didn't read the whole thing yet… it's just that in America people think that star is satanic, you know, evil."

"What! No, that cannot be! Why?"

"They really do and now I wonder even more why they think that."

"Aamir likes you," Helena said. We were in our hotel room, everyone had gone to sleep. The drive had been many hours. Meryem and her daughter stayed in one room, the boys in another.

"No he doesn't!"

"Yes girlfriend, he does, the way he looks at you … "

"I never noticed," I said.

There was a knock at the door and then Aamir came into our room.

"I've got a balcony off of my room, do you guys have one?"

"No, it doesn't look like it," Helena said.

"Come over to my room and check it out. You can see the whole city of Marrakesh."

"Okay," I said.

"I'll see it tomorrow," Helena said, "I'm exhausted."

In Aamir's room, Muhammad was sleeping on one of the beds. We tiptoed through the darkened room and went to the balcony.

The minaret tower stood high over the small adobe houses, glowing with soft light.

"This is spectacular," I said.

"Yes, it is."

Then he stepped towards me, taking my hand and kissing me. I would have been shocked if Helena had not told me about his interest.

We sat down on the floor of the balcony and talked.

"Where are you from in America?" he asked.

"I'm from New York State, near the mountains."

"The Catskills?"

"How do you know that? I've met southerners, err, Americans, who had never heard of the Catskills."

"Do you live near the Hudson Valley?"

"Yes!"

"I know all about Henry Hudson and I've studied the geography. I learned a lot about America in college when I studied English."

We heard the sound of doors opening and closing and I quickly went back to my room. Meryem was at my door a minute later.

"I brought you some apricots, we usually eat a little bit before the sun comes up since we are fasting."

"Thank you," I said, relieved she didn't know I had visited the boys' room.

"You were right," I told Helena later. "Aamir, I guess, likes me."

She laughed, "I can't believe you didn't notice."

"Yeah, I can be so clueless."

We spent the morning roaming around the markets of Marrakesh in a small group, while hucksters tried to sell us things from every direction. There were beautiful things: lanterns, antiques, clothes, and of course, rugs. Large outdoor stalls stuffed with apricots, dates, almonds, oranges, and lemons filled the center square, along with towering palm trees.

The buildings were made of a kind of red adobe that seemed to grow right out of the sand. Helena got her guitar and played music for us while we sat in the sun, the air was chilly but people came out to listen and applaud. When she stopped playing, a man approached her.

"I would love to offer you a job," he said. "I own a café and you can play music there."

"I'll think about it," Helena said, coolly.

"I can give you a beautiful house with a garden that you can live in while you're here, your friend too." He handed her a business card.

"Yeah, okay, I'll think about it," she repeated.

When he left she turned me and said, "No way in hell am I staying in this country, women aren't even allowed out at night! I'm going to play for a bunch of men who think I'm a whore? We've got to get to West Africa, that's our plan!" she said, tossing his card in the trash.

Back in Casablanca, we decided to check on the ship again. It *still* had not arrived.

"We're going to start calling this boat the mythical Pagaso!" Aamir said.

We had checked out of the hotel before Marrakesh so we needed to go back and get another room.

"Why don't you just stay at my apartment?" Aamir said. "You can stay there for free."

So we moved into Aamir's apartment, sneaking in as usual.

Aamir began teaching me Arabic phrases like *la tuhawil 'ayu hyl ealiin,* a snappy phrase to say to taxi drivers so they would not inflate their rate because I was a tourist. We fed him daily, taking him out to dinner with us, or we shopped and I cooked. His friends came by his apartment regularly. He said he wanted us to meet his friend Rashida, but we would need to meet her out because he did not want her to face prison for coming here.

"Me, I can leave the country. I am in the process right now of getting a visa to go to Hungary. I have some friends there."

"What are you going to do there?" I asked him.

"I want to be an actor and I want to get to America … and I definitely want to get out of here before I go to jail."

We met Rashida at the market, her father had dropped her off. We walked around together through the busy streets.

"You don't know how lucky you are!" she said, "I am so angry, every day I just I'm full of rage." She clenched her jaw in a grimace, she was slightly shaking.

"I'm so, so, sorry Rashida! I don't know what to do for you, but I can't even imagine!"

"Luckily, I have a good father and he's going to help me go to France, Inshallah!"

"Praise God for that," I said, "I'm sorry it's so hard here. I wish I could take all of you home with me!"

Driss chimed in, "I am so angry also, but I am a journalism student. I want to stay here and report on the government."

"Yes that is good for you," she said, "because you're a man."

"Driss you need to be careful, can't you get years in prison for reporting on the government?"

"Forget them!" he said. "I am not afraid."

"I've seen the Color Purple, and a number of banned movies. What is it really like in America?" Rashida asked.

"Well, it has its problems like any country, but I have to say I didn't realize how truly free I was until I left."

"Me either!" Helena chimed in, "We kind of live in a bubble. We can do most anything, and we can say anything—we don't really have censorship. And everyone dresses differently. I get mad at our government all the time but I can't get in any trouble even if I go out and march on the Capitol."

"You've been on marches?" Driss asked.

"Yes, and Sena slept in front of the White House trying to stop the Persian Gulf War. She was there for months."

"And they just let you sleep there?" Rashida asked.

"Mostly … yeah," I said.

"I want you both to meet my friend Khalida. I will bring her tomorrow. Can you be here again?"

"Yes, we will," we said, and she left us as her father had returned to pick her up.

Driss turned to me. "You know, you are like a great … a great … mother… yes, yes, you are mother Sena!"

"Oh my God girlfriend!" Helena said. "How did he know, how does everyone know that you are Mama Sena?"

The next day we met Khalida. Tall and willowy, she was shy and younger than Rashida. She walked alongside Helena and Rashida walked alongside me. At one point, we sat down on the steps of a closed business. Aamir walked away to get tobacco.

Khalida said, "Men say mean things to me on the street, they say I'm ugly and that I'm too tall and too skinny. Does that ever happen to you?" she said to Helena.

"No, that never has but Sena keeps getting her butt pinched on the street at night and it doesn't happen to me, but listen, in America, I swear, you could be a model!"

"Yes it's true," I said "you have the ideal look in America."

"Really?" she said, her eyes wide.

"Oh yes, have you seen many American films?"

"Only a few," she said.

"You have to be tall and super skinny to be an American actress or model," I said.

Helena continued to talk to her like a big sister, explaining about beauty and culture and how different it is everywhere.

"Khalida, will you ever get to go to Europe?" I asked.

"I don't think so," she said. Her eyes looked frightened and sad.

"You see? You see what we have to put up with. She's a prisoner here and I can't help her, only her father can!" Rashida said.

"You mean she can't travel without her father's permission?" I asked.

"Of course not, she can't even get a passport unless a man gets it for her; it must be her father, husband, or her brother."

Helena and I looked at each other, sharing a silent moment of assent over the horror of what we were hearing: these women are prisoners!

Later we walked home in shocked silence, while Aamir and Muhammad chattered away in Arabic.

Aamir and I were getting closer. We wrote poetry, we read poetry together, and we had long conversations about culture, religion, and politics. He was worldly and his English was so good he sometimes corrected mine! I asked him if Muslims do circumcision like Jewish people do.

"Yes we do but not as an infant, we do it at puberty."

"Wait, no, that can't be!"

"Oh yes, they tricked me. They said there was a special party for me when I turned thirteen and when I went to the party my uncles were all there, and they tackled me and held me down and circumcised me."

"Did they shoot you up with painkillers?"

"No, no painkillers."

"That's so barbaric! How could you even live through that?"

"I don't even know how to describe the pain but somehow, I'm still here."

"I'm traumatized even hearing about it. I know they do that to women but I didn't know they did it to men too."

"Yes, they do. It is very cruel ... listen, my dear, there is something else I want to tell you. The first person I had sex with was our maid. Maybe I was twelve? She came in my room and got on top of me and said, 'If you tell your parents or anyone, I will kill you.' I was really scared of her, I never told anyone."

"Oh my God, I'm so sorry! That's child molestation, that's rape!"

"I know, but I never told my family. I'm not sure they would believe me."

I have been hearing stories like this from others since I was a teenager so I was not surprised, but it sickened me. Humans can be so evil, no matter where they are from.

On one of our daily walks to the market, I reached over and took Aamir's hand.

"I love you, don't touch me." Aamir said, brushing away my hand. "Six months in jail."

"Lord, is everything here six months in jail?"

"No. My crazy neighbor burned an apartment building down because he was obsessed with the girl who lived there. She was killed. He got ten years."

"Ten years! Ten years? In America you can do most anything you want, but if you burn someone's house down and kill them, you're going to do life in prison! The laws are just so different here …"

Helena and I went out alone some days while Aamir was visiting his family. They owned the apartment he lived in but they lived out in the country. He would take the train to go and see them.

We went to a bus station thinking maybe we could find a bus that would take us to West Africa, but it turned out there were no buses that left the country.

Helena started getting really upset. "We're never getting out of here! You just want to stay here with Aamir and we're not even going to go to West Africa!" she said.

"Yes, we are, we are gonna go!" I said, but before I could stop her, she was lying on the floor, stamping her feet and crying like a toddler having a tantrum.

"Come on, you have to get up," I said. We were drawing a crowd around us. She sat up and I sat down on the floor next to her. Tears streaked her rosy cheeks.

"I know you want to just stay here with him but I don't want to stay in this country, Sena."

"I don't want to stay here either, Helena, and I'm not going to. I promise! We are going to keep traveling soon as we figure the best way out of here."

Long before coming here, I railed against oppressive cultures, many of them theocracies. I had read books on Saudi Arabia and Iran, and I learned about Iraq and Kuwait while I was protesting the Persian Gulf War. I knew there were cruel regimes that were especially hard on women, but being here was even worse than I imagined. Still, a man who sat next to me at dinner had assured me this was "liberal Islam."

"We tell our women how to dress, not the government. I decide if she covers her face or not. That is freedom! In other places, the King decides. Here, we are free." he told me one evening over the ubiquitous sweet mint tea drunk here at a dinner party we attended. We were often invited to the homes of people who wanted to meet us.

Free? I thought. *The restaurants are filled with men, as are the teahouses and most public places. Women are rarely seen except in the afternoon at the markets. Nights the only women out besides us were prostitutes, recognizable by the direct eye contact they made with passersby, and the fact that they were out at night.*

"Why do you want to go to West Africa? Everyone there is black." he continued.

"What! But you're black!" I said.

"No, I am brown, but down there the people, they are very black!"

"Well, in America, you'd be considered black!"

Later, a group of us sat in Aamir's living room, I said, "Listen, you guys, the UN sought to abolish the use of the word "race" after World War II because it was used incorrectly to promote genocide. There is only one race, the *human* race, and every human on earth belongs to it! We are all one human family. Please tell me you all agree!"

"We do!" they said.

"Of course we do," said Driss, looking thoughtful.

Aamir kissed me and told his friends I was upset, then he switched to Arabic and they all shook their heads in understanding.

"You must forgive us for this ignorant man," Muhammad said, "do not think all Moroccans are like him."

The month had passed by and now it was *Laylat Al Qadr,* one of the holiest nights of Ramadan. Aamir took us out to the Medina late one night and we walked all over the old city. It was crowded with families and we were happy to see women and children out. There was energy in the air, a feeling of excitement. The booths were lit with candles and people were eating sweets and candy.

"This holiday is magic," Aamir said, "it's called the Night of Power, it's the night Muhammad received the Koran."

Ramadan was over, and restaurants were open again during the day. We went with Aamir to meet one of his friends named Samira. She was a clerk in a large insurance agency in the center of Casablanca. Dressed in a simple suit of a gray jacket with a matching long skirt and turtleneck top, she was one of a few women I had seen not wearing a headscarf or a djellaba. Her long brown hair was in a loose braid falling down her back. Now that Ramadan was over, a small percentage of the population wore conservative western dress.

Aamir waved to her through the glass door where we could see women at their desks working. She came outside. "Come to lunch with us," he said, "these are my American friends, I want you to meet them."

"Oh my, you are Americans? I am so happy to meet you," she said.

"Your English is very good," I said.

"Oh, thank you. I speak a few languages, I learned in school."

We walked with her towards a café where we all sat and ordered mint tea.

Her manner was gentle and she seemed shy, but her soft-spoken voice belied a rebellious side we would soon see.

"I am not allowed to socialize or leave the house except for work, but since I only have two hours for lunch I cannot go home. It is nearly forty minutes away. My father does not like it but it means I can see friends at lunchtime."

The café was brimming with professionals on their lunch break, which lasts two hours.

"I'm so curious about you. What brings you here from America?" Samira said.

"We wanted to see places, other cultures," said Helena, "and we wanted to meet people and talk with them, learn about them, hear what they think, you know?"

She shook her head then flooded us with questions, blurting them so rapidly she sounded breathless.

"But how did you get your fathers to let you go?"

"We didn't ask them," Helena said.

"What do you mean? I don't understand. How did you get a passport?"

"At the post office," I said.

"I don't understand," she said. Her eyes were wide with curiosity and filled with questions.

I recalled the conversation with Khalida. "In America, once you are eighteen, or even younger in some states, you can do whatever you want. You can leave home and you don't have to be with your parents anymore or do what they say." I said.

"Oh, I see," she said, fiddling with her bracelets. "My father, well he decided I should marry later. My mother died and he remarried and had a new family of small children. I must stay and help my new mother take care of the children. He lets me work since it's good money and I took languages in school. He takes the money, of course—it's for the household."

Helena and I were silent. I glanced at her and the pain of the conversation was clearly written on her face.

"What do you mean you will marry later?" she asked Samira.

"Well, he said he will marry me in my thirties to an older man, a widower or something ..." she trailed off and a sadness passed over her face like a shadow. Then, she flashed a grin.

"My father he, uh, he ... he wants to make sure I am a virgin for marriage, of course. He brings me to work in the morning and picks me up at the end of the day. But what he does not know is that I have already lost my virginity. On my lunch break at a hotel with a French boy whom I loved."

"But are you gonna do it?" Helena asked. "Are you going to marry a man you father chooses?"

"Of course," she said. "What else would I do?"

It was as if she had never thought about the question. Her life was fated by her father and she was born a citizen of a country that endorsed his power and stole hers away.

I held my breath thinking of my life in the United States, thinking how this girl was a bit like us; delighting in rebellion, interested in the larger world, craving freedom. *What if I were born here?* I thought. *What if I was the person I am inside and I was born into a life like this. How would I survive?*

Helena and I walked through the city with Aamir after Samira went back to work. We were still absorbing the shock of the conversation we'd had over lunch.

"Why is it like this, girlfriend? Can we help her?"

"No," I said, "I mean, I don't know how. She was born in prison. It's a cruel, horrible, unfair fate."

Helena took my hand and gripped it tightly.

Late that night, when the tinny voice of the *muezzin* broadcast the call to prayer, Helena called for me. I was sleeping in Aamir's bed, Helena was on the couch.

"What's up?" I asked, walking to the living room and sitting on the couch next to her.

"We have to get out of here! We have to get the fuck out of this place! I don't feel safe. I just want to leave. Fuck the boat, it's never coming, let's find out if we can fly. I'll get some money out of my trust fund, I don't care, I just don't want to be here!"

Tears filled her eyes and I held her close, "Okay," I said, "let's see about flying."

The next day we went to a travel agency to look into plane tickets. They only flew to two countries in West Africa: Ivory Coast and Nigeria. The price was the same.

We asked Aamir how to make a phone call. I had not seen a phone the whole month we were here!

"Oh, you have to go to the central building … I will show you."

We went to a large municipal building with an open floor plan ringed by tiny wooden phone booths. At the desk, we gave the clerk the phone number we wanted. He asked how many minutes and we paid up front in cash. Then he directed us to one of the phone booths where he sent the call.

Helena got her uncle to wire money to the Citibank. We picked up the money, went back to the travel agent, and chose Ivory Coast because that went on Tuesday, which was sooner. For Nigeria, we had to wait until Thursday.

We walked out of the office with plane tickets in hand and I tried to steel myself for separation from Aamir.

TWENTY-FOUR

April 1992
Abidjan, Ivory Coast
West Africa

Allons! through struggles and wars!
The goal that was named cannot be countermanded.
Have the past struggles succeeded?
What has succeeded? yourself? your nation? Nature?
Now understand me well—it is provided in the essence of things that from any fruition of success, no matter what, shall come forth something to make a greater struggle necessary.
My call is the call of battle, I nourish active rebellion,
He going with me must go well arm'd,
He going with me goes often with spare diet, poverty, angry enemies, desertions.

***

"That was like the fucking *Handmaid's Tale*!" I said to Helena as we sat together on a stuffy, tiny plane flying out of Morocco.

"Oh my God, that book! It was, it was so like that! Did you read her other book, *The Edible Woman*?"

"No, but I think you're the only person I've ever met who understands everything I say!"

We stepped off the plane into the blazing afternoon heat and onto the tarmac. The air was moist and heavy, slight breezes offered little relief. The bags were unloaded from the plane as we waited and we grabbed ours and headed into the terminal.

Immediately, people approached asking where we were going.

A petite muscular man with dreadlocks came forward.

"Sisters, sisters, let me help you," he said, taking our bags from our hands. "I am Ras Kaya, I can take you in my cab."

"We are going to stay at the auberge," I said.

"How much you pay to stay there?" he asked.

"I think maybe five dollars?"

"I know a great place you can stay for five dollars, a room with two beds. It's in the building where I stay. I am here visiting also, I am here from the Congo."

"Wow, from the Congo?" Helena said.

"Yes, I am reggae musician so I came here to make a record. Who plays the guitar?"

"I do," Helena said.

"Oh so good! You can play music in my hotel, we love all music in Africa!"

We went with him.

"All I want is a hot shower. Do you have hot showers there?"

"Oh yes, yes we do!"

When I finally got into the tiny concrete stall, I took the longest shower of my life!

When I went back into our room I was in tears.

"Oh girlfriend, are you okay?"

"I'm just sad to leave Aamir. I gave him Louis's number and address but I don't know if I'll ever get to talk to him again. I am just really sad."

When Ras Kaya returned from driving, he asked us to come listen to music with him. "I have a cassette player," he said.

"Oh that's so awesome," I said, "I haven't heard my cassettes in months!"

We listened to Linton Kwesi Johnson's *Dread Beat An' Blood*, and Hugh Mundell's *Africa Must be Free*.

"I've missed my music so much! I said, singing and dancing in the hall his door was open to.

"Sister you have the best reggae music! Helena, get your guitar and let's practice playing along."

She sat on a tiny carved wooden stool in his room, he sat on the bed, and they strummed along with the music.

When we went back to our room Ras said, "Here my sister, take my tape player to your room. You can use it a time."

"Thank you so much!" I said.

"Oh do not worry, you are in Africa now! We share everything, we never worry."

We spent a lot of time with Ras Kaya, and soon we nicknamed him, "Ras Cuckoo." He was sweet and generous, but also frenetic, distracted, and unpredictable. I suspected he was bipolar, like my father, who would eschew sleep for weeks while he dreamed up schemes to get money, or to free animals from the zoo.

We found out we needed a visa to go to Ghana, the country just east of this one. We applied, and were told it would take a few weeks.

Ras offered to take us to meet his friend who he said loves Americans and speaks English. We walked down a dusty dirt road that snaked through a small village. Women with bare feet hurried by with scarves wrapped about their heads, framing their faces with bright gold cloth. Many balanced large parcels on top of their heads.

A massive mound of garbage sprawled across the dirt road yet people, sometimes with bare feet, walked over the mound like it was not there. They maintained a straight-ahead gaze and did not even look down. Helena and I stopped and stared in disbelief.

Past the village was a widening dirt lane leading down to the water. We walked along fenced-in properties. The fences were hand-fashioned from what looked like bamboo, though it might have been sugarcane, as it grew plentiful here. We stopped at one gate that looked like it had a compound within—the fencing was so high and the door so well-fashioned.

"We are here," Ras Kaya announced, and he began to knock on the door. A man opened it and gestured for us to come inside. We followed him to where a small group of men sat in a circle on the ground, while one man sat in a large wicker chair. We were introduced to him, the owner of the compound. His name was King I Live.

Helena and I each took a seat next to him on rusting folding chairs. He looked at us, smiling, and pulled on his long beard.

"So, my sisters, tell me, what's happening on General Hospital?"

"What! Wait, how do you know what General Hospital is?"

"Because I'm from Georgia. I've been away twelve years now and I wonder what's happening on my stories."

"We don't watch television." I said.

"What! Really? I'd do anything for American television, hell, I'd do anything to get home. I don't have the money so I'm trapped here, stranded. All I have is this bit of land. It's not even worth enough to get a plane ticket home."

"We were thinking of moving here, Sena wants to," Helena said.

"Moving here? I don't know why you'd want to do that."

Later he offered to walk me to the river.

I took my sandals off and waded into the water, first lifting my skirts then letting them skim the top of the water, dampening the edges of the cotton gauze.

"Oh come on now, woman, I can't go in the water! I'm like a cat, come back here."

"No, I like the water," I said, moving further into the current. I saw an island in the distance covered with tiny homes.

"People live there?"

"Yes," he said "there is a bridge and they drive over there."

"That looks so amazing! I want to live on an island."

"Yeah, you can live here with me if you want," he said.

"Oh, I don't think so. I'm just passing through. I'm going to Ghana."

I dipped my hands in the water and splashed my face to cool off. It was blazing hot. The water was lukewarm.

"What are you doing there?" he asked.

"I just want to see it. I want to travel. I'm hoping to see many more countries, yet so far things take forever here. It's hard to move around."

He took out a knife and cut stalks of sugarcane sprouting near the river's edge. "These are good to chew on," he said, offering me one.

I bit into the green stalk and cane juice filled my mouth.

"Yeah, you are in Africa now. Everything moves slow, even compared to the south back home!"

"I need to get back to my sister," I said, wading out of the water, wringing the water out of my skirt with my hands.

We nicknamed him "King-I'm-crazy."

We went to an outdoor restaurant one afternoon and got a meal of pasta with peanut butter sauce, a spicy sauce that I often made after I learned it from Sa'eed.

"White pasta? This is insane," I said, "this is American aid food, it has to be!"

When I left my corporate job, I became the director of a nonprofit hunger organization and later became the assistant to the director of the Martin Luther King Center. She gave public talks on different subjects involving Africa. One of the things we learned is that American aid, though it is measured in dollar value, often comes from our surplus food.

It made me think of a reggae song called "Aid Travels with a Bomb."

The girl waiting on us was no more than fourteen, she was carrying a baby, as people did here while they worked. They were usually tied onto the lower back with a large cloth but occasionally they would be tied to the side, over the hip.

"How old is your baby?" I asked her.

"Oh she's just a few months, but she is my sister."

"Your sister? And you bring her to work with you?"

"Oh yes I take care of her since my parents went to America."

"Your parents are in America?" Helena said, "And you are here alone?"

"I am with my brother and sisters," she said, "we are war refugees from Liberia."

"You're from Liberia?" I said, "Oh, so that's why your English is so good!"

"Liberia is a former American colony," I said to Helena.

She smiled and began collecting our plates.

"You are from America?" she said

"Yes," I said, "I'm from New York."

"And I'm from Florida," Helena said. "So your parents left you with the baby?"

"Yes, I can explain it to you in a little bit. My brother will come to pick me up, will you wait?"

"Yes, we will," we said.

A tall boy, no more than sixteen, and another sister, about nine, came to get Alphia after her shift. She quickly told them about us, and the whole family sat down at our table.

"Do you know where Maryland is?" the boy asked.

"Of course!" we said.

"That is where my parents went. They got the visas and went to get jobs, they said they would send for us later."

Alphia broke in and said, "When my mother was boarding the plane they said 'You cannot bring the baby' and she said 'My baby is only a few weeks old' and they said 'No, you need a separate visa.' My mother, she was crying and she put her into my arms and said, 'You take care of your baby sister.'"

Helena and I sat in silent shock a moment then asked, "Where do you all live?"

"We live in a small apartment and our parents send us money." the boy said, "We were happy in Liberia. My favorite thing was books, and school."

"Me too," I said, "I love books."

"They all were lost when they burned my school down, I was very sad," he said.

"Well, I brought a lot of books with me and if you want to look at them you can meet me here tomorrow and I'll bring them."

"Oh, I would love that!" he said.

We handed them a few dollars because even though we were living on a shoestring, they needed it more than we did.

The next day I emptied my backpack of most of my clothes, leaving them on top of my tiny twin bed. I brought all the books I felt I could part with. The only books I left on the bed with the clothes were my small books by Yogananda, *Leaves of Grass* by Walt Whitman, given to me by my father on my nineteenth birthday, and *The Way Out*, given to me by Red Wolf.

At the restaurant, the kids waited excitedly for us to show up. Helena brought her guitar and played some music while Alphia was waiting on tables. People smiled, clapped, and encouraged her to play more.

The boy's eyes were wide as I unzipped the backpack and my small pile of books sat there.

"Go ahead," I said, "you can look at them."

He reached for the *Itations of Jamaica and I Rastafari* book. He flipped through the pages, filled with color pictures from Jamaica.

"This book is so nice," he said.

"Isn't it?" I said, "it's one of my favorites. I want to give it to you, in fact I want to give you all of these books."

"Oh really? Really? This the nicest thing, I am so happy, so very happy!"

I gave him *Peace is Every Step* by Thich Nat Han, *For Your Own Good* by Alice Miller, the Koran translated into English, and *The Aquarian Gospel*.

"Listen," I said to him, "I didn't get to finish high school either but books have made me very knowledgeable and taught me all about the world. They gave me an escape. Just keep reading books, read as many as you can get, as many as you can find. When you go to America with your parents, we have libraries."

"Yes, yes, I know of this, you can get the book for free right?"

"Yes, there are thousands of books you can borrow and then return them and borrow more."

"Yes we had that in Liberia before the war but everything got burned, everything, my whole town is gone."

"I am so sorry," I said, squeezing his hand and choking up. "War is so unfair, and I'm so sorry you went through that, but I'm so glad you're safe with your family and if you love books that will help you make sense of this crazy world."

Later, when we walked back to our hotel we passed so many people on the street despite the blistering heat; women with giant baskets on their head full of wares for sale; like combs, hair cream, and aspirin, and men in suits, and small groups of children playing.

"Children are always the victims of war and it's not fair!" I said.

Helena clasped my hand, "No, it isn't!" she said, "It's friggin' heartbreaking. Are those kids going to be okay all by themselves? How are they going to raise a baby?"

"I don't know but they're doing it. I can't believe they wouldn't let her bring her newborn when she was going to the United States as a war refugee! And why does she have to leave all her kids behind? This war is our fault, we colonize these countries in order to take natural resources and then when war breaks out we leave."

"It's disgusting," Helena said.

We announced to Ras Cuckoo that we were leaving Ivory Coast and taking a bus to Ghana. Our plan was to see many countries. We also thought we might fare better in a country that spoke English, in terms of moving around.

"No! My sisters, you cannot go! It is not safe. I brought you to my producer's house, don't you want to stay and make a record?" he said.

"Here we go again," I said to Helena.

I walked out of his room and then Ras slammed his bedroom door shut and used the key to lock it from the inside.

"I will not release you from this room. It is my duty to protect you!" he said to Helena, who was now locked in.

I pounded on the door, yelled, and generally freaked out. I went outside and, looking up at the second-floor window of his room, I yelled to Helena and she came to the window.

"I'm okay Sena, I'm fine. He's just trying to talk me out of leaving."

"What the hell with these people locking you in rooms? I never heard of that! It's probably illegal in America!"

"He's going to have to let me out, he's got to drive his cab in the morning."

I looked around and saw scads of people sleeping alongside the sidewalk. "I'm going to sleep out here," I told Helena, "then you can call me if you need me. Plus it's like a hundred degrees in our room!"

I went and got my blanket. Imitating the locals, I spread out my blanket and lay down on the cool concrete.

The man across the street from me popped up awake.

"Hello," he said, "a white lady is lying down in the street? This I have never seen!"

"Well, all of you do it," I said.

"Yes, but not white ladies. I have to get my wife, she will want to see this."

He got up and walked down the road, returning a few minutes later with a diminutive woman by his side. He spoke to her in a tribal language and she smiled and waved to me.

"Say something, she wants to hear you speak English," he said.

"Nice to meet you, it's a beautiful evening," I said.

She giggled then and teetered back to her home.

"How come you speak English so well?"

He sat back down on his blanket. "I travel for buying trips, I go to the UK and France often."

"What do you buy?"

"Ladies' brassieres."

I asked him no more about his work and somehow, I slept.

The next morning we were on a bus to Ghana. People were friendly and cheery, and reggae music played over the bus stereo system.

"Can you imagine the Greyhound playing reggae in America? People who didn't like it would freak out!"

"I know," said Helena, "but it seems like everyone here likes it."

She reclined back into her seat and we settled into the long ride to Ghana.

TWENTY-FIVE

May 1992
Accra, Ghana
West Africa

The bus rolled up to the border of Ghana. It was noontime, and we had skipped breakfast and brought no food with us. We were starving.

A young boy approached us as we stepped off the bus. "Fried egg?" he said, holding out a wax paper wrapped sandwich he took from a basket.

"I'm going to get one," I said to Helena.

"It's so hot I don't think I can eat, I don't want any, plus it looks disgusting!"

I bought the sandwich and ate it while we stood on line for Customs. When it was our turn, we handed the agent our papers.

"Let me have your vaccination papers," she said.

"We don't have them," we said.

She began hollering at us, "Why you don't have vaccination! Why don't you go to doctor and get vaccination?"

Helena tried to explain to her that we were allergic and she mimed getting an injection and falling over sick.

A group of onlookers that had formed all burst out laughing.

"Ma'am," I said, "they weren't required by the United States for us to come so we didn't get them, we have a note from the doctor giving us an exception..."

She went back to hollering. Despite the fact she was speaking English, it was incredibly hard to understand her. Ghanaians speak British English far removed from Great Britain; it is very different than any English we'd heard. After a lengthy scolding, she stamped our passports and let us into Ghana.

There were banks of cabs waiting to take people from the bus. We went over to one of the drivers and asked him if we could go to Accra.

"Oh yes," he said, "welcome to Ghana!"

We got in the backseat, putting our packs in the trunk and just as we started to relax, more people got in the cab, and then more, and more, until Helena was on my lap and I was half on someone else's lap! People were overwhelmingly warm and friendly—they were all smiles while the crushing heat pounded down on the small car.

I questioned whether the car itself would fall apart from this many people. There were six people in the backseat, and three people up front including the driver. When I finally thought we could not get anyone else in, they put people on the roof. On the roof! There was a rail along the edge on both sides, and they sort of hung on. We started to drive incredibly slow; the roads were pocked and pitted and even broken apart in places though we were on a main highway.

"What are those castles?" I asked Helena. "I keep seeing these buildings on the shore, I don't know they look like Dutch forts or something. Look there's another one."

No one in the car understood our American English, and we were surprised to find that once again we could have private conversations whenever we wanted.

I was nauseous. I get carsick and the holes in the road made the car jump and lurch.

"I feel so sick," I said, "and I'm really scared those are prisons where they kept slaves. They are right on the coast, the old Gold Coast. It's where the British shipped slaves from, I think it's also called the Slave Coast."

"Oh no! Sena, it reminds me of that sad song you love so much."

"*Hateful, hate.*"

"Yes!"

More than six hours later we arrived in Accra. It was nighttime and I was seriously doubtful about how we would travel by land in the future. Places on a map that look an hour away could really be five hours of extremely slow driving away.

Everyone got out of the car and Helena started to dig through her bag to pay the cab but a man dressed all in white surprised us and paid our fare.

"My sisters," he said, "welcome to Ghana! You will always remember that we welcomed you as travelers and friends! I paid for your trip, we are so happy to have you visit here."

"What? Oh no, you shouldn't do that! It's too generous," we said.

"We always help travelers and strangers. I am so happy to do it. Welcome to Ghana!" he said again, with a slight bow.

As always, we used our guidebook *Africa on a Shoestring* to find the cheapest hotels and places that the locals stayed. We didn't want to be in a commercial hotel with tourists.

We ended up in a small rooming house where they rented rooms by the week or the month. The room was at the end of a long hall on the second floor just adjacent to the shared bathroom. It was five dollars *a week* and had two twin beds and a couple of windows. The first night, I got up to use the bathroom and when I opened the door to the hall, the entire hall was full of sleeping boys who worked in the restaurant downstairs. They were each wrapped in a blanket, asleep on the wooden floor, and lined up in an orderly way.

The manager of the hotel, Kwame, was warm and friendly like most everyone here. He made himself our unofficial tour guide. Every day he gave us advice about where to go and told us about the culture.

We walked around the city meeting people. It was easy to do, once a couple across the street from us started waving at us as if they knew us. Then, they crossed the street and introduced themselves.

"So, where are you from?" they asked.

"America," I said.

"What! You are American? I thought you'd be tall, and blond!" the woman said to me.

"Well, she is," I said, and we all laughed.

"Can you visit a bit?" the woman asked us, and we four sat down together at an outdoor restaurant.

I told them about how in America homelessness is such a huge problem and in New York City there are entire families living outside, and lots of Vietnam veterans. Also, the mentally ill that Reagan tossed out of institutions in the '80s.

"No!" she said, "it cannot be true! If you were not American, I would never believe you. It is so wealthy there, how is that possible? We don't have that here unless somebody you know, if they are not right in their mind, if they are crazy maybe we can't get them to come inside."

"It's hard to imagine," Helena said, "and people here wouldn't die if they were outside, in much of America you can die from exposure from the weather."

They continued to shake their heads in disbelief. "Everyone here would like to go there, we dream of going there it is so wealthy and grand."

"I guess it is but not everyone there is wealthy," I said, "in fact, it is very few," but I was becoming aware that even poor Americans might seem 'wealthy' in comparison to some of what we had seen traveling.

"Kwame, people keep saying that they can't believe I'm American, and that they thought I'd be tall and blond! Why do they think that?"

"Oh they watch American television. The favorite shows here are *Dallas* and *Santa Barbara*."

"Really? They watch nighttime American soap operas?"

"Yes and they think that all Americans are wealthy, even I would think that if I did not meet you. You don't have a sports car back in America?"

"No, definitely not."

One evening we were sitting at a table with him and some other people watching them play a game of *oware,* where small stones were shuffled between depressions on a carved wooden board.

"My sisters," he said, "you should go walk down the block, go two blocks to the tobacco stand, you will see something."

We did tend to walk in the evenings because it was so brutally hot during the day, so we went. The air was close; we wore sleeveless African dresses with sandals, and tied our dreads up on top of our heads. Again, we had met people who literally gave us the clothes off their backs, women who insisted we take dresses of theirs; well-worn frocks with bright colors and beautiful patterns. They showed us how to tie skirts and head scarves. When we walked about dressed like Africans it delighted passersby. They told us it was a compliment to them that we wore their clothes.

In addition to that, women kept offering to fix us up with their brothers!

We walked the two blocks as Kwame instructed, and we saw a group of Africans sitting in folding chairs. Some were just arriving and setting up their chairs. They were all facing a television set sitting high atop the counter of the tiny tobacco stand, and sure enough, they were watching *Santa Barbara*!

At the outdoor market, we bought mangoes and avocados. Women, usually with their children, cooked food with small gas cans over a single burner. Sometimes we bought fried plantains from them.

One morning when Kwame was with us, I saw a regal-looking man who wore only a white loincloth. The women walking with him wore the same cloth but as a wrap dress, similar to how we would wear a bath towel in the west.

At stands that sell fabric abound in Ghana, you can pick fabric then have it made into clothing for you by tailors sitting nearby hunched over sewing machines, ready to take your measurements. Dozens of multicolor designs filled the tiny shops but I had not once seen white fabric, or anyone dressed in all white.

"Those are the Fetish people," Kwame said, lowering his voice. "They know magic. They can put herbs on you so that a bullet cannot penetrate your body."

I had heard this before from Gambians talking about their tribal people.

"Really?" Helena said, "You mean can't be shot?"

"The bullet will not penetrate the skin. I have seen it," Kwame said, "they are very powerful and very wise. They live far out in the jungle, a few days' walk. They live a traditional way of life. They are not Christian the way we are but we still highly respect them."

We talked to someone one day who told us about apartments for rent. We went to look at one and it was thirty dollars a month!

"We could live here so cheap," Helena said.

"Yeah, but we'd have to work here to pay for it. Plus we can't live in a city!"

We marveled at how inexpensively you could live in such an amazingly beautiful place and the city people here were warm, friendly, and laid-back. The issues that plagued us back home seemed far away. We were the minority here, yet the people were so magnanimous.

Kwame was concerned about our lack of eating. We mostly sat at the tables downstairs and ate mangoes.

"You are eating those wrong," he said, laughing, "why are you biting them?"

"In order to eat it?" I said.

"No, no, you do not bite, you just suck the juice out, like this," he said, taking one and making a small cut and slurping out the juice.

Then he turned serious. "Listen my sister, you are not eating enough. Are you trying to get small?"

"No," I said, laughing.

"Please do not get small, you do not want to do that. Look at your friend, she is too skinny! Also, I really like your teeth! Do not fix them."

"What, why?" I said. I have tooth-sized gap in my bottom teeth I was born with.

"Because they have spaces, I love them," he said.

"But your teeth are perfect! People in America pay to have teeth like yours. In fact most everyone I've met here has perfect teeth."

"Yes and it is very plain, not special like yours."

"Kwame, what's that building over there?" I said, turning around in my chair one afternoon and pointing in the general direction. "It looks like some weird old prison. I saw bunch of them on the way here."

"Oh yes," he said, "that is where they kept the slaves before they put them on the ships."

"Is that what they fucking are? I knew it!"

"Yes, this is the old Gold Coast. People go there, they go to those buildings, and they cry, they cry so much, they fall down on the floor crying. They have rooms there that they put the slaves inside of, they put the people into the darkness, and then if they were still alive some days later, they put them onto a ship and they never came back again."

My eyes filled with tears and he took his hand and placed it over mine.

"You have family that came through here, relations?"

"No, I... I mean I am not sure of all my family but yes, my human family came through here, all humans are originally from Africa. I've read books on the slave trade and the suffering ... it's unbearable ... I can't even think about it!"

He patted my hand with his. "You will be alright. I will get you some Fanta."

He left, then returned and handed me the ice cold can, pulling the tab for me.

"There," he said, "you will feel better soon."

I nodded.

Helena walked up to us at the table and sat down. "Oh my God, Sena, are you drinking orange soda?"

I smiled, laughing at myself. "It was easier than saying no," I said in my quick American English.

She nodded her head in agreement. One thing we had learned here is unlike in America, you can't really say, "no thank you." It is almost impossible. I tried it at first and Kwame said to me, "Why, why are you saying no" and I said, "because I'm not thirsty," and he said, "why are you not thirsty?"

"Girlfriend, those fucking buildings are what I thought, they are prisons built by slave traders ... for people who were kidnapped and sold."

"Oh no! No! That is so disgusting. It makes me ill!"

"Yeah, it's evil, so evil."

We sat in silence for a long time, a rare thing for us.

Later Helena and I talked about how it was so different to be raised in an individualist culture where your personal choices are allowed, and often unnoticed, but here it was extremely noticeable to people when we didn't follow along.

Sometimes they even scolded us mildly saying things like, "What is wrong with you? Why you will not eat this?"

"America is a big experiment," I said to Helena, "I think most places tend towards homogenization, even in the west."

"Yeah and there's something to be said about that because then there's tradition and culture and maybe they are more bonded then we are in our country?"

"That may be true, I mean, Americans don't even say they're American, they say they're Irish or Italian or Scottish or whatever."

"Well, the only Americans would be the Native Americans."

"Yeah, that's true," I said.

One night while we were out walking about the city I fell into a hole. It was in the road and it was so big that I needed help climbing out. I didn't expect it so I wasn't looking down.

"Man, I said, I can't believe Americans think we have bad roads. This hole is bigger than me and it's right on a main road, in the capital!"

We needed to go to the bank during daytime hours but it was way on the other side of the city so we jumped into a cab. It was easily a hundred degrees; we had spent the morning sitting near the open windows of our room listening to Michael Jackson blasting out of a neighbor's window.

"I haven't listened to this much pop in years," I said.

"I know, me either, I was on Dead Tour for the last few years!"

"I had no idea we would be listening to mostly American music! People here just love anything American," I said.

When the driver arrived at the bank he said, "I'll wait here for you," turning off the engine.

"Really, you're going to wait?"

"Of course! You just relax, you are in Africa now!"

He offered us some kola nuts, and then decided he would go in with us.

Inside, there was a long line leading to the teller and he simply guided us up to the front of the line.

"We can't cut all these people," Helena said

"What?" he said. "You must relax, just relax, you are in Africa now, I told you, no one minds."

We looked behind us and people smiled and waved.

"Is this really happening?" I said to Helena.

"I guess whoever is in the most hurry is allowed to go to the front? I can't even imagine in a million years doing this in the US!" she said.

"But wouldn't it be nice? Like people cared about each other and weren't just thinking about themselves all the time."

We approached the smiling teller and once again created excitement by changing American money.

On a blistering evening, we lay on our beds and talked in the dark, our windows were open but there was no breeze, the air was still and heavy. The city was quiet at night, much more than any city I had visited.

"You know, I've thought of going back," I said, letting out a sigh.

"Really? Girlfriend, you have? How come?"

"I just want to talk to someone who will get my *Gilligan's Island* references."

She let out a flurry of laughter. "No, but really, do you really think about it?"

"Yeah, I do, because of so many reasons. It takes forever to travel around here and I'm so tired. Pretty much everyone we've met has asked us about coming to America and it makes me think so much about why America could become a shining star of light, it could be a beautiful example, if it changed. If it became humane and compassionate and cared more, and wasn't run by corporations... and if the elections weren't fixed."

"Wait, girlfriend, you think the elections are fixed?"

"Hell yeah, a regular person can't get elected, you have to have tens of millions or more behind you of corporate money, it's for the upper echelon, but somehow, if we could get rid of that system and get something that was really about community and human needs ... I don't know. It just keeps blowing my mind how everyone, bar none, asks about coming to the United States. I thought people in Morocco would be mad about things like we armed both sides in the Iran-Iraq war, that's fucking genocide! "Everyone is so enamored with America, everyone, it's like being a celebrity just being from there and that makes me think if we could be a better example and people want to emulate us, we could save the world! We could be, like, using solar power, and housing all our veterans and homeless, and having the best school systems teaching reconciliation and peaceful conflict resolution."

"I know, I've thought that too, it is so different here. You can't get all the books we have, they don't have the freedom of information like we have. I don't know, maybe I'm just a little homesick too," Helena said.

I went to the public phone center to call my mother, Joan. I had not spoken to her in months and I had given Aamir her PO box so he could write to me. I really wanted to find out if he had written and if he had left Morocco yet for Hungary.

"Hey," I said, "I'm in Ghana and I have a place you could send stuff so I was wondering if I've gotten any mail?"

"No," she said, "but I got mail from your friend Sharon."

"Wait, what? What are you talking about?"

"Yeah, she wrote me a letter and she said to tell you that you better not be using her passport and that she is now with Grace and they are a family and they adopted some dogs. She also said that you're a whore… "

"What! What are you talking about?"

"That's what her letter said, I don't know. I just threw it away."

"But why would she write to you?"

"I don't know," she said.

I marched across town in a fury and I burst into our room and blurted out to Helena, "Sharon wrote a letter to my mother and said all this crazy stuff including she has a family with Grace now and that I am a whore. Why would she say that to my mother? She knows we have almost no relationship, it's not like she could damage anything but why would she do it? Couldn't she just send me hate mail directly!"

"Oh my God, girlfriend, she totally sounds like a jilted lover!"

"Damn it! I was right! I *knew* she was mad at me!"

I felt nauseous, I thought it was the heat but it seemed like it was something more. I started looking in my guidebook to see if there is anything about illnesses and there was. Reading through the list of symptoms I started thinking I might have hepatitis!

I told Helena and she scoffed at the idea. "No, I don't think so girlfriend, I mean, wouldn't I have it too?"

The next day I got a small plastic cup and I peed into it, my urine was dark orange. I walked into our room holding it in my hand.

"Girlfriend, where did you get a glass of orange juice?"

"It's not orange juice, it's my urine!"

"What! Oh my God, what does that mean?"

"I means I have hepatitis A. That goddamn frigging egg sandwich!"

"But that was weeks ago!"

"It can take that long, and it's the only thing I've eaten that you have not eaten and it comes from food, from people not washing their hands. I am so illin'… I can't even think about it!"

"What do you have to do for it?"

"Nothing, it clears up on its own but it takes a few months. I was thinking a fruit fast, like if I could get some melons, and not eat any fat at all because that goes through the liver. It's a liver thing."

"Oh shit, that's crazy!"

"I was thinking we could go to Lou's back in New York, my juicer is there and then I could juice watermelons. We would have to break into your trust fund again, though, and I'm betting the tickets are going to be crazy expensive."

We left West Africa. We paid a thousand dollars each for one-way tickets on British Airways, which was a fortune. We flew to JFK via Heathrow. It was an eighteen-hour flight with a one-hour layover in London.

When we finally landed in New York, we got on the line for Customs and saw a large sign saying that any items must be declared. We had little money left and the few items we brought back from Africa were given to us as gifts. Helena had bought me a gorgeous carved mask for only five dollars, but it had much greater value in America.

"Muñeca, what are we gonna do? Are we gonna have to claim all the stuff?"

"Let's try not to," I said, and when the agent put my bag in front of him and began unzipping it, he asked if I had anything to declare.

"No," I said and he shuffled through my djellabas, two wooden masks, strands of beads and shell necklaces, and African clothes and fabrics.

"Okay," he said, looking up at me, "you can go now."

He did the same with Helena's bag, then we left Customs and we were back in America, just like that.

"Does he think that I just fly around with African masks and strands of cowrie shells in my backpack? That was hilarious, I was sure he was gonna make us pay duty!"

"Girlfriend, I have no idea, but I am just so happy that we're back in New York! I'm so excited to talk to people!"

"I know, me too!"

We walked through the cavernous airport, passing a family who appeared to be from Saudi Arabia. The women were heavily veiled with sweeping black *niqabs*; only their eyes were revealed through a narrow slit. The men beside them wore pressed white *thobes*. *Was there a girl like Samira under all that fabric?* I wondered.

I had not shaken off thoughts of her, and scary imaginings of myself in her position. I whispered to myself, *There but for the grace of God go I.*

We reached the front doors of the terminal then walked outside into the bright sunlight. We crossed the wide access road jammed with cars, walking towards a field of green. An outsized American flag waved overhead. I threw off my backpack, kicked off my sandals, dropped to my knees in the grass, and began kissing the earth.

"Thank you God!" I called out, "Thank you, God, thank you! I was born in America! I'm American! I can read any book I want, marry who I want, go wherever I want! I was born free!"

I had known this from nightmarish books I read on women's lives the world over, and from the study of global politics, but I now understood in my gut that those born in theocracies are truly born imprisoned; they lack basic freedoms in areas of life we hardly think about.

Their country *is* a prison; a place where people cannot choose their religion, their books, their way of dress, the length of their own hair! A place where your opinion could cost you years in prison, and disobedience can cost your life.

I sat down on the grass and Helena dropped her bag and sat next to me, putting her arm around me.

"We've essentially hit the lottery being born here," I said, "and now we have to fight for Samira ... and Khalida, you know, set the captives free!"

"You right, girlfriend, you're so right!" she said.

TWENTY-SIX

June 1992
Suburbs, NY

Allons! after the great Companions, and to belong to them!
They too are on the road—they are the swift and majestic men—they are the greatest women,
Enjoyers of calms of seas and storms of seas,
Sailors of many a ship, walkers of many a mile of land,
Habituès of many distant countries, habituès of far-distant dwellings,
Trusters of men and women, observers of cities, solitary toilers, …

***

At Louis's I was obsessively playing the new KRS-One record *Edutainment*.
"Look at this girlfriend, he is wearing rudraksha beads on the cover! Maybe he's Hindu?" I said to Helena.

We camped out in his living room and I juiced watermelons and fasted on only the juice. I wrote a letter to Aamir and told him where I was and gave him the phone number.

I called the Tree House and talked to my dear friend Jessie. "Listen Sister," she said, "are you friends with Lemongrass?"

"I love her so much, she's one of my favorite people on earth!"

"I know, me too, she's amazing, but I have some bad news … she is in a lot of trouble—"

"What trouble? How? What happened?"

"She was driving some herb in a van ... I'll tell you more when I see you. It was in one of those mandatory minimum states so she was facing life in prison."

I started to cry. "Oh my God, my poor Lemongrass! There are murderers that don't get life! Rapists!"

"I know, it's true, but listen, her father is a judge in Mississippi, he pulled a lot of strings and now she's in rehab for five years but then she has to stay there, with him. He will have some kind of legal custody."

"Can you get me a phone number and address? How do I get in touch with her?"

"I think Diego knows how to reach her."

I called Lemongrass, asking for her at the rehab by her charmingly sweet southern name, Maribelle.

"Lemongrass!" I said, "it's Sena!"

"Oh my beautiful Sena!" she said with a heaviness in her voice that I had never heard. I wished I could reach through the phone and hug her.

"My sweet girl, this is terrible, I'm so sorry Sister, I've been through it, I've been in jail. Can I do anything to help you?"

"Keep doing what you do, these laws have to change. I was facing a life sentence for basil ... oregano ... you know, a simple herb. I won't be staying here long; they're gonna move me to a rehab in Mississippi, near my parents. They're gonna try to make me cut contact with my Rainbow family, but that won't happen," she said.

But that was the last time I ever spoke to her.

Helena and I spent the weeks swimming, chilling out, and listening to music. Louis is a DJ; I gave him all of my records when I went on the road. I had a big collection but he had a huge collection that took up half his bedroom. We looked through the new stuff and found *Hypocrisy is the Greatest Luxury*, the debut album by The Disposable Heroes of Hiphoprisy. We listened to it dozens of times until

Helena declared, "The guy who made this, Michael Frente, we have to meet him! He is family, he wrote these incredible lyrics!"

"Agreed," I said, "he's a fellow activist!"

"I think I'm in love with him," she said.

"Samira? This is Sena. I'm back in New York."

I had gotten the phone number for her agency from information, and asked for her by first name as that was all I knew.

"*Salaam*, Sena, how are you? Is Helena with you?"

"Yes, we are together. Listen, sorry to bother you at work, but can I give you a phone number for Aamir to call me?"

"Of course," she said.

"Shukran," I said.

The next day he called.

"My love, what are you doing back in New York?"

Before I could reply, the phone disconnected.

"What did he do," I said to Helena, "just pay for one minute?"

"He never had any money, Sena, he probably just couldn't afford it."

"Yeah what's up with that? How come he didn't work? I never even asked him."

I never heard from him again. He never wrote or called. I cried to Helena about him.

"Do you think he was some kind of gigolo?"

"What! No, why do you think that?"

"Because we fed him every day, and paid for the cabs."

"I was there, he really liked you, but now you're on the other side of the globe and he's broke. I'm sure he wants to call and talk to you, girlfriend."

"He's not even writing to me, and he has a master's in English!"

"Muñeca, he's not worth it, he's not worthy of you anyway."

I felt better after my watermelon juice fast, though the smell of food still made me nauseous. Helena and I borrowed Lou's car to go to the city and walk around the Village. We stopped at a rest area on the way down and when we walked into the bathroom, there was a group of young Latina women.

"Oh my God," they said, "look at your hair!" They crowded around us and one girl asked, "Can I touch it?"

"Sure" I said.

She held one of my dreads and noticed the ringlet on the end of the lock.

"Is this what your hair was like?"

"Yeah," I said

"So you mixed?"

"I don't think so ..."

"Well, your hair look so cute. Yours too," she said to Helena, "I didn't know you can get dreads with that kind of hair."

"Well, you just stop combing it so even though my hair was straight, it still knotted up."

We drove to the Village and parked Lou's car so we could walk around. It was early summer so we wore sleeveless long dresses and sandals. The color and the diversity of the Village always enamored me, but now it was with new eyes.

"I love the freaks of America!" I said.

"Yes, I know, it's so lively and varied and full of art! But has the city always been this friendly?"

"I'm not sure, maybe we just didn't notice before?"

We were planning to travel west next, across the top of the US so we could see the Dakotas, Montana, and Iowa, then land in Washington. Most likely, we would go by Greyhound.

"You know, I thought the patriarchy at Rainbow was bad, and insurmountable, and now it seems like nothing compared to what we saw in Morocco."

"I know, I don't know how I'm ever going to get over that. I still feel traumatized," Helena said.

"I know, I do too, but maybe I should've stayed and fought harder at Rainbow, I don't know."

We walked around smiling and talking to each other and sometimes to others who would jump out from the blur of gray wearing tie-dyes, bells, and handmade jewelry. African people stopped us to ask about our jewelry and clothes and we would tell them we had just returned from Ghana. Everyone we spoke to was warm, friendly, and interesting.

"Nanga def," we would say, a Senegalese greeting, or, "Agoo," to the Ghanaians we met. People would laugh with delight!

Eventually, we walked by a table on Saint Mark's Place, in the heart of the Village, where a man sat at a folding table selling marijuana grow books.

"Oh my God, Red!" I said, hugging him. It was a Brother from Rainbow named for his long dreadlocks of bright red hair.

"I am so happy to see you, Sister!" he said. "What are you guys doing?"

"We're just hanging out," we said and he invited us to sit with him for a while at the table. He had a second folding chair and we sat on it together.

"We can help you sell books," we said, and he loved the idea.

"You wouldn't believe how many books I sell. People are desperate for this information."

Then he offered us some candy from his backpack.

"Do you want a Snickers? I know that's your favorite."

"You will not believe this, but I have not eaten a Snickers since January. There aren't any in Africa!" I said, taking the candy.

"I'm headed east to an apartment I'm staying at. Do you guys want to come?"

"Yes," we said, "we can drive you."

We went and got the car and pulled up to where he was and put his folding table, chairs, and books in the trunk.

We arrived at a three-bedroom apartment where a group of college guys who were attending FIT lived. They were artists and musicians, and they also had a ska band. They invited us to come see them perform.

After the show, we hung out on the roof of the building until the wee hours. Rob told us we could crash with him so we slept on the floor of his room since we had not brought our sleeping rolls.

The next day he said, "I can totally hire you guys, I make a lot of money selling books. You could come sell books with me and you could live here. You need to come live in New York City!"

"Oh my God, Muneca, let's live here!" Helena said.

"I don't know, let's think about it. I don't know if I can live in a city but the music, I just love all the music that's here, I mean everybody we are meeting are musicians!"

"I know! I totally want to stay, I could study with musicians, I could play with bands. Let's do it!"

"Well, why don't we say we will do it for the summer? I can spend the summer in the Village. Then we will see what happens."

A few days later, we moved into the apartment.

TWENTY-SEVEN

July & August 1992
East Village
New York City

The Soul travels;
The body does not travel as much as the soul;
The body has just as great work as the soul, and parts away at last for the journeys of the soul.

All parts away for the progress of souls,
All religion, all solid things, arts, governments—all that was or is apparent upon this globe or any globe, falls into niches and corners before the procession of souls along the grand roads of the universe.

***

"Excuse me ladies, but when you clothe yourselves in the cloth of our ancestors you bring great offense. Haven't you taken enough from us?"

"What?" I said. Helena and I were arm-and-arm in full African regalia: dresses, headscarves, and necklaces made of shells and tiny carved masks.

The tall black man wore a simple suit and bowtie; he was sitting at a folding table along the sidewalk giving out pamphlets and selling incense.

"Where did you get these clothes you are wearing?" he asked.

"In West Africa, from our friends," Helena said.

"Oh ... " he said, then he returned to his table and said nothing more.

"I can't believe in Africa everyone wants to dress us in their clothes, but we're offending people here?" Helena said.

"I can't even imagine how hard it must be as a black American, I mean their culture was stolen and then they've had to live in a racist country for generations. The people in Ghana do not. It's just so unfair."

We made many friends that summer. I got close to one of the band members, a musician named Mike. We were walking around the Village together, talking. The air was hot and humid, and the people around us were from so many places, it was like a global village. I was meeting a couple of Ghanaians a day just based on the clothes I was wearing.

I kept quoting song lyrics to Mike, and finally he said, "I have never met a girl who knew as many Public Enemy lyrics as you!"

"Hey, they are so political I worship them. I really want to meet Chuck D."

He laughed, "I bet you will, I bet you will. What you going to talk to him about?"

"This evil form of capitalism we have, I want there to be no profit made on housing, food, or medicine. Those are necessities, they're not luxury items. He's definitely an activist who I think will agree. I am so tired of all the homelessness ... all the veterans on the street. I ran a hunger organization for a couple of years and I brought emergency food to people who had nothing in their cabinets... I mean totally empty cabinets!"

"She's on her soapbox again!" he said, laughing.

"I know, I'm sorry," I said, "it just drives me crazy when so many things are broken in our system, and the poorest people always get screwed!"

"I know, you're right," he said.

We continued walking on St. Mark's Place.

"Hey, how do you feel about meeting Lady Miss Kier?" he asked.

Before I could answer she walked over with her bandmates and began talking to Mike.

Later, I told Helena, "Oh my God, girl, I met Deee-Lite today!"

"What do you want to eat today muñeca?" Helena would ask me every morning as she was always planning our meals.

"Pizza," I said.

"Pizza? You say pizza every day!"

"I know, it's my favorite food, and we're in New York, with the best pizza on earth!"

"I'm gonna start calling you Indra-pizza," she said, laughing.

Evenings I made dinner at the apartment for everyone who was there; the nine of us who lived there, and the visitors. I found the Vaishnavas and went to Kirtan on Saint Mark's where they had a small temple, and sometimes I went to their main temple in Brooklyn to cook with them. Afterwards, they would give me a box of produce to take back for the dinner I was making. Some afternoons I traveled with them in their van to help feed the homeless *Prasada*, the holy food we prayed over while cooking.

Helena and I would go out at night, after dinner, just to walk around the Village. With the warm nights, plenty of people were out also. We talked to people everywhere we went, people from all over the world. Late one night as we walked down MacDougal Street towards Washington Square Park a few men approached us.

"Hey *'dere*, what's up my Sistren? Do you worship the one true God, Jah Rastafari?" one man asked us, he had dreadlocks and a Caribbean accent.

"No, we worship the Goddess," Helena said, disarming them with her ever-present grin.

"Wait now, yuh worship di what?"

We laughed and continued walking, almost bumping into a man leaning over a guitar outside a shop, smoking a cigarette.

"Can I bum a cigarette?" Helena said. She was committed to never buying them thus not being a 'real' smoker.

"Of course," he said, and he smiled at her. We learned his name was Zev, and from that night on I'd be dealing with him daily.

Helena lingered, talking to him about frets and scales, then he began to walk with us and soon we were in the park, where we sat down on wooden benches lining wide pathways lit by decorative streetlamps. Within a few minutes, a man approached and asked if he could sit next to me.

"Sure," I said, smiling.

"I've been trying to figure out if you were maybe Puerto Rican?"

"No," I said.

"Okay, so you're mixed race?"

"Nope, but I just got back from West Africa."

"Well, but what race are you?" he said.

"I'm human, from the human race, but you mean my ethnicity? I'm half Irish," I said, which was always confusing to people.

He sighed, "Oh no," he said, "now I'm sitting here with a white woman?"

I laughed and said, "And you're black American?"

"No, no, I am a true Israelite."

"Wait, really? Some of my family is Jewish."

"No, that's incorrect, white people cannot be Jewish."

"Oh lord, are you a Five Percenter?"

"Good God woman, no, I am a black Hebrew Israelite, the real Israelites, the original chosen people. I am from the Nation of Yahweh."

I still gave him my phone number even though I thought the whole conversation was strange. I'd always been fascinated with people's ideologies, especially if they were not standard, or something I had not heard or read about.

He told me there were regular rallies of the Nation of Yahweh by the Port Authority. I went soon after that night with Helena just to see what was happening and it kind of blew our minds. It was a black supremacy rally.

"Well, I guess it's better than having the Ku Klux Klan here," I said.

"Yeah, I mean it is their right, but the signs are so weird."

"I know, and I really like this guy but how can I go out with him? Like, he's so brilliant, he knows all this history and culture stuff, but if this is what he's part of how can I be with him?"

He called me at the apartment and I told him I had gone to the rally.

"I'm so glad to hear that," he said, and we talked for a while then he asked if I would want to go to dinner.

"I would love that," I said, "but are you allowed?"

"Not really," he said, "but you're so different from any white person I've ever met. I'll call you tomorrow and we'll figure out where we should meet."

The next day he called and said, "I've decided I can't socialize with you, I can't go out with you. I talked it over with my spiritual advisor and I have to respect my religion … this will not turn out well for me."

"I understand," I said, even though his philosophy was something I could never understand.

We went to Club S.O.B.'s in SoHo lots of nights to hear live reggae music. I met a producer there named Junior, a Jamaican man. I told him that I had met Israel Vibration briefly and I was a huge fan. He offered me free tickets for different shows he was producing, and sometimes he met me there and got me and Helena in as his guests.

"Listen, Junior, I have to ask you, do you know KRS-One?"

"I know him a little, Kris you mean, Kris Parker, right?"

"Yes!"

"He was going to produce an album for your friends there," he said, pointing to the reggae group on the stage with a few of the guys we lived with. "You should ask them … why, what do you want to talk to him about?"

"I'm just such a huge fan and I always think I could meet him or Chuck D and have some really interesting discussions about politics."

Kathy from DC called Louis', trying to track me down, and he gave her my number in the city. When she called me, she could not believe I was living in New York City.

"I already told Diego, and he totally wants you to set up a business there for him. I'm doing computer graphics for him, you could be doing sales in New York. You're always hanging out with musicians, right? You could sell logos and stuff to them. And we'd get to work together!"

"I don't know, I said, "I wasn't planning to stay here."

But I knew Helena was dying to stay and I felt comfortable in New York State, plus we had a fun summer in the city.

Before I knew it, Diego had wired us money, and we were on a train to DC where we hung out with old friends at the Tree House, and talked business with Diego.

"I'll give you fifty thousand to start any kind of business you want, just get me a business plan," he said, "but mostly I'm looking to seed new businesses. The graphics business is exploding and we've been doing really well here. Kathy said you might wanna do that with her?"

"Yes," I said, "maybe, I do want to think about it a little."

"Sure, stay as long as you want, or call me when you're back in New York, I'll come up there and we'll go to dinner."

Helena and I talked the whole way back on the train about what to do if we stayed in New York.

"The thing is, I can't stand Diego," I said.

"I know, he's kind of smarmy, but you'll be working with Kathy and she is awesome!"

"I know, I love her so much!"

"Why don't you try it and if it doesn't work out, we will continue on our journey west?"

"Maybe I can save up money for a farm, that's always been one of my dreams! I want to plant gardens, and orchards, and nut trees."

"Nut trees?"

"Yeah, you can grow pecans here, it takes about fifteen years before the tree makes nuts, though."

"Oh my God, I can't believe I'm with a woman who wants to wait for nuts to grow!"

We told Happy, one of the sweet boys we lived with, that we were staying in NYC, but we were going to rent an apartment.

"Brrrp," he said, his signature sound, "I'm sad ... this means that the summer of love is over!"

"The summer of love?" Helena said, laughing.

"Yeah, that's what we call it, ever since you two came to live here! The summer of love!"

TWENTY-EIGHT

September 1992
East Village
New York City

Camerado, I give you my hand!
I give you my love more precious than money,
I give you myself before preaching or law;
Will you give me yourself? will you come travel with me?
Shall we stick by each other as long as we live?

***

Helena and I walked briskly through the mild end-of-summer afternoon. We smiled at the dappled sunshine trickling through the leaves above us. We walked hand-in-hand and I was so happy, I could have died right then.

We were out looking at apartments and by the day's end we rented one. Soon, I wore the shackle I thought I'd sworn off forever when I vowed never again to be bound by rent, and bills, and *stuff*.

We moved onto 13th Street near 2nd Avenue in the East Village to a small one-bedroom on the second floor of a large building. Helena made the living room her bedroom. I took the tiny bedroom; it was dark, with one window looking out at a brick wall. The kitchen and entrance were in the center of the apartment, so it worked well.

How did this happen? I thought, sitting on the floor of my empty room with a sleeping bag and backpack as my only possessions.

I got a futon, then a standing lamp. I walked all through Manhattan carrying that lamp home, not knowing that it was yet another marker of the end of my freedom, but it was; later I had another apartment and later still, a house full of things. It all slipped past me, those first broken vows, those tiny cracks hinting that the end of the carefree existence I was living was imminent.

We heard there was a picnic in Central Park for Rainbow Family and we went with Zev. In seconds, I felt at home. Tie-dye swathed people surrounded us, and we sat down a hodge-podge of quilts and blankets. A man smiled at me from a few feet away and for a moment I thought I knew him. He came over to me.

"Are you from Senegal?" I asked him.

"People always ask me that," he said. "I'm Troy, I'm American, and from Harlem, but you look so familiar to me."

He wore a loose blue batik shirt over his slim frame, and a gold bangle bracelet I'd seen many West Africans wearing. Turns out we hadn't met before, but we spent the rest of the day talking. His voice was a gorgeous, deep baritone, with notes I could feel in my belly.

The picnic broke up as evening descended on the park. Troy and I went to dinner together, walking and talking the whole way downtown to Dojo, where we ate tofu burgers.

Now connected with local Rainbow Family, Helena and I started having Monday night potlucks at our apartment. I cooked vats of veggie stew for the crowds that came while I was fasting; I had finally mastered fasting and was now able to not eat on Mondays and to fast for 24 hours daily, eating only one meal. It had a dramatic effect on my stomach and I was much better.

Once back in the US, I realized we hadn't eaten a drop of sugar in over four months, or any kind of junk food, and I found I could simply give it up (including my beloved Snickers bars). Noticeably, I had not had a stomachache the whole time we were away so I also started eating much healthier, besides pizza.

One day at lunch with Troy, I ordered rice and beans with a cheese enchilada and when the server left Troy said, "I can't believe you're going to eat that! Aren't you a vegetarian for animals?"

"Of course I am!" I said.

"Then how the hell can you eat dairy? You know exactly the suffering that goes into that food. It's an evil industry!"

"You're right," I said, and the next day I went vegan and never ate New York City pizza again.

Troy showed me around the city, taking me to different neighborhoods to see the architecture. We would walk hand-in-hand. Once as we walked towards a corner a black girl came around it and almost bumped into us. She squealed and said, "Oh my lord—it's jungle fever!"

I burst out laughing as she strode past us.

"Do you think that's funny?" he said.

"Yeah, I kinda do."

"I'm gonna go talk to her right now," he said, turning to walk after her.

"No, no, don't!" I said, grabbing his arm. "You can't chase after her! And who cares anyway, I don't."

"I do," he said, "and I can't believe you don't!"

"Whatever, it was a great movie," I said. "Just laugh it off."

We heard there was a Rainbow picnic happening in Brooklyn, and Troy and I took the subway there with Helena and a teenage girl we had adopted named Asa. Her strict Persian mother kept punishing her for being "alternative."

We were in Prospect Park and there were more trees than I'd seen the whole time I'd been in Manhattan. It was so nice to sit down on green grass and look up at the clouds and not see buildings. I was having fun with people but I didn't think I was ever going to adjust to being in a city. Nature has always been my panacea.

Asa sat next me to me, her pitch-black mane falling over her face. Her intense pale-green eyes were troubled.

"My mother wants me to cut my hair, and shave my legs, or she's going to take me to a psychiatrist!"

"What? What the hell Asa, that sucks! I'm sorry little Sister, she just doesn't understand your lifestyle, that's all."

"I don't know what I'm gonna do. I'm still only sixteen so I can't leave. Can she get me locked away? I'm scared of her!"

"It's possible honey, though I don't think she can for those reasons. You might find an ally if you get a therapist— "

"I had one and he said I was using it to rebel and I'm not!"

"She just doesn't want you to be an outcast. Ask her if you can get a woman therapist, I know one that's cool, maybe she can help?"

"I don't know, I don't need to go, I mean, I asked my mother 'why should I shave?' and she said it is because of bugs and I said, 'So all men have bugs?' Then she just started screaming at me."

"My friend Kathy went to college for marketing and she says shaving armpits was introduced by an ad campaign from a razor company trying to sell razors to women during World War I, while the men were away."

"What! You mean it's some bullshit marketing thing so that we buy more crap?"

"Yeah, I think that's the way it goes in capitalism," I said.

She sighed and then looked off into the distance. "Oh, look, there's Star, with baby Golden Ra! I love her so much!"

She jumped to her feet wiping grass off her long corduroy skirt.

"Wait, Star, Star who is with Uncle John?"

"Yeah," she said. "Come over and see them."

"I can't believe this, the last time I saw them they weren't even pregnant!"

I went over to Star and crouched down behind her. "Hey Sister," I said, putting my hand on her shoulder.

"Hello Sister," she said back without looking and then she turned and said, "Oh my God, Sena! My beautiful Sister, I am so happy to see you! I can't believe it… look, this is my son! Uncle John and I had a baby!"

"He is so gorgeous! I missed you so much, you don't know how happy I am to see you! What are you guys doing in New York?"

"We live in New York now!"

"Oh my God, so do I! I just got an apartment with Helena."

"I don't think I know her... "

"She's over there," I said, pointing to her, "we just came back from Africa!"

I told her about our Monday night potlucks, and she showed up with Uncle John and Papa Dave in tow.

"Sister Sena," Papa said, "so this is you running this potluck?"

"Yeah, this is my apartment," I said, reluctantly hugging him.

People went into my bedroom to smoke pot because it was closed off in the back of the apartment. A few of us were sitting on the floor in a circle when Papa Dave came in, taking some marijuana out of his backpack. "I grew this on my farm back in Tennessee, it is all organic," he said, rolling some up.

As the night wore on people trickled out and finally it was just Papa Dave and me in my bedroom. He stretched out luxuriously making himself at home, and put his head on my futon.

"I miss you at the Gatherings, Mama Sena," he said, looking at me softly.

Just then the door to my room opened, and in came Troy.

I sprang to my feet and kissed him. He sat down, smiling and greeting Papa Dave. It was the three of us. Troy took my hand and held it on his knee. I saw Papa Dave absorb the situation.

"So, I'm gonna get going, it's pretty late," he said.

"Yeah," I said, "we'll see you again."

"Oh, I'm going back down south. Are you going to be at the Gatherings this year?"

"No, I'm gonna stay here and work. I don't really like to socialize with rapists anyway."

"Man, you're still on that, huh?"

"Yes, and I always will be."

He sighed deeply. "Okay Sena," he said, turning as he left my bedroom, and tapping the brim of his hat, "Peace!"

Helena and I walked around our new neighborhood evenings, buying chocolate-covered rice dream bars at the corner bodega and talking to everyone we met. Happy rented an apartment one floor down from us and we were thrilled to have him so close. Our Monday potlucks expanded to his apartment and still there was often a long line to get into our apartment!

These were the halcyon days, but I didn't know it then. I believed I had found my white horse, my blessing. I didn't see all the darkness coming for us both.

I didn't know that soon both Helena and I would be devoured completely; her by hard drugs, and me by my father's suicide ... and my demons.

I was blissfully unaware that this would be the apex of my love life, that I would never feel this way again, and I would lament for years the things I did—and didn't—do back then.

It turns out this was *my* summer of love; the only summer I've ever had, the only love I've ever known.

AFTERWORD

In the years between my first and second books, I also spent a lot of time working on my third. It starts in 1999, when my father committed suicide and my whole life came apart. Helena was hooked on heroin and I was in one of my now notorious bad relationships. My father had killed himself, and I felt like I had the freedom to do the same. But while I was planning different methods, it seemed like a miracle happened. I thought I found a savior of sorts, a man sent to me by God, an angel—but really, I was back where I started, in the arms of evil, and it would take me years to learn that.

BOOKS IN MY BACKPACK

The Way Out and *The Impersonal Life*
by Joseph Benner

For Your Own Good: Hidden Cruelty in Child-Rearing and *The Roots of Violence*
by Alice Miller

You Can Heal Your Life
by Louise Hay

Meet it with Faith
by Martha Smock

The Qur'an translated into English

Itations of Jamaica and I Rastafari
by Millard Faristzaddi

Scientific Healing Affirmations and *How You Can Talk with God*
by Paramahansa Yogananda

The Aquarian Gospel of Jesus the Christ
by Levi

Present Moment, Wonderful Moment
by Thich Nhat Hanh

Bhagvad Gita—As It Is
by His Divine Grace A.C. Bhaktivedanta Swami Prabhupada

Leaves of Grass
Walt Whitman

MUSIC IN MY BACKPACK

Hail H.I.M., *Marcus Garvey*, and *Dry & Heavy*
Burning Spear

Blackman's Foundation and *Africa Must Be Free By 1983*
Hugh Mundell

Dread Beat An' Blood
Linton Kwesi Johnson

Djam Leelii
Baaba Maal & Mansour Seck

Babylon By Bus and *Survival*
Bob Marley & The Wailers

It Takes A Nation Of Millions To Hold Us Back
Public Enemy

Ghetto Music: The Blueprint of Hip Hop
Boogie Down Productions

Walt Whitman (1819–1892), *Leaves of Grass*
Song of the Open Road

1
AFOOT and light-hearted, I take to the open road,
Healthy, free, the world before me,
The long brown path before me, leading wherever I choose.

Henceforth I ask not good-fortune—I myself am good fortune;
Henceforth I whimper no more, postpone no more, need nothing,
Strong and content, I travel the open road.

The earth—that is sufficient;
I do not want the constellations any nearer;
I know they are very well where they are;
I know they suffice for those who belong to them.

(Still here I carry my old delicious burdens;
I carry them, men and women—I carry them with me wherever I go;
I swear it is impossible for me to get rid of them;
I am fill'd with them, and I will fill them in return.)

2
You road I enter upon and look around! I believe you are not all that is here;
I believe that much unseen is also here.

Here the profound lesson of reception, neither preference or denial;
The black with his woolly head, the felon, the diseas'd, the illiterate person, are not denied;
The birth, the hasting after the physician, the beggar's tramp, the drunkard's stagger, the laughing party of mechanics,
The escaped youth, the rich person's carriage, the fop, the eloping couple,

The early market-man, the hearse, the moving of furniture into the town, the return back from the town,
They pass—I also pass—anything passes—none can be interdicted;
None but are accepted—none but are dear to me.

3
You air that serves me with breath to speak!
You objects that call from diffusion my meanings, and give them shape!
You light that wraps me and all things in delicate equable showers!
You paths worn in the irregular hollows by the roadsides!
I think you are latent with unseen existences—you are so dear to me.

You flagg'd walks of the cities! you strong curbs at the edges!
You ferries! you planks and posts of wharves! you timber-lined sides! you distant ships!
You rows of houses! you window-pierc'd façades! you roofs!
You porches and entrances! you copings and iron guards!
You windows whose transparent shells might expose so much!
You doors and ascending steps! you arches!
You gray stones of interminable pavements! you trodden crossings!
From all that has been near you, I believe you have imparted to yourselves, and now would impart the same secretly to me;
From the living and the dead I think you have peopled your impassive surfaces, and the spirits thereof would be evident and amicable with me.

4
The earth expanding right hand and left hand,
The picture alive, every part in its best light,
The music falling in where it is wanted, and stopping where it is not wanted,
The cheerful voice of the public road—the gay fresh sentiment of the road.

O highway I travel! O public road! do you say to me, Do not leave me?
Do you say, Venture not? If you leave me, you are lost?

Do you say, I am already prepared—I am well-beaten and undenied—adhere to me?
O public road! I say back, I am not afraid to leave you—yet I love you;
You express me better than I can express myself;
You shall be more to me than my poem.

I think heroic deeds were all conceiv'd in the open air, and all great poems also;
I think I could stop here myself, and do miracles;
(My judgments, thoughts, I henceforth try by the open air, the road;)
I think whatever I shall meet on the road I shall like, and whoever beholds me shall like me;
I think whoever I see must be happy.

5
From this hour, freedom!
From this hour I ordain myself loos'd of limits and imaginary lines,
Going where I list, my own master, total and absolute,
Listening to others, and considering well what they say,
Pausing, searching, receiving, contemplating,
Gently, but with undeniable will, divesting myself of the holds that would hold me.

I inhale great draughts of space;
The east and the west are mine, and the north and the south are mine.

I am larger, better than I thought;
I did not know I held so much goodness.

All seems beautiful to me;
I can repeat over to men and women, You have done such good to me, I would do the same to you.

I will recruit for myself and you as I go;
I will scatter myself among men and women as I go;
I will toss the new gladness and roughness among them;

Whoever denies me, it shall not trouble me;
Whoever accepts me, he or she shall be blessed, and shall bless me.

6

Now if a thousand perfect men were to appear, it would not amaze me;
Now if a thousand beautiful forms of women appear'd, it would not astonish me.

Now I see the secret of the making of the best persons,
It is to grow in the open air, and to eat and sleep with the earth.

Here a great personal deed has room;
A great deed seizes upon the hearts of the whole race of men,
Its effusion of strength and will overwhelms law, and mocks all authority and all argument against it.

Here is the test of wisdom;
Wisdom is not finally tested in schools;
Wisdom cannot be pass'd from one having it, to another not having it;
Wisdom is of the Soul, is not susceptible of proof, is its own proof,
Applies to all stages and objects and qualities, and is content,
Is the certainty of the reality and immortality of things, and the excellence of things;
Something there is in the float of the sight of things that provokes it out of the Soul.
Now I reexamine philosophies and religions,
They may prove well in lecture-rooms, yet not prove at all under the spacious clouds, and along the landscape and flowing currents.

Here is realization;
Here is a man tallied—he realizes here what he has in him;
The past, the future, majesty, love—if they are vacant of you, you are vacant of them.

Only the kernel of every object nourishes;
Where is he who tears off the husks for you and me?
Where is he that undoes stratagems and envelopes for you and me?

Here is adhesiveness—it is not previously fashion'd—it is apropos;
Do you know what it is, as you pass, to be loved by strangers?
Do you know the talk of those turning eye-balls?

7
Here is the efflux of the Soul;
The efflux of the Soul comes from within, through embower'd gates, ever provoking questions:
These yearnings, why are they? These thoughts in the darkness, why are they?
Why are there men and women that while they are nigh me, the sun-light expands my blood?
Why, when they leave me, do my pennants of joy sink flat and lank?
Why are there trees I never walk under, but large and melodious thoughts descend upon me?
(I think they hang there winter and summer on those trees, and always drop fruit as I pass;)
What is it I interchange so suddenly with strangers?
What with some driver, as I ride on the seat by his side?
What with some fisherman, drawing his seine by the shore, as I walk by, and pause?
What gives me to be free to a woman's or man's good-will? What gives them to be free to mine?

8
The efflux of the Soul is happiness—here is happiness;
I think it pervades the open air, waiting at all times;
Now it flows unto us—we are rightly charged.

Here rises the fluid and attaching character;
The fluid and attaching character is the freshness and sweetness of man and woman;
(The herbs of the morning sprout no fresher and sweeter every day out of the roots of themselves, than it sprouts fresh and sweet continually out of itself.)

Toward the fluid and attaching character exudes the sweat of the love of young and old;
From it falls distill'd the charm that mocks beauty and attainments;
Toward it heaves the shuddering longing ache of contact.

9

Allons! whoever you are, come travel with me!
Traveling with me, you find what never tires.

The earth never tires;
The earth is rude, silent, incomprehensible at first—Nature is rude and incomprehensible at first;
Be not discouraged—keep on—there are divine things, well envelop'd;
I swear to you there are divine things more beautiful than words can tell.

Allons! we must not stop here!
However sweet these laid-up stores—however convenient this dwelling, we cannot remain here;
However shelter'd this port, and however calm these waters, we must not anchor here;
However welcome the hospitality that surrounds us, we are permitted to receive it but a little while.

10

Allons! the inducements shall be greater;
We will sail pathless and wild seas;
We will go where winds blow, waves dash, and the Yankee clipper speeds by under full sail.

Allons! with power, liberty, the earth, the elements!
Health, defiance, gayety, self-esteem, curiosity;
Allons! from all formules!
From your formules, O bat-eyed and materialistic priests!

The stale cadaver blocks up the passage—the burial waits no longer.

Allons! yet take warning!
He traveling with me needs the best blood, thews, endurance;
None may come to the trial, till he or she bring courage and health.

Come not here if you have already spent the best of yourself;
Only those may come, who come in sweet and determin'd bodies;
No diseas'd person—no rum-drinker or venereal taint is permitted here.

I and mine do not convince by arguments, similes, rhymes;
We convince by our presence.

11

Listen! I will be honest with you;
I do not offer the old smooth prizes, but offer rough new prizes;
These are the days that must happen to you:

You shall not heap up what is call'd riches,
You shall scatter with lavish hand all that you earn or achieve,
You but arrive at the city to which you were destin'd—you hardly settle yourself to satisfaction, before you are call'd by an irresistible call to depart,
You shall be treated to the ironical smiles and mockings of those who remain behind you;
What beckonings of love you receive, you shall only answer with passionate kisses of parting,
You shall not allow the hold of those who spread their reach'd hands toward you.

12

Allons! after the GREAT COMPANIONS! and to belong to them!
They too are on the road! they are the swift and majestic men; they are the greatest women.
Over that which hinder'd them—over that which retarded—passing impediments large or small,

Committers of crimes, committers of many beautiful virtues,
Enjoyers of calms of seas, and storms of seas,
Sailors of many a ship, walkers of many a mile of land,
Habitués of many distant countries, habitués of far-distant dwellings,
Trusters of men and women, observers of cities, solitary toilers,
Pausers and contemplators of tufts, blossoms, shells of the shore,
Dancers at wedding-dances, kissers of brides, tender helpers of children, bearers of children,
Soldiers of revolts, standers by gaping graves, lowerers down of coffins,
Journeyers over consecutive seasons, over the years—the curious years, each emerging from that which preceded it,
Journeyers as with companions, namely, their own diverse phases,
Forth-steppers from the latent unrealized baby-days,
Journeyers gayly with their own youth—Journeyers with their bearded and well-grain'd manhood,
Journeyers with their womanhood, ample, unsurpass'd, content,
Journeyers with their own sublime old age of manhood or womanhood,
Old age, calm, expanded, broad with the haughty breadth of the universe,
Old age, flowing free with the delicious near-by freedom of death.

13

Allons! to that which is endless, as it was beginningless,
To undergo much, tramps of days, rests of nights,
To merge all in the travel they tend to, and the days and nights they tend to,
Again to merge them in the start of superior journeys;
To see nothing anywhere but what you may reach it and pass it,
To conceive no time, however distant, but what you may reach it and pass it,
To look up or down no road but it stretches and waits for you—however long, but it stretches and waits for you;
To see no being, not God's or any, but you also go thither,
To see no possession but you may possess it—enjoying all without labor or purchase—abstracting the feast, yet not abstracting one particle of it;

To take the best of the farmer's farm and the rich man's elegant villa, and the chaste blessings of the well-married couple, and the fruits of orchards and flowers of gardens,
To take to your use out of the compact cities as you pass through,
To carry buildings and streets with you afterward wherever you go,
To gather the minds of men out of their brains as you encounter them—to gather the love out of their hearts,
To take your lovers on the road with you, for all that you leave them behind you,
To know the universe itself as a road—as many roads—as roads for traveling souls.

14
The Soul travels;
The body does not travel as much as the soul;
The body has just as great a work as the soul, and parts away at last for the journeys of the soul.

All parts away for the progress of souls;
All religion, all solid things, arts, governments,—all that was or is apparent upon this globe or any globe, falls into niches and corners before the procession of Souls along the grand roads of the universe.

Of the progress of the souls of men and women along the grand roads of the universe, all other progress is the needed emblem and sustenance.

Forever alive, forever forward,
Stately, solemn, sad, withdrawn, baffled, mad, turbulent, feeble, dissatisfied,
Desperate, proud, fond, sick, accepted by men, rejected by men,
They go! they go! I know that they go, but I know not where they go;
But I know that they go toward the best—toward something great.

15
Allons! whoever you are! come forth!
You must not stay sleeping and dallying there in the house, though you built it, or though it has been built for you.

Allons! out of the dark confinement!
It is useless to protest—I know all, and expose it.

Behold, through you as bad as the rest,
Through the laughter, dancing, dining, supping, of people,
Inside of dresses and ornaments, inside of those wash'd and trimm'd faces,
Behold a secret silent loathing and despair.

No husband, no wife, no friend, trusted to hear the confession;
Another self, a duplicate of every one, skulking and hiding it goes,
Formless and wordless through the streets of the cities, polite and bland in the parlors,
In the cars of rail-roads, in steamboats, in the public assembly,
Home to the houses of men and women, at the table, in the bed-room, everywhere,
Smartly attired, countenance smiling, form upright, death under the breast-bones, hell under the skull-bones,
Under the broadcloth and gloves, under the ribbons and artificial flowers,
Keeping fair with the customs, speaking not a syllable of itself,
Speaking of anything else, but never of itself.

16

Allons! through struggles and wars!
The goal that was named cannot be countermanded.

Have the past struggles succeeded?
What has succeeded? yourself? your nation? nature?
Now understand me well—It is provided in the essence of things, that from any fruition of success, no matter what, shall come forth something to make a greater struggle necessary.

My call is the call of battle—I nourish active rebellion;
He going with me must go well arm'd;
He going with me goes often with spare diet, poverty, angry enemies, desertions.

17
Allons! the road is before us!
It is safe—I have tried it—my own feet have tried it well.

Allons! be not detain'd!
Let the paper remain on the desk unwritten, and the book on the shelf unopen'd!
Let the tools remain in the workshop! let the money remain unearn'd!
Let the school stand! mind not the cry of the teacher!
Let the preacher preach in his pulpit! let the lawyer plead in the court, and the judge expound the law.

Mon enfant! I give you my hand!
I give you my love, more precious than money,
I give you myself, before preaching or law;
Will you give me yourself? will you come travel with me?
Shall we stick by each other as long as we live?

www.ingramcontent.com/pod-product-compliance
Lightning Source LLC
Chambersburg PA
CBHW081352040426

42450CB00016B/3408